Hard Disk Management in the PC and MS DOS Environment

Thomas Sheldon

McGRAW-HILL BOOK COMPANY

New York St. Louis San Francisco Auckland
Bogotá Caracas Colorado Springs Hamburg Lisbon
London Madrid Mexico Milan Montreal New Delhi
Oklahoma City Panama Paris San Juan São Paulo
Singapore Sydney Tokyo Toronto

Library of Congress Cataloging-in-Publication Data

Sheldon, Thomas.
  Hard disk management in the PC and MS DOS environment.

  Includes index.
  1. File organization (Computer science)
2. PC DOS (Computer operating system)   3. MS-DOS
(Computer operating system)   4. Magnetic disks.
I. Title.
QA76.9.F5S47   1987   004.5'6   87-26069
ISBN 0-07-056556-2

1DIR is a trademark of Bourbaki, Inc.
Bernoulli Box is a trademark of Iomega, Inc
dBase III is a trademark of Ashton-Tate
Disk Optimizer is a trademark of Softlogic Solutions
Disk Technician is a trademark of Prime Solutions
Disk Test is a trademark of Peter Norton Computing
DSBackup is a trademark of Design Software
FastBack is a trademark of Fifth Generation Software
Fixed Disk Organizer is a trademark of IBM Corporation
Flash is a trademark of Software Masters
Lightning is a trademark of Personal Computer Support Group
Lotus 1-2-3 is a trademark of Lotus Corp.
Norton Commander is a trademark of Peter Norton Computing
Prokey is a trademark of Rosesoft
Rbase is a trademark of Microrim
SpeedStor is a trademark of Storage Dimensions
Superkey is a trademark of Borland International
Vcache, CONDENSE, HTEST/HFORMAT, and HOPTIMUM are
     trademarks of Paul Mace Software
Vfeature is a trademark of Golden Bow Systems
Windows Presentation Manager is a trademark of Microsoft
WORD is a trademark of Microsoft Corp.
WordPerfect is a trademark of WordPerfect Corp.
WordStar is a trademark of Micropro
XTree is a trademark of Executive Systems Incorporated

   34567890 DOC/DOC 892109

Printed and bound by R.R. Donnelley & Sons Company.

DEDICATION

To my wife, Alexandra,
for all her help and support.
May we live long and prosper.

Special thanks to Richard Bonati
for editing this text. His ideas helped
make it more accessable to a wider
range of computer users.

Thanks also to Gordon and Julia Held
for their support and friendship.

and of course . . .

Thanks to my Mom,
for so many countless things.

In memory of my Dad,
the electronics wizard
and basement mad scientist.

This book was produced on
an Apple desktop publishing system.

Contents

Introduction

*A little help at the right time
is better than a lot of help
at the wrong time*

- Tevye

Hard Disk Management in the PC and MS DOS Environment is written for new and existing users of hard drive computer systems who are using either IBM Personal Computer Disk Operating System (PC DOS) or Microsoft Disk Operating System (MS DOS). New computer users will benefit from the step-by-step approach that helps them do the right thing with their system from the start. Existing users will find this book helps them refine their skills; they can improve the efficiency and organization of a hard drive system already in place. Part One kicks off with an introduction to the operating system by explaining what it is and how to use it. Those who already have a fundamental idea of what DOS does and how it is used can simply skim through these chapters. Don't miss the many tips and techniques designed especially for hard disk users, however. You'll see how to organize your system through menus, directory structures and various operating system commands.

Part Two covers topics of special interest for all users. Chapters 12 and 14 are written for those contemplating the purchase of a hard drive or those who simply want to know more about the operation of their system. Chapter 13 will be useful to almost everyone who uses a hard drive because it explains various steps you can take to keep your drive operating at peak performance levels. Occasionally, the text tends to get a little technical due to the nature of the material, but don't let that stop you from reading. You'll be rewarded with the knowledge to make your system more organized and efficient. I use plenty of illustrations and easy-to-understand descriptions. Chapter 15 discusses the new optical (laser) disk storage and data backup units that are just coming on the market and will dominate the storage of data in the near future.

Why Organize?

Most new users of hard drive systems are either not familiar enough with their computer to organize it properly from the start, or are previous PC users operating in the "floppy disk mode." I have seen hard drives with absolutely no file organization. Files were stored in the bottom level ROOT directory and files for programs like LOTUS 1-2-3 and Microsoft Word were stored in the same directory along with hundreds of data files. This is like a motel making everyone stay in the lobby overnight! Reorganizing these hard drive systems to operate more efficiently can be quite a task, especially after a period of time when many files have been written and stored on the drive. That's why it's important to organize early on.

When a new filing cabinet is purchased for a busy office, a filing structure using folders and alphabetical or numeric tags is usually established before the actual files are placed in them. The same should be true for a hard disk filing system. One way to look at how files on a hard drive might be organized is to make a comparison to

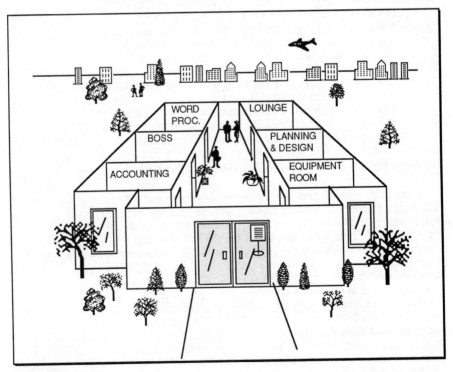

Figure 1. How you organize a hard disk filing system can be compared to the layout of an office building.

the way an office building might be organized. You can create special areas on your hard drive known as **directories** that can be compared to the individual offices in the building. Let's say that you own a business and occupy a building like that shown in Figure 1. Each office is occupied by people who perform a specific function like accounting or word processing. Assume also that you have planning and design personnel, and an office for yourself. In addition to your own office, there is a recreation room and a utility room where office machines, supplies and maintenance material are kept. Last, but not least, is the reception area, where employees check in and guests are received.

Now let's look at how this office environment compares to the organization of a hard disk filing system. You can subdivide your hard drive into separate areas, just like the office is divided into separate rooms. In each area, you can place files related to specific tasks. For example, you can place the word processing applications in a directory called WORD. If you use the Lotus 1-2-3 spreadsheet program, you could create another area on the disk called LOTUS since you might be using Lotus to develop business plans or projections, just like the planning department of the office. Further, you could store games software in a subdirectory called GAMES, and utility software in a subdirectory called UTILITY. These directories can be compared to the lounge and utility rooms in the office. Since you are the main user of the system, you might want to create a directory called PERSONAL to store your personal letters and private information. Figure 2 shows how the office layout has been translated to a hard drive directory structure.

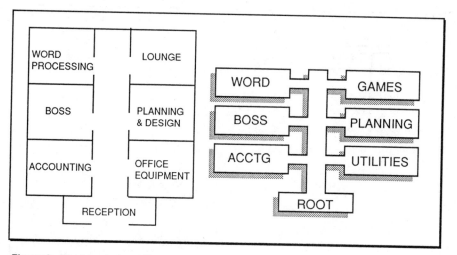

Figure 2. The layout of an office can be compared to the way you will be organizing your hard drive filing system.

Just as the office building has a reception area, your hard drive has a special area that the operating system checks into every time you boot your system. When you arrive at the office, you check with your receptionist for messages and other important information. Likewise, the operating system reads several very important files in its reception area. In fact, if these files, known as the "start-up" or "boot" files, are not available, your system won't start properly.

The designers of DOS like to refer to the way hard drives can be organized with directories as "tree structuring," rather than the office building analogy I use. This tree structure can vaguely be seen in the diagram on the right in Figure 2. Because the designers used the tree analogy, the bottom level directory (reception area, if you will) has become known as the **ROOT** directory. All other directories branch from the ROOT directory. Since every directory can have its own branching directory (we'll be calling these **subdirectories**), you can end up adding a lot of limbs to the tree. Personally, I prefer to think of my hard drive as being organized like an office building.

The reason for separating a hard drive filing systems into directories is the same reason for organizing the various functions of your business into separate areas. Some work simply needs to be kept separate from other work to avoid confusion. You wouldn't want to put your planning staff in the recreation room! In a similar way, the files on your hard drive need to be separated into categories and that is where directories come in handy.

Dividing a hard drive into directories does not create a barrier between files, however. In the office, if you want to review a

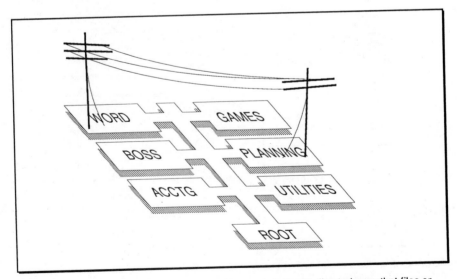

Figure 3. Temporary or permanent links can be made between directories so that files or programs can be accessed and used without duplicating them in other directories.

customer file or have a letter written, you can simply pick up the phone and ask the appropriate person. DOS offers a feature called **pathing** that allows you to set up a link to other directories, just like the phone provides a link between offices in a business. Now you can write letters in your personal directory using the word processor stored in the word processing directory. You don't need to have a copy of the program in each directory. This saves disk space and helps you organize better.

If you're setting up a new business, you could simply place all of your files in a shoe box or a filing cabinet to start, but as your business grows so will the number of files used until eventually you'll need to reorganize the filing system. The same holds true of a hard drive filing system. Organizing now can save you a lot of headaches later.

Just as an office will outgrow itself, so too will a directory. Assume that you take on a new project that requires additional staff and the preparation of special documents that need to be kept separate from those of your regular business. In your business, you might consider building or attaching another office to the word processing department. Under DOS, you simply create a subdirectory that branches from the word processing directory. Figure 4 shows how a subdirectory can be attached to the word processing directory. Note that this new directory branches from WORD and not the ROOT directory. Technically, it is a subdirectory of WORD.

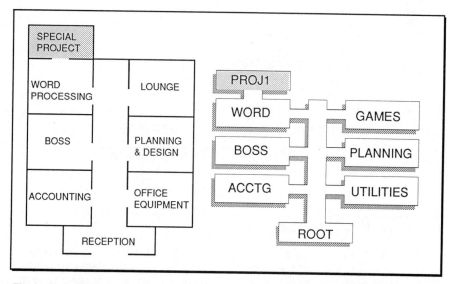

Figure 4. Each directory can have its own branching subdirectories so you can separate files created by each program, just as an office may need to expand to accommodate new projects.

Since each directory that branches from the ROOT directory can have its own branching subdirectories, we need to make a comparison to an even larger office building. The elevator to each floor can be compared to the ROOT directory of a hard disk filing structure. You can take the elevator to any floor and once on that floor, you simply walk down the hallway to any office. Each floor then becomes a directory branching from the ROOT and each office becomes a subdirectory.

Occasionally, an office building is so large that several companies may use the same building with each company occupying several floors. Likewise, if your system is being used by several people, you can set up separate storage areas for each person. When a hard disk filing system gets this large and complicated, you will need menus like Figure 5 to help you and other users move around in it, just like a large office building has an occupant directory in its main lobby. Creating menus that allow you to easily move through your system is one of the main topics of this book. Sometimes, a company occupying an office building may even have its own private elevator that goes directly to a specific floor, not stopping between floors. Likewise, in DOS, you can create special one-key commands that zip you directly to a subdirectory or start an application. This book will show you how to integrate all of these features into an organized and well tuned hard disk filing system.

```
          M A I N   M E N U

          1. WORD PROCESSING
          2. PLANNING
          3. ACCOUNTING
          4. GAMES
          5. UTILITIES
```

Figure 5. Just as an office has a listing of occupants in its lobby, your hard disk filing system can use menus to guide you and other users.

Organize Now, Not Later

With the potential to organize your hard disk filing system in so many ways, you'll want to make sure you do the right thing from the start. That is the purpose of this book. If you are a new user who is still trying to understand some of the simplest DOS commands, how are you to know the best way to organize your system? Will it be the best organization for future use? Will you have to start all over if you create a monster that is too hard to handle later as your system and needs grow? Fortunately, this book will help you determine the best course of action to take now.

Methods of Organizing

There are, of course, many excellent programs available to help you organize your system and make it easier to use. Programs like *The Norton Commander, Fixed Disk Organizer, XTREE, DOS 4 DOSSHELL,* and *1DIR* provide user-friendly menus and automatic organization for a small price. These programs tend to hide the user from the operating system or at least make it easier to use by providing on-line help. The drawback is that you may never learn or become familiar with it. A day will come when you are forced to do so, usually under the pressure of a deadline. So, a little help now will save you a lot of trouble later.

There are advantages to learning and using the operating system properly, rather than using programs that "hide" it like *Fixed Disk Organizer.* Learning the commands and functions now will make you an expert in their operation and help you recover from the occasional problems that come up. Using the DOS commands and batch file operations, you can customize your system to make it work faster and more efficiently than the packaged software. The price will be less since everything we describe in this book can be done with DOS.

What This Book Will Do For You

Part One of this book will lead you through a process that, in the end, will organize your computer system. The methods I use to do this are taken from the various commands and features of the operating system. I first describe how to set up a hierarchical file system, showing you several ways to create directory and subdirectory structures. You'll then create menus that will serve as guides to help you or other users "navigate" through the system. Batch files that automate the menus are then covered. I'll even show you how to assign various keys on your keyboard to make your custom system even easier to use.

Since the book is a step-by-step guide, it's best to read the chapters in order. You will benefit, however, no matter how much material you cover. If you are an intermediate user, you can skim through much of the material in the first few chapters. Part Two contains many "special interest" topics that describe hard drives and give pointers on how to select one for your system if you haven't done so yet. You may want to skip there now.

What You Should Know and What You Will Need

This book is about using hard drives on MS DOS and PC DOS systems. Although many topics are covered, there is simply not enough room to talk about every feature of the operating systems. You can refer to my first book on DOS, *Introducing PC-DOS and MS-DOS*, which is an excellent guide for beginners. It explains commands and concepts in much more detail that can be covered here. This book, however, does cover hard drive topics in more detail. In Chapter 2, I cover the preparation of your fixed disk for use unless you have a non-standard system or a hard drive that has special set-up requirements. If you're not sure what to do, refer to an experienced user or the place where you bought the system or drive. Normally, the installing dealer formats the hard drive; if so, you will be able to skip this chapter.

As far as hardware is concerned, you should, of course, have a hard drive system or access to one, unless you are reading this book in advance of buying. I do urge you to buy the latest version of DOS. If you have one of the new Personal System/2 machines from IBM, chances are you already have the latest version of DOS (Version 4). This book assumes that your system is set up and ready to go. You'll start out using the original floppy disk that is supplied with your operating system, so you may want to get the disk ready.

What Version of DOS?

This book covers features of DOS 2.0, DOS 2.1, DOS 3.0, DOS 3.1, DOS 3.2, DOS 3.3, and DOS 4, either from IBM or Microsoft. Because of the added features in DOS 3.3, especially for hard drive users, I would highly recommend that you purchase this version although DOS 3.1 or 3.2 will do just fine if you own a non-IBM system. Throughout this book, I will refer to all versions of DOS 2.x as simply DOS 2. All version of DOS 3.x will be referred to as DOS 3, and DOS 4.0 will be referred to as DOS 4. Whenever there is a feature specific to any version, I will mention that version by its true version number.

If you own one of the new Personal System/2 machines from IBM or an AT class computer, you can use both DOS 3.3 or 4, and Operating System/2. Most IBM DOS commands and utilities are also IBM Operating System/2 commands. Note that OS/2 will only work on advanced personal computers using the Intel 80286 and 80386 processors. These machines include the IBM PC XT Model 286, the IBM Personal Computer AT and the Personal System/2 models 50, 60 and 80. Operating System/2 is covered in Chapter 16.

Some very important features were added to DOS with the announcement of DOS version 3.3 by IBM and Microsoft in April of 1987. New and improved commands allow you to access information on hard drives through improved file handling techniques. In addition, you can use hard drives over 32MB in size and organize your directory structure in a more efficient way with new commands. Backing up the hard drive is also faster. DOS 3 offers the ability to store more information on a hard drive than DOS 2. This has to do specifically with the way files are stored on the disk. A hard drive of the same capacity will store files more efficiently and use less space under DOS 3 than under DOS 2.

DOS is extensively documented in the IBM PC DOS manual and in other DOS manuals, but it may not be immediately comprehensible to beginning users. You should be aware that most DOS manuals supplied with computers are simply reference manuals and are not intended to help you develop your DOS skills. This book, however, will help you learn more about your computer and DOS while organizing your system. In fact, this book can be read in place of all but a few sections in your DOS manual.

Determine Your Level

One of the problems with writing a book like this is trying to determine the starting point of each reader and how to best present the information to that reader. The first section of Chapter 2 will help you determine where you should start reading and what to do first. A convenient flow chart will help you determine the best course of action based on your system hardware and how it is installed. The DOS manual supplied with your system may not be the most helpful guide if you are just starting with your system since it was designed as a reference manual. This book will lead you through a step-by-step process that helps you use your system properly from the start.

Working With The Examples

Throughout this book, you'll be working through a number of example exercises that will help you get to know DOS. Each example will appear as it does on your screen as closely as possible. Keep in mind, however, that various versions of DOS will display messages that are slightly different from the versions used here. Usually, this won't cause a problem. The example on the next page illustrates one of these examples.

```
C>DIR↵
C>
```

You should only type the part in boldface. The rest of the characters represent what is displayed on the screen. The ↵ symbol indicates that the carriage return or Enter key on your keyboard should be pressed. This sends the command to DOS for processing. Occasionally, DOS will produce a list that is too long to print in this book. The listings will be shown with a vertical ellipsis to represent missing text, followed by at least the last three lines of the listing.

There are several key combinations on your keyboard that perform various tasks. For instance, you can stop a scrolling display by holding down the Ctrl key while pressing S or the Break key. These will be shown as Ctrl-S or Ctrl-Break. In listings they will be shown as <Ctrl-S> or <Ctrl-Break>. Just press the keys, don't type the brackets. After creating files in DOS, you will be asked to press the F6 key, which places an end-of-file marker in the file. If you don't have an F6 key, you can press Ctrl-Z. These keys will be shown in examples as <F6> or Ctrl-Z. Once again, just press the keys, don't type the brackets.

Books and Disks Available

A diskette with a menu-driven directory system is available from the author. The system can be run from the diskette to get an idea of how it works, or the complete system can be installed on a hard drive. In addition, individual parts can be copied to help save time when creating your own customized system. The disk contains most of the menus and batch files discussed in this book. The price of the disk is $25 including shipping and handling. California residents should add $1.50 tax. Send a check, or a Visa or Master Card number, to the address below. Specify 5.25" or 3.5" diskette. Your order will be shipped promptly.

Sheldon Publishing
P. O. Box 90524
Santa Barbara, CA 93190-0524

Organizing and Maintaining Your System

DOS for Hard Drive Users

You're about to learn some very important techniques for handling the files and resources of your computer. If this is your first time on the system, you're starting at the right place. This book will remove a lot of the mystery of your computer by making it easier to use. At the same time, you'll install a system that keeps it running efficiently. For now, you can set aside the DOS reference manual. This book will help you with the basics of getting started. Later, you can refer to the reference guides for additional information.

If your computer is set up and all of the cables are attached, you're ready to start reading this book. If your system hasn't been set up, Chapter 2 of this will provide you with useful information for preparing your system. This chapter will cover a few basic concepts related to DOS, and how to use your computer. For now, we'll just be working with the floppy drives using the DOS disk supplied with your DOS manual, so you'll need to have it ready. In the next chapter, you'll begin working with the hard drive.

What is DOS?

DOS is an acronym for Disk Operating System. It is the connection between you and your computer. It can be compared to a translator, converting commands that you type, to commands that the computer understands. It also translates messages from your computer to messages that can be read on the screen. DOS does a lot more, however. There are approximately 40 to 60 command files stored on the original DOS disk that let you perform various housekeeping chores on your computer system. How you interact with your computer through these commands is the subject of this chapter.

Starting DOS

You can start working with DOS right away, whether your hard drive is installed or not. DOS 4 users should refer to Appendix E at this time. Locate the original DOS diskette in the plastic or paper envelope at the back of your DOS manual. If there are two diskettes, use the one labeled "DOS" or "DOS Startup," not the "Supplemental" disk. By placing this disk in the "startup" floppy drive, the system will load DOS when it starts. If your system has one floppy drive, that drive is the startup drive. If two drives are available, the startup drive is usually the one on the left or on top.

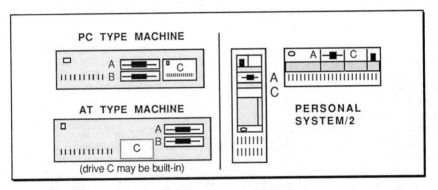

Figure 1-1. DOS refers to each of your floppy or hard drives with a device name. The startup floppy drive is always drive A, and is usually located on the left, or on top, in a two drive system. The first hard drive is known as C. IBM Personal System/2 machines use 3.5" floppy diskettes, and PC type machines use 5.25" disks.

After a few moments, you'll see the following date message appear on the screen. If your system has a built in clock that has been installed by the dealer, the date is probably correct. If not, type in the date and press the Return key. You can simply press the Return key at this point to keep the date as shown, but it is important to set the correct date, since all files you create are date tagged for sorting and organizing purposes.

```
Current date is Mon 5-25-1987
Enter new date (mm-dd-yy):
```

Important: Enter the correct date and time or make sure your internal system clock is set. DOS tags all files with the date and time of their creation. Later, this will help you determine file contents and other important information about the file. You can also sort a file listing by either date or time.

Next, DOS will ask you for the current time, which you can enter or simply press Return to keep the current time.

```
Current date is Mon 5-25-1987
Enter new date (mm-dd-yy):
Current time is 8:13:00.14
Enter new time:
```

After you press Return, the DOS version number and copyright message should be displayed, depending on your version of DOS. The DOS prompt A> then appears with a blinking cursor next to it.

```
Current date is Mon 5-25-1987
Enter new date (mm-dd-yy):
Current time is 8:13:00.14
Enter new time:

The IBM Personal Computer DOS
Version 3.3

A >
```

That is how most of your interactions with DOS will be. DOS asked you a question, you type in a response and press the Return key, then DOS asks another question or displays text. The **Return** key is always used to send a completed command or response to DOS. Later in this chapter, you'll learn how to alter or correct your responses before sending them to DOS.

It is important to start your system with a disk that contains DOS, otherwise, you'll get a message saying "Insert the system disk." In the next chapter, you'll install DOS permanently on your hard drive, so you'll be able to start from there every time without having to insert the original DOS disk. The DOS disk currently in your floppy drive contains several important files known as the **DOS System Files**. The system files contain the DOS program code and translation features that turn your typed commands into responses the computer understands. Just a moment ago, DOS found the DOS files on the disk in the floppy drive so it started your computer from there, displayed the copyright screen and then the prompt.

The DOS system files are three separate files that are placed on the disk in an area equivalent to the reception area of the office building discussed in the introduction. When DOS boots, its checks into the reception area for instruction code and special messages. If it doesn't find these files, your computer won't start-up properly. As you see in the next chapter, you can leave special messages in the reception area that instruct DOS on how you want it to behave. These instructions are placed in two files I'll refer to as the **start-up** files.

Keeping track of the drive that DOS boots from is important because this is the drive that DOS will automatically use when you are saving or retrieving files. The boot drive becomes the **default drive**. When you booted your system with the DOS disk in the floppy drive, the floppy drive became the default drive. When you boot from the hard drive in the next chapter, that drive will become the default drive. If you look at the DOS prompt you will see the characters A>, followed by a blinking cursor. DOS is telling you that the current

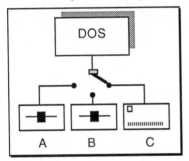

default drive is A. All commands you type will go to that drive, not drive B or C. You can, however, log onto any other drive by simply typing its device name with a colon and pressing the Return key. This essentially switches you to another drive.

Figure 1-2. Throwing the default drive switch by typing **C:** logs you onto another drive, in this case, drive C.

Important: The drive you boot from becomes the default drive. All commands related to disk will take place on the default drive unless you specify otherwise. To specify an operation on another drive, you can either make it the default drive by switching to it or specify the drive name in your command.

By the way: You can create a special area on your hard drive called a **directory** that DOS can treat as if it were another disk drive. Files stored in the directory are separate from files stored in other directories. If you wish to refer to a file in that directory, you must place its name in your DOS commands.

Next to the A prompt (the drive indicator) is an arrow that points to the flashing cursor. The flashing cursor indicates the position where you can type commands you would like to send to DOS. This line is known as the DOS **command line**. You can type anything you want on the command line, however, DOS will only respond to specific requests that are within its "vocabulary." DOS interprets each statement or string of text you type on the command line as soon as you press the Return key. If the string is a valid DOS command, it is carried out. There are from 40 to 50 commands in Disk Operating System, some of which you will find useful in your work. Other commands, like the public domain utilities are available.

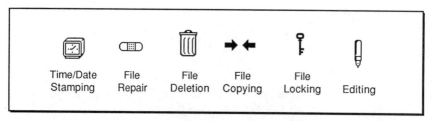

| Time/Date Stamping | File Repair | File Deletion | File Copying | File Locking | Editing |

Figure 1-3. DOS contains a complete toolbox of commands for performing various tasks and maintenance routines on your computer. One set is designed just for working with files.

Interacting with DOS

 DOS is like a traffic cop or intersection light in that it directs the flow of information through your computer. It also checks to make sure your commands are valid and won't do damage to other files. In the latter case, DOS will warn you if you are about to delete a group of files or completely erase a disk. If you type in a command and leave spaces out that separate parts of the command, enter invalid options or simply reverse the order of parts of the command, DOS complains by displaying an error message on the command line.

You should still be logged onto drive A so you can try entering a few commands to get an idea of how DOS talks back. Enter the following disk directory (DIR) command, but type it wrong to see if you can fool DOS. Remember that you should type only the boldface portions of the screen example below. The ↵ indicates that you should press the Return key.

```
A>DER↵
Bad command or file name
A>
```

DOS tells you that you've entered an unfamiliar command. Notice that the disk drive light came on indicating that DOS looked on the disk for a command called DER. Because some commands are less important than others, DOS simply keeps them tucked away on disk, rather than in its internal memory. When you need one of the commands, DOS loads it into memory from disk. In the example above, DOS looked for a command on disk called DER but did not find it, thus the error message. Now, type the DIR command the right way, as shown below. This time DOS recognizes the command and produces the list of files stored on the disk in floppy drive A.

```
C>DIR↵
·
·
·
TREE     COM     3357   12-30-85   12:00p
VDISK    SYS     3307   12-30-85   12:00p
XCOPY    EXE    11200   12-30-85   12:00p
       39 File(s)        22528 bytes free
A>
```

You may have noticed that the screen scrolled by faster than you could read it. There are ways to control the screen scroll when using the DIR command by adding **options** on the command line before pressing Return and sending the command to DOS. Options are used in many DOS commands to request special handling procedures. You can think of them as switches or flags. In the case of the DIR command, you can add the **/P** option to tell DOS to "page" the directory listing to the screen. The paged listing will show 23 files with the message "Strike a key when ready . . ." on the last line. Another option with the directory command is **/W**, which prints a wide listing of files. When the directory is listed in this way, the date and time of creation are not shown, but you will see most if not all of the complete file list. Try either of these commands now.

```
A>DIR /P↵          (One page at a time is listed)

A>DIR /W↵          (Wide listing of files)

A>
```

Take a look at the files just listed on the screen. Most of these files are used for various housekeeping chores, but some can be used for more practical uses. For example, the file called **EDLIN.COM** is a word processor you can use to create or edit small files. All you have to do is type **EDLIN** on the command line. Try it now:

```
A>EDLIN↵
File name must be specified

A>
```

I misled you so you could see how DOS responds to another type of command error. In this case, you must specify the name of the file you want to edit, so try the command using TEST as a file:

```
A>EDLIN TEST↵

Write protect error writing drive A
Abort, Retry, Ignore?

A>
```

Once again, another mistake produces a different kind of error message. This time DOS is telling you that the disk is write protected (assuming you still have the original DOS disk in the floppy drive). EDLIN is trying to write a file to a disk that is protected against such things. Whenever the notch on the upper right corner of a disk is covered by a piece of metal or plastic tape, the files on that disk are safe from accidental erasure or alteration. In some cases a disk may be permanently write-protected by the absense of a notch. You'll get a chance to use EDLIN in the next chapter, so don't worry about completing this command for now. The message **"Abort, Retry, Ignore?"** is a common message you will see as you deal with DOS. This message will appear if a drive door is open, a disk is missing or a disk is write protected, as in the example above. If you removed the write-protect, you could type **R** to **R**etry your command, but for now, just press **A** to **A**bort the example. You'll get a chance to work with EDLIN later.

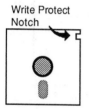

Write Protect Notch

Many of the commands listed in the directory can be executed directly on the command line by typing the filename, just like the EDLIN command. Each of the commands you see listed on the disk are known as the **external** DOS commands because you must have the disk holding them in the drive before they can be executed. DOS will give you a "Bad command or file name" message if you try to execute an external command that is not on disk. To recover from this type of error, simply place the correct disk in the drive and try again. Once you place all of your files on the hard drive in the next chapter, you won't have this problem, unless you work with floppies occasionally.

In addition to the external commands, DOS has a full set of commands that are used so often that it places them in the internal memory of your computer every time it loads. These **internal commands** are grouped in the file **COMMAND.COM,** which you can see in the DOS directory listing. The DIR command, as well as COPY, ERASE and others are internal commands that are part of COMMAND.COM. Your system will not boot properly if COMMAND.COM is missing, so in the next chapter, you'll be placing this file on your hard drive.

DOS Command Syntax

You've already seen how to enter the DIR command with its /P and /W switches. DIR is one of the simplest of DOS's commands since it consist of a command and only two options. Most commands, however, consists of several components that must be properly placed on the command line, a process that is often confusing to new computer users. If you take the time to understand the five basic syntax groups discussed here, you'll gain a good feel for how DOS works in almost any situation. Each syntax type will be discussed separately, starting with the simplest.

The DOS command is always typed first on the command line, followed by other components of the command. Each component should be separated by a space, otherwise DOS displays an error message becuase it can't interpret the command.

Figure 1-4. Spaces must be typed in between each component of a command. They are used by DOS to separate each part for processing.

Before attempting to run any DOS command, you must first make sure the command itself will be found. Currently, you have the DOS disk in the floppy drive and are logged onto that drive, so all DOS commands are available. If you need a command that is stored on another drive, you will need to specify the drive where that command is or switch to the drive.

In the next chapter, you'll set up your hard drive and store all of your DOS files in a special area called a **directory**. As discussed previously, a directory can hold files on your hard drive as if they were stored on a separate diskette.

Important: Directories holding files that need to be used while you are working in other directories can be flagged as special directories. The system PATH holds the list of special directories. DOS will then "look in" the directories on the PATH listing when searching for a command. Detailed coverage is in Chapter 3.

Commands for Controlling the Computer

The first type of command is used to directly affect your computers operation (as opposed to affecting a file or external device like a printer). A space is required after the command and before the option or parameter in most cases. You can try any of the examples below without harming your computer. Simply type the command and options, if any, on the command line next to the the DOS prompt, which should still be A> if you did not turn your system off. Note how the command is entered. First the command name is typed, then any optional parameters, followed by Return.

Syntax:

COMMAND   PARAMETER

└ Switches, flags or options as required

└ The DOS command performing the task

Examples:

```
A>DATE↵

Current date is Fri   5-29-1987
Enter new date (mm-dd-yy) ↵

A>
```

```
A>CHKDSK↵

     362496 bytes total disk space
      45856 bytes in 3 hidden files
     294912 bytes in 39 user files
      22528 bytes available on disk

     655360 bytes total memory
     463520 bytes free

A>
```

```
A:>CLS↵
```

Typical commands of this type are the DATE and TIME commands, used to set the internal calendar and clock of your system. The CHKDSK command (Check Disk) is used to check disk drive file use. The CLS command clears the screen. MODE is another command of this type that can be used to adjust printer and monitor settings.

Commands to Control Your Disk Drive

These commands instruct DOS to perform specific actions on any floppy or hard drive of your system. You must specify the drive name following the DOS command along with any options or parameters the particular command uses. If you leave out the drive name, DOS will use the *current default drive*. Recalling the DIR command from earlier, you can see how the drive designator and optional parameters are placed on the command line.

In the next chapter you'll get a chance to run several commands of this type. Note that the CHKDSK (Check Disk) command is used here as well as in the previous example. You can specify another drive to check, or simply have the command check your current default drive.

The examples below assume that you have a second floppy drive called B. If you have only one drive, simply type A in place of B to execute the commands on the default drive. Normally, when executing commands on the default drive, you do not need to specify its drive. Before starting, place a disk in the B drive, like your *DOS Supplemental Programs Disk*. If you don't have a B drive, just keep the DOS disk in the A drive and execute with that disk.

Syntax:

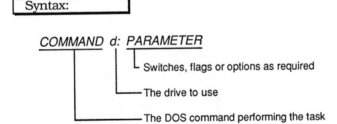

COMMAND d: PARAMETER
- Switches, flags or options as required
- The drive to use
- The DOS command performing the task

Examples:

```
A>DIR B:↵
      •
      •
      •
SAMPLES   BAS      2363   12-30-85   12:00p
SPACE     BAS      1851   12-30-85   12:00p
VDISK     LST    136315   12-30-87   12:00p
          18 File(s)     107520 bytes free

A>
```

```
A>CHKDSK B:↵

    362496 bytes total disk space
     45856 bytes in 3 hidden files
    294912 bytes in 39 user files
     22528 bytes available on disk

    655360 bytes total memory
    463520 bytes free
A>
```

Commands using this format also include those for making, changing and removing directories in a hard drive directory structure. The MD (Make Directory) command, the CD (Change Directory) command and the RD (Remove Directory) are commands you will work with in Chapter 4. The names of directories are used in much the same way you would use drive specifiers. Remember that DOS will treat a directory as if it were a separate and distinct diskette. As an example, the following command would move you to a directory called LOTUS. Drive C is the default drive. *You don't need to type these examples.*

C:>**CD LOTUS**

In next example the user changes to the RBASE directory on the D drive. Drive C is the default drive. In this case, the drive specifier for drive D is placed in front of the directory name.

C:>**CD D:RBASE**

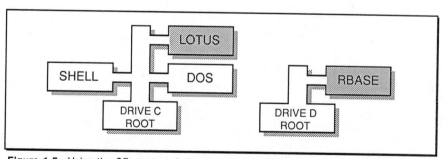

Figure 1-5. Using the CD command changes the default directory, either on the current default drive or on another specified drive. In this case, LOTUS becomes the default directory on the C drive and the RBASE directory becomes the default for drive D.

Commands to Manipulate a Single File

Single files can be edited, displayed, deleted, or checked with commands in this category. To work on files in other drives, place the drive specifier before the filename.

Remember: DOS will always issue a command on the default drive unless you specify a different drive.

Because you've still got the original DOS disk in the A drive and because it is write protected (presumably), there aren't many commands of this type you can execute now. Below is a short listing of commands you will be able to try when you get the hard drive running in the next chapter. The second command, **TYPE**, is used to display the contents of a file on the screen. Since COMMAND.COM is a computer program, it does not contain recognizable text, except to your computer. COMMAND.COM is not a file you would normally TYPE. It does produce an interesting display, however. In the next chapter, you'll create standard text files that can be displayed on the screen using the TYPE command. These files contain normal alpha-numeric characters and are created with the EDLIN editor or your word processor.

Syntax

COMMAND d: FILENAME

            └ The file to work with

         └─The drive holding the file

       └─ DOS command

Examples:

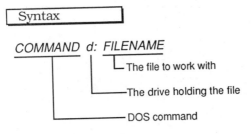

```
A>DIR  COMMAND.COM↵

  Volume in drive A has no label
  Directory of A:\

COMMAND   COM     23791   12-30--85  12:00p
          1 File(s)     22528 bytes free

A>
```

```
A>TYPE  COMMAND.COM↵

  (garbage)

A>
```

Most of the commands listed below will be covered in more detail as you go through this book. ATTRIB can be used to lock a file against accidentally erasure. Two interesting commands available are FIND and SORT . FIND allows you to locate strings of text in a document or count the appearance of a word in a document. Sort allows you to change the order of lines in a file. TYPE and MORE are used to display any DOS file to the screen, with MORE providing a paged listing.

```
ATTRIB options filename      (lock/unlock a file)
ERASE filename               (remove a file)
EDLIN filename               (edit a file)
FIND options filename        (find text in a file)
MORE filename                (list file by pages)
SORT filename                (sort a file)
TYPE filename                (display a file)
```

Some DOS commands can be combined to provide "enhanced" display output. For example, you've already seen how the DIR command lists the contents of a disk. If you combine the DIR command with the SORT command, DOS will display the file listing in alphabetical order. To combine two commands on the command line, a feature known as "piping" is used. You can imagine a pipe being fitted between the two commands, so that the output from the first is used as input by the second. In the example below, the symbol I is the pipe specifier; this key is usually located above the backslash on most keyboards. The file listing from DIR is piped to the SORT command and is then displayed on the screen in sorted order.

```
A:>DIR  |  SORT↵
   .
   .
   .
A:>
```

Commands to Manipulate Multiple Files

When working with multiple files, the most important thing to keep track of is which file is the source and which is the destination. The most common command of this type is COPY. You can make a duplicate of a file using COPY by specifying the file to be copied (the source) and the filename of its duplicate (the destination). If you want to copy a file to a different drive, you specify the file to be copied (the source) and the drive to copy it to (the destination). This is a very common procedure since files are usually copied from a hard disk to a floppy disk for backup or transfer to another system.

Remember: The *source file* and the *destination file* are important features of DOS commands. The source file always goes on the command line first, followed by the destination file. The source file is the file you want to duplicate or rename. The destination is the new file or target file. If you don't specify a destination filename, DOS will use the source filename.

Syntax:

COMMAND d: SOURCE-FILE d: DESTINATION-FILE

— The file to work on

— The drive to work on

— The file to work from

— The drive to work from

— The DOS command

At this time, commands of this type cannot be executed because you are logged onto the original DOS disk, which is write protected. In Chapter 3, you'll get a chance to work with this type of command after the hard drive has been prepared. Look over the following examples to see how commands of this type are built:

COPY OLDFILE NEWFILE	*NEWFILE is the destination file. It is a copy of the source file OLDFILE.*
COPY OLDFILE A:	*OLDFILE is copied to the A drive.*
COPY OLDFILE A:NEWFILE	*Oldfile is copied to the A drive as NEWFILE.*

Commands to Copy Files Between Directories

The last type of command is similar to the previous, except that a path name is specified. The path name specifies the directory that a file "lives in." You'll find a complete description of this command type in Chapter 4 where you'll learn about the use of the hierarchical filing system of DOS. *Hierarchical directory structures*, sometimes referred to as *tree structured directories* allow you to place groups of files in separate and distinct areas called *subdirectories*. The path portion of the command syntax above allows you to specify the subdirectory where a file is located so you can execute a command such as ERASE or TYPE on the file from another directory. You must also specify the path when copying files between directories.

Syntax:

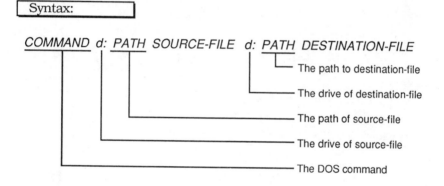

```
TYPE \WORD\MYFILE.DOC

DIR WORD

COPY A:YOURFILE.DOC \WORD

COPY \WORD\MYFILE.DOC \ARCHIVE\OLDFILE.DOC
```

In the first example, the file MYFILE.DOC in the WORD directory is listed using the DOS TYPE command. This is a single file command and MYFILE.DOC is the source file. In the second example, a directory called WORD is listed with the DIR command. This is a drive command, but in this case a directory is specified. In the third example, the file YOURFILE.DOC on the disk in the A drive is copied to the WORD directory on the default drive. YOURFILE.DOC on A is the source file and the directory WORD is the destination. In the last example, the file MYFILE.DOC in the WORD directory is copied to the ARCHIVE directory and renamed OLDFILE.DOC in the process. As you can see from these examples, the destination of a command can be either another drive, a directory, or a new file.

File Naming Strategies

How you name your files is just as important to keeping things organized as creating the shell system described in this book. The name of a file can clue you in to its contents later when you may have forgotten. If you don't establish a file naming strategy now, you'll become more and more disorganized as files are added to the hard drive.

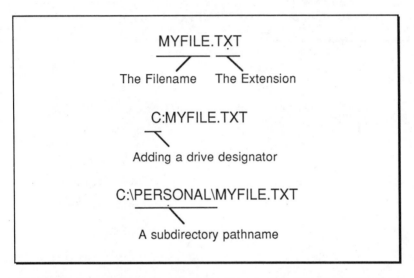

Figure 1-6. A filename consists of its name, the extension and can also include the drive and directory path where the file lives.

A file name consists of a name that may not exceed eight characters, an extension that may not exceed three characters and two optional components, the drive name and the pathname. A period usually separates the file name from the extension, however, a file name does not have to have an extension. You can leave it out at the expense of becoming more disorganized, as you'll see in a minute. Figure 1.6 illustrates the parts of a filename. The drive specifier as well as the directory can be considered as much a part of the name of a file as the filename and extension.

The basic strategy for naming files is to use the extension to group files into categories like letters, mailing lists or spreadsheets. The filename can then be used as a more descriptive tag. For example, the extensions TXT and DOC can be used for text and document files produced by a word processor. The extension DAT or DTA can be used for data files such as a mailing list or inventory listing. Within these groups, you can use the filename to further divide groups as shown in Figure 1-7. Table 1-1 lists the most common DOS file name extensions. Many programs automatically put filename extensions on your files. For example, Microsoft Word appends the extension DOC, Lotus 1-2-3 the extension WKS and Ashton-Tate's Dbase III the extension DBF. This makes it easy for you to determine what files belong to what programs.

Ext.	Meaning	Explanation
BAK	Backup	A backup of a file
BAT	Batch file	User created DOS command file
COM	Command	A DOS command file
DAT	Data	A file containing data
DAT	Data	Another type of data file
DBF	Data Base File	Dbase III data file
DOC	Document	A word processing file
EXE	Execute	A DOS executable file, like COM
HLP	Help	Help instructions
LET	Letter	A letter
LIB	Library	A program library file
MNU	Menu	A DOS menu file
MSG	Message	A message file
SYS	System	DOS system file/device driver
TMP	Temporary	A temporary hold file
TXT	Text	A text file (usually ASCII)
WKS	Worksheet	Lotus spreadsheet file
$$$	Defective	Incorrectly stored file

Table 1-1. Common DOS File Name Extensions

The importance of using a systematic file naming procedure becomes more important as the number of files on your system grows. For example, the DIR command can be used to selectively list the files on your disk, if you have them grouped into filename and extension categories. You can list just the files that end in DOC or just those that end in DAT. If you're copying groups of files to other disks or to other directories on your hard drive, or if you are deleting groups of files, applying common group names and extensions to files is even more important since you can use one command to work with a group rather than executing a copy or delete command for each file individually.

There are a couple of tricks you can use in DOS to work with groups of files. In the examples below you get a chance to list some of the files on the DOS disk using what DOS calls **wildcard characters**. Wildcard characters can be placed on the DOS command line in place of filenames and extension or as parts of those filenames and extensions. These characters consist of the asterisk (*) which can substitute for one or more characters, and the question mark (?), which substitutes a single character in a specific location.

Using wildcards in your commands is sometimes referred to as **global** referencing since your commands specify a large group of files instead of a single file. Although the examples use the DIR command to list files, keep in mind that wildcard characters can be used with almost any DOS command that works with groups of files.

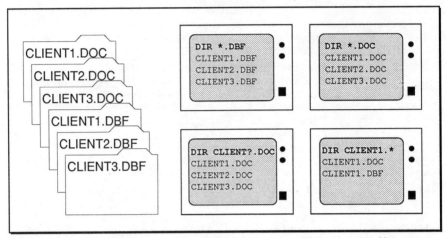

Figure 1-7. The six files above can be subdivided into many different groups. You can then work with these groups when copying, deleting or listing files. The first screen example shows a listing of all files with DBF in the filename extension. The second shows files with DOC in the extension. The third lists all DOC files with CLIENT in the first 6 positions and anything in the seventh position of the filename. The last screen shows a listing of files that contain a 1 in the seventh position and any extension.

Place your DOS disk in floppy drive A and boot your system if it is not already on. In the first example, the asterisk is used to substitute the filename so that the DIR command will list all files that have the extension EXE. By using the asterisk in place of the filename, DOS will list *any* filename. Because the extension of EXE has been specified, DOS only displays the files with the EXE extension. On my disk, the files FIND.EXE and SORT.EXE match the request. They are a subgroup of all filenames on the disk.

```
A>DIR *.EXE↵
   Volume in drive A has no label
   Directory of A:\

FIND       EXE        6416   12-30-85   12:00p
SORT       EXE        1408   10-20-83   12:00p
        2 File(s)        28672 bytes free

A>
```

You may see more or less files, depending on the version and distributor of your DOS. The asterisk tells DOS that any group of characters may occupy its position. Note that DIR *.* has the effect of listing all files on the disk because any filename will work and any extension will work.

The next wildcard character is the question mark (?). It can be used in place of a single character and tells DOS that any character may occupy its position. For instance, the following command will list all files that have *DISKCO* in the first six positions of the filename. The last two positions may be occupied by any character. There should be two files on your DOS disk that match. They are shown in the listing below.

```
A>DIR  DISKCO??.*↵
   Volume in drive A has no label
   Directory of A:\

DISKCOPY COM     5792   12-30-85   12:00p
DISKCOMP COM     6724   12-30-85   12:00p
        2 File(s)       28672 bytes free

A>
```

In this example, two similar files are displayed. The asterisk was used in place of an extension so that DOS would display any extension, however, in this case, only two COM files were listed. The ? wildcard is typically used to list, copy or delete files that have a common character in their filenames. Some accounting packages, for instance, create files for each day of the month and code those files with a character that represents the month and another that represents the day. The filename APC21.DAT is an example of an accounts payable file for March 21. The AP stands for Accounts Payable, the month is coded using the alphabet so that March becomes C and the date is simply specified as is. To list all accounts payable files for March, you could type **DIR APC*.DAT**, where the asterisk is used to tell DOS that any date will do.

In summary, there are several important things to remember when working with DOS on your hard drive system. First, remember how DOS refers to files:

- If you are in the same directory as the file, you can call it by its normal filename. Example: MYFILE.TXT.

- If you are in another directory besides the one holding your file, you must attach the path of that directory to the filename when referring to it. Don't forget to put the ROOT symbol at the start of the path if the directory branches from ROOT, otherwise, DOS will assume the path branches from your current directory. Example: \DATA\MYFILE.TXT

- If you want to refer to a file on another drive, place the drive specifier before the filename. Example: A:MYFILE.TXT.

The following list discusses the most common tasks you'll perform on your system during normal computer operations.

- *Listing Files:* The DIR command can be used to list the files on your system.

- *View File Contents:* The DOS TYPE and MORE command can be used to view the contents of a DOS file, assuming it is a text file.

- *Copying Files.* The COPY command is used to copy files between directories and drives, and to make duplicates of files in the same directory or another directory. COPY can also be used to write new files, as you'll see in Chapter 3.

- *Backing Up Files.* The DOS BACKUP or XCOPY command can be used to back up the files on your hard drive to floppy disk.

- *Deleting Files.* The hard drive must occasionally be "purged" of old or unnecessary files. This can be done with the DEL (delete) command.

- *Create and Remove Directories.* As you add new software or work with new projects, you'll need to create directories- and eventually remove them. DOS has commands for doing this.

- *Optimizing Your Drive.* There are various steps you can take to make your drive run faster and more efficiently. These steps can be done at the DOS level and are covered in Chapter 13.

2

Preparing Your System

Now that you've seen how DOS works, you can begin using the hard drive. The first thing to do is determine where to begin. Does your drive need to be installed? Is it installed, but won't recognize DOS?. Is its storage capacity of the drive larger than DOS will recognize without special software? The flowchart in Figure 2-1 will help you determine where to begin. You can then refer to the appropriate section in the text for instructions on the task you should perform to get your system up and running. DOS 4 users should refer to Appendix E.

A Is The Drive Physically Installed?

If your drive has not been mounted in your system unit, you will need to do so now. Proceed to step B for instructions on installing your hard drive. If the drive is installed, jump directly to Step H.

B Installing the Hard Drive

To properly install your hard drive, you should refer to the instruction manual supplied with your system. You can also refer to Appendix A, which has information on installing hard drives in PC and AT type machines, and how to work with some controller cards and hard drives.

PC and XT Type Machines:

PC and XT type machines will require the installation of a drive controller card which must have its on-board switches set to designate the type and size of drive you are installing. You can only set these switches accurately if you have the owners manual for the drive controller card on hand, since each board is different. Once the switches are set, simply install the board in one of the card slots and install the hard drive in one of the bays using the proper mounting kits. Connect the cables and proceed to step D.

AT Type Machines:

If you are installing a hard drive in a AT type machines, you can use the existing controller card or install a new controller card, depending on the type of drive you have selected. Normally, there are no dip switches to set on controller cards for AT type machines, unless you are replacing the board supplied with the system. When installing the drive, jot down the drive type, usually a number from 1 to 14 on a label stuck to the front or top of the drive. This number will be important in the next step for telling DOS about the type of drive you are using. If you're not sure of the drive type or it is not labeled on the drive, you can refer to Appendix D for some help in this area. If attempts to determine the drive type are unsuccessful, you should call the manufacturer. Once installed, you can proceed to step C.

C Running SETUP On AT Type Machines

On AT type machines, there are no dip switches to be set on the controller card. Instead, a hard drive installation program normally called SETUP and located on the DIAGNOSTICS diskettesupplied with your system is used to set memory switches on the computer system board. These memory switches use a battery backup to maintain their setting when the power is off settings. Place the DIAGNOSTICS disk in drive A and re-boot your system. After a moment, the diagnostics menu will appear and you can follow the simple instructions. If you make a mistake, you can simply run the program again to make alterations.

Once the setup program is complete, you should refer to step D if the storage capacity of your drive exceeds 32MB. If not, jump to step E to run the FDISK command.

Figure 2-1. *Opposite page.* Flowchart for determining your level and where you should begin.

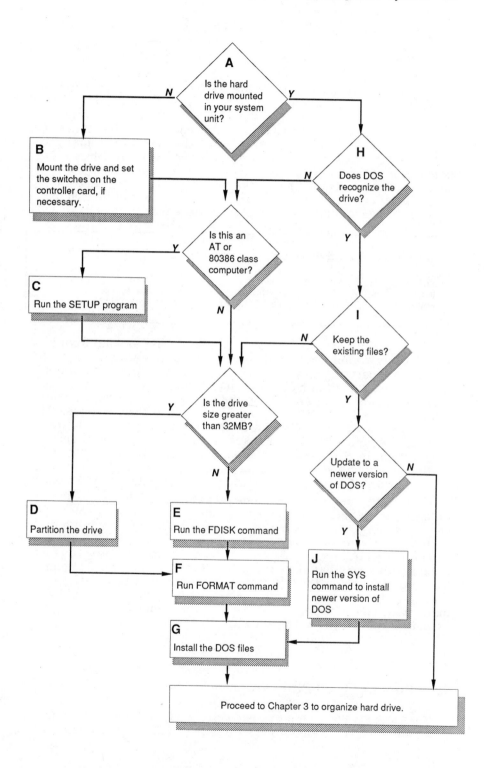

D Working With Drives Larger Than 32MB

If your drive is larger than 32 Megabytes, all version of DOS below IBM PC DOS version 3.3 will not recognize the full capacity of the drive unless you take extra steps. The 32MB limit is a built-in problem with DOS that goes all the way back to the original design of DOS version 2. You will need to divide the disk into several partitions so that "sees" your hard drive as several smaller drives. For example, if your drive is 60MB in size, you can divide it into two 30MB partitions. The first partition will become drive C and the second will become drive D. This is an acceptable solution, since separate drive can help you organize your system.

DOS 3.3 and DOS 4 Users:

The DOS FDISK command can be used to partition your drive into separate logical drives. At this point, you should go to step E; otherwise, continue reading the rest of this section. DOS 4 users can refer to Appendix E.

If you purchased your large-capacity hard drive as a kit from a systems integration house or mail order, chances are it came with software for partitioning your hard drive. At this point, you should refer to the installation manual for more details. If you don't have such a program, there are two on the market that can be used successfully. The first is *Vfeature Deluxe* by Golden Bow Systems. This program allows you to either partition your drive, or use the whole drive as one unit (by increasing sector size.) The second program is *SpeedStor* by Storage Dimensions, which allows high-capacity hard drives to be partioned. A combination of disk tests are also available with the package. Both programs are listed in Appendix C.

If you set up multiple partitions on your hard drive, you will need to format or initialize each partition individually. This is covered in step F, which you should refer to after you've finished running the partition programs. Many new AT type systems and 80386 based computers with large capacity hard drives come with programs for handling the partitioning of the drive. For example, the Compaq Deskpro 386 uses a program called DISKINIT that performs partitioning and formatting automatically. The program asks you how many partitions you prefer and handles the complete task of preparing your drives automatically.

E Running the FDISK Program

The DOS FDISK commands lets you specify how much of your disk should be set aside for DOS. It is not to be confused with the partitioning procedure used on drives over 32MB covered under D above. Once you've established partitions, you can place other operating systems like CP/M or UNIX on your drive, not just DOS. If you plan to do this on your machine, you should refer to the operating system instructions that discuss co-installation in a DOS environment. For this discussion, we will assume that you are preparing a hard drive with a single DOS partition. If you set up multiple DOS partitions as discussed in step D above, you will need to perform this step and the formatting step (Step F, below) for each partition, unless your partitioning program performs this task automatically.

IBM PC DOS version 3.3 is used in the examples below, since this version allows for partitioning of high capacity drives into a "primary partition" and several "extended partitions." The primary partition can be up to 32MB and becomes the C partition that DOS boots from. The extended partition can be subdivided into multiple areas called logical drives that can be up to 32MB each in size. Each subdivision takes on a successive drive name starting with D and can go up to Z, depending on the size of the drive. Remember that each partition created must be individually formatted, covered later in step F.

1: Place your original DOS disk in the floppy drive and start your system. If you want to use the latest version of DOS, you should insert this version now. As in the last chapter, the date and time request appear on the screen. After entering the correct date and time, the DOS prompt (A>) will appear. Type the FDISK command on the command line as shown below.

```
A>FDISK↵

IBM Personal Computer
Fixed Disk Setup Program Version 3.30
(C)Copyright IBM Corp  1983, 1987

FDISK Options

Current Fixed Disk Drive: 1

Choose one of the following:

     1. Create DOS partition
     2. Change Active partition
     3. Delete DOS partition
     4. Display partition information

Enter choice: [1]↵
```

2: DOS places the default selection 1 in the "Enter choice" brackets. Simply press Return to select this option and the next screen will be displayed. This screen has two choices, the first of which allows you to create the primary DOS partition and the second allows you to create the extended partition.

3: At this point, you can choose 1 to create the primary partition. DOS will ask you if you want to use the entire disk. If you don't intend to create an extended partition, simply say yes and the system will restart, at which point you can proceed to the formatting procedures in Step F below. Go to step 4 if you intend to work with extended partitions.

4: (optional) You are at this step because you want to create an extended partition to divide your hard drive into two or more logical drives. This procedure is recommended for large capacity drives that exceed 20MB to 30MB of storage area and is required if your drive is larger than 32MB.

Hard Drive Cylinders Explained

Before proceeding, you will need to know about cylinders since FDISK will ask you how many cylinders you want to allocate to the primary partition and to the extended partition. At this point, you can refer to Chapter 12 for an in depth discussion of cylinders. Briefly, data is stored on a hard drive in many concentric rings that extend around the circular platter or platters of a hard drive. A hard drive with 1 platter has a top and bottom side and each ring on the top is duplicated on the flip side of the platter. The two of

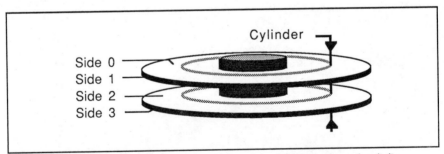

Figure 2-2. Cylinder of a hard drive. Note: Only one set of tracks is shown for clarity.

these tracks make up a cylinder. The reason these two tracks are linked is because the recording heads always move together as one assembly. If the drive has two or more platters, a cylinder extends through the same track number on each cylinder. Almost all hard drives are different, some having more platters or number of tracks per side than others. You can refer to Appendix D to determine the number of cylinders your drive has, depending on what its drive type is. If your drive is not listed, you'll need to refer to the owners manual or call the manufacturer.

After you have successfully run the FDISK routine, DOS will recognize your hard drive. You are now ready to run the formatting procedures in Step F.

F   Formatting Your Hard Drive

Formatting is a procedure that prepares the hard drive to receive files. It divides each platter of the drive into "sectors" that hold a specific amount of data, typically about 512 bytes or characters. Each of these sectors is given an address depending on the type of drive you are using. The address of the sectors can be compared to the street address of your house or business. Formatting can be compared to creating a "street grid" on your hard drive so that DOS can easily find files.

The DOS **FORMAT** command is used to format the drive unless you are using DOS 3, in which case you can use the **SELECT** command to automatically prepare the hard drive. If you will be using DOS 3, continue in the next paragraph. If you're using an older version, skip to *Using FORMAT* below.

Using SELECT:

Using the SELECT command involves specifying the country and keyboard code, which can be found in the COUNTRY section of your DOS manual. The country you select will determine the date and time formats used by your system and the keyboard selection determines the keyboard layout you want to use. The SELECT command takes the form:

`SELECT xxx yy`

where xxx is the country code and yy is the keyboard code. For the US, you can simply specify 001 for the country code and US for the keyboard code. Type the following command to format your hard drive if you have version 3 of DOS and live in the United States:

```
A>SELECT 001 US↵
```

In a minute, you will see two messages appear, one describing the SELECT command and the other warning you that all data on the hard drive will be erased. You can ignore these massages if you are sure there is nothing on the hard drive to save. Press the

Return key to continue with the hard drive preparation, then skip to "Completion of SELECT or FORMAT" below.

Using FORMAT:

If you use a version of DOS prior to version 3, you must use the FORMAT command to prepare your hard drive. Type in the command shown, which formats drive C and places a copy of the DOS systems files on it. The /S parameter copies the system files from the original DOS disk and the /V parameter instructs DOS to ask you for a volume label when formatting is complete. Formatting takes about 10 to 20 minutes, depending on the size of the drive.

```
A>FORMAT C:/S/V↵
```

Completion of SELECT or FORMAT:

When the formatting of the hard drive is complete, you will see the following message:

```
Format Complete
System transferred

Volume label (11 characters, ENTER for none)?
```

You can enter a volume name for your drive that can be up to 11 characters. This name can be anything you want, such as your company name but it doesn't really matter since it is only used as a header whenever you get a directory listing. After entering the name, you will see some drive statistics and the DOS prompt will return. You can go on to Step G.

G Copying The DOS System Files

Now that the hard drive is prepared, you can copy the DOS files on the original DOS disk to it. These files will be used on a regular basis to perform various housekeeping chores and to build the shell around your hard drive. It is common practice to copy the DOS files to a subdirectory called DOS, where they will be separated and not mixed with other files on your system. You can think of the DOS directory as you would the utility room in the office building discussed in the introduction. Just as the office utility room contains the office machines and tools to run a day-to-day business, the DOS directory contains the tools you will need to maintain your computer and its hard drive.

Before creating the directory and copying the files to it, you should "log" onto the hard drive. When you ran the SELECT or FORMAT command in Step F, DOS copied three essential files to the hard drive as part of the routine. These files are everything DOS needs to boot from the hard drive, so you can do so now by re-booting your system. First, remove the DOS disk from the floppy drive and then a "soft-reboot" by holding down the **Ctrl** key, the **Alt** key and **Del** key at the same time. Your system will completely re-set itself and start over, this time booting from the hard drive.

In a moment, the date and time messages will appear on the screen, then the DOS version message. Notice that the DOS prompt now shows the default drive to be drive C. You have suc-cessfully completed installing your hard drive!

Now you can copy the DOS files to it. First, create the DOS di-rectory using the MKDIR (Make Directory) command. MKDIR can actually be shortened to MD to get the same results. To use the command, type it on the command line, followed by the name of the new directory as shown below. Note the backslash character in the command. This will be covered in more detail later, but for now, I'll suffice to say that this symbol indicates that the directory is to branch from the ROOT or bottom level directory.

```
C>MD  \DOS↵
C>
```

Once the directory is made on drive C, you can copy all of the files on the original DOS disk to it by typing the COPY command shown below.

```
C>COPY   A:*.*   \DOS↵
      37 File(s) copied

C>
```

Recall the command syntax discussed in Chapter 1 to under-stand how this command copies all of the files on the A drive to the DOS directory on drive C. The first part is the COPY command. The second part indicates the "source" of the files to be copied, which are on drive A. All files are specified on the A drive by using the wildcard characters (*.*, often pronounced star-dot-star). The destination for the files is specified as \DOS. Since drive C is now the default drive, the drive device name does not need to be speci-fied in the destination portion of the command.

In a future chapter, you will need some of the programs on the Supplemental Disk that comes with IBM DOS versions 3 and above, so its a good idea to copy them now. Locate the disk in the DOS manual and place it in the floppy drive. The command you typed above to copy the DOS files is the same command you need to copy the files on the Supplemental Disk. All you need do is press the F3 key and DOS will re-type the command. (The F1 through F6 keys are assigned special editing functions in DOS; refer to your DOS manual for details.) When all of the files have been copied, return the diskettes to their sleeves and store them in a safe place. You are now ready to move on to Chapter 3.

H   Does DOS Recognize Your Installed Drive?

You are here because your hard drive is installed but you're not sure if it has been prepared. There is a simple way to find out. You should currently be logged onto drive A since you booted your system with the DOS disk in the floppy drive. Type the following command to attempt to log onto the hard drive.

```
A>C:↵
C>
```

If the message "Invalid drive specification" appears, your drive is not prepared. Go to Step B above but disregard the discussion regarding physical installation of the drive. If, however, you see the C> prompt as in the example above, you system has been prepared and you can go on to Step I at this point.

I   Keep Or Remove The Existing Files?

The hard drive is recognized by DOS, but if you know that the data stored on the drive is no longer of any use, you may choose to format the drive, thus completely erasing the existing information and placing new DOS files on it. Perhaps you have purchased this system used and do not have a use for the files left on the drive by the previous owner. If that is the case, go to Step D above. If you want to keep the existing files but upgrade the DOS to a newer version, continue with Step J below.

J   Upgrade To New Version of DOS

You are here because you have decided to keep the existing program files that have been left on the hard drive by someone else or were installed by your dealer. You have a new version of DOS that needs to replace the existing version. The following steps will assist you in the process of upgrading any system to a higher level of DOS.

Important Consideration: There is one important thing to consider before preceding with this step. There is a difference in the
way DOS-2 and DOS-3 store files on hard drives. DOS-2 actually
uses 4K of disk space for each file stored, even if it only has one
character in it! This has to do with a design trade-off made necessary by early hard drives. DOS-3 is more efficient, using a minimum
of 2K per file, unless you are using a 10MB drive, in which case it
uses 4K. The point to be made here is that if you are upgrading
from DOS-2 to DOS-3, you should follow the formatting routine of
step F in order to take advantage of the more efficient storage
techniques of DOS 3. The procedure described *here* only copies
the new DOS-3 system files, retaining the old format 4K file format
of DOS-2. If you decide to reformat, make sure to backup your files
first as described in Chapter 10.

Place the latest version of the DOS disk in the floppy drive and
soft-boot your system by pressing the **Ctrl** key, the **Alt** key and the
Del key at the same time (Ctrl-Alt-Del). This completely restarts
your system and loads the new version of DOS on the disk in the
floppy drive. When you see the A prompt, enter the SYS command
shown below to copy the new system files to the hard drive.

```
A>SYS C:↵
System transferred successfully
A>
```

The new version of the system files are copied to the hard drive.
The last step is to copy the DOS command files to a subdirectory
called DOS. Refer back to Step G for a complete description of this
process. After completing that step, you will be ready to move on
to Chapter 3.

Creating the Startup Files

The purpose of this chapter is to introduce you to the process of creating short, simple files using the COPY command, and to introduce you to two start-up files you will need to operate your hard drive. To get an idea of the file creation process, you'll first create a simple menu that is displayed on your screen every time you turn your computer system on.

Before beginning you should become familiar with the different types of files you will be working with as you use DOS. There are four basic groups:

PROGRAM FILES

Program files contain code used only by your computer. They make it perform various tasks, usually in a specific order. A program might ask you for numeric values, then produce a loan repayment schedule based on those values. Microsoft Word, for example, has a complete set of routines and utilities for writing letters and documents. Referring to Table 1-1, most program files use an extension of COM or EXE, so if you are listing the contents of a disk, you can tell which files are program files by these extensions. If you were to look inside a program file like COMMAND.COM, as you did with the TYPE command in Chapter 1, you would not be able recognize its contents. Computer code would be displayed on the screen as a series of random characters. Your computer, however, knows how to interpret this code to perform useful tasks.

Note: Programs like Microsoft Word, dBase III and Lotus 1-2-3 are used as examples throughout this book. These programs will be referred to as *applications* or *applications programs*.

DATA AND TEXT FILES

Most files in this group are those created by you when using applications like Microsoft word. These files usually contain standard alphabetical characters instead of computer code so you can use the DOS TYPE command to display their contents. The menus you'll be creating to organize your system are text files. Text files use file name extensions, such as DAT, DOC, LET and TXT.

BATCH FILES

Batch files are like program files, except that you create them as if you were typing a standard text file. They are used by DOS only, and always have the extension BAT. Basically, a batch file contains a group of DOS commands that are executed one-by-one when it is "run." Running a batch file involves typing its name on the command line and pressing Return. Batch files simplify your interaction with DOS by executing long or repetitive commands automatically. This helps eliminate mistakes and increases productivity.

SYSTEM FILES

System files contain information that DOS or your programs refer to in order to alter their operation. DOS has its own system file, called CONFIG.SYS. You can place special operating parameters in CONFIG.SYS to customize your system. In addition, if you are using special equipment like an optical laser disk or 3.5" floppy drive, the CONFIG.SYS file holds commands that tell DOS where to find instructions on how to operate those devices.

Creating Simple Files with DOS

Here's your chance to see how a menu system works by creating a menu and a batch file to automate it. First, make sure you're logged onto the ROOT directory of drive C by typing the command **C:** at the DOS prompt, then **CD **.

Note: The menu file created here is a good example of how you can create files directly at the keyboard while in DOS. You can use these methods to create and edit many types of files, such as notes, appointment schedules, and mailing labels.

To create the menu, type the following at the DOS prompt:

```
C>COPY CON MENU.TXT↵
```

When you press Return, the cursor will jump down below the C in the DOS prompt, giving you a blank line to type on. The command essentially tells DOS to "COPY whatever is typed at the CON (keyboard console) to the file MENU.TXT." Type the text shown below, or make up your own message. After the last line, press the F6 key and Return to close the file and write it to disk. Note that if your keyboard does not have an F6 key, type Ctrl-Z instead.

```
C>COPY CON MENU.TXT
GOOD MORNING, MR. PHELPS↵
↵
WHAT SHALL WE DO TODAY?↵
↵
<F6>↵

C>
```

When the C> prompt returns, you can display the file on the screen using the DOS **TYPE** command. First clear the screen by typing **CLS** (clear screen) at the DOS prompt, then the TYPE command as shown below:

```
C>CLS↵

C>TYPE MENU.TXT↵
GOOD MORNING, MR. PHELPS

WHAT SHALL WE DO TODAY?

C>
```

The text is displayed on the screen just as you typed it. Assume now that you want to add another line of text to the file. If you want to make a change to a file like MENU.TXT, you can't use COPY CON since it only creates new files and doesn't allow you to edit the existing file. You can use the DOS **EDLIN** line editor to make changes. To edit the file, type the following:

```
C>EDLIN MENU.TXT↵
Bad command or file name
```

You're probably getting tired of seeing error messages every time you try to start EDLIN. Don't worry, this will be the last one I'll lead you into. If you recall from the previous chapter, we attempted to run EDLIN and got an error message, but that was because a filename wasn't specified. This time we've attached a valid filename to the command so there must be a different kind of problem. If you recall, the DOS files, including EDLIN.COM, were copied from the DOS diskette to a directory called DOS on the hard drive. This is where the current problem is. Remember, DOS treats individual subdirectories as if they are completely separate and distinct diskettes. You are now in the ROOT directory trying to run a program (EDLIN) that is in the DOS directory. Before continuing, you'll need to tell DOS where to find EDLIN.

Previously, I discussed the links that can be made between directories so DOS can use programs from any directory. The **PATH** command is used to establish this link. The following command will make the DOS directory a "global" directory. In other words, you'll be able to run the commands in DOS from any other directory.

```
C>PATH \DOS↵
C>
```

Now you can re-issue the EDLIN command to fix the MENU.TXT file. Later, I'll show you how to make the PATH a permanent part of your system so you won't have to type it every time. For now, type:

```
C>EDLIN MENU.TXT↵
End of input file
*
```

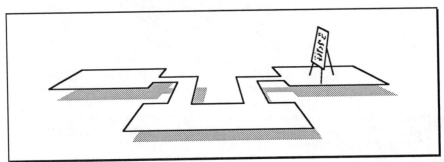

Figure 3-1. Setting a path to a directory makes its files visible from other directories on the system.

The PATH Command:

Let's say that you're looking for another person in an office building. When you ask the receptionist where to look, she says "Look in his office first. If he's not in there, look in the lounge and if he's not there, take a look in the computer room." Someone has just given you a path to follow in order to find your missing person. The PATH command does the same thing for DOS. You can create a search path that DOS will follow when you execute a command.

The most important reason for setting search paths is to eliminate multiple copies of programs and commands on your hard drive.

It doesn't make sense to place a second copy of a command in your current directory that is already stored in another directory. This wastes valuable disk space. Instead, the PATH command can point to each of your directories that hold commands you may want to use while in other directories. The command takes the following form, where [d:path] is the name of each directory that you want DOS to search through. The semicolon is used to separate each individual path.

```
PATH    [d:path];[d:path];[d:path]  .  .  .
```

The following path command example would place the ROOT (\) directory and the DOS directory on the search path:

```
PATH  \;\DOS
```

When you press Return, the message "End of input file" appears. This message means the complete file, up to its end has been loaded into memory. An asterisk appears, (the EDLIN prompt) waiting for you to enter a command. The lines of the file are not visible because you must first tell EDLIN to list them. EDLIN has about 11 single character commands for manipulating the text inside a file on a line by line basis. Line by line editing means that you can only work with one line at a time. Since each line is numbered, you have to specify the number of the line you want to work on. Table 2-1 provides a brief description of the EDLIN commands.

For now, type **L** next to the asterisk to list the file. The contents are listed, with a number in front of each line. Try deleting the third line by typing **3d**. List the file again to see the changes and notice that line 3 is gone and line 4 has moved up into its place, changing its line number to 3. Next, type **3i** to insert a new sentence just before the blank line. On this new line, type "Hard drive C is available." After typing the text and pressing return, DOS gives

A	(Append Lines)	Merge lines from another file
C	(Copy Lines)	Duplicate one or more lines
D	(Delete Lines)	Delete one or more lines
[line #]	(Edit a Line)	Enter a line number to edit
E	(End Edit)	End editing and write file to disk
I	(Insert Lines)	Insert a new line
L	(List Lines)	List one or more lines
M	(Move Lines)	Move a one or more lines
P	(Page listing)	List file a page at a time
Q	(Quit Edit)	Quit without saving changes
R	(Replace Text)	Replace a string with another
S	(Search Text)	Locates a string in the text
T	(Transfer Lines)	Merges a complete file with text
W	(Write Lines)	Writes specified lines to disk

Table 2-1. The EDLIN editor single character command set

you another line since you're in the insert mode. Press the **F6** key (or Ctrl-Z if you don't have such a key) and press Return. The asterisk reappears. Last, press the **e** key to end editing and write the file to disk. These activities are shown below. Note the use of capital L so as not to confuse it with the number one.

```
*L↵
        1:*GOOD MORNING, MR. PHELPS
        2:
        3: WHAT SHALL WE DO TODAY?
        4:
*3d↵
*L↵
        1: GOOD MORNING, MR. PHELPS
        2:
        3:

*3i↵
        3:*Hard drive C is available.↵
        4:<F6>↵
*e↵

C>
```

After the DOS prompt returns, try listing your file to the screen using the DOS TYPE command. First, however, clear the screen using the CLS clear-screen command.

```
C>CLS┙

C>TYPE MENU.TXT┙
GOOD MORNING, MR. PHELPS

HARD DRIVE C IS AVAILABLE

C>
```

That should give you a good idea of how files can be created from DOS. Most of the files created in this book will be small so EDLIN is an ideal tool for editing them. You can use your own word processor, but in most cases, EDLIN is much faster for small files since it loads quickly. The next step is to create the two startup files that will be essential to the operation of your system. Both files will be created using the COPY CON command as above. Later, you'll be able to alter and add to them using the EDLIN command.

The DOS Startup Files

The files you are about to create are called the *start-up files* because they supply information to DOS when it first loads. They must reside in the ROOT directory of your hard drive. Recalling the analogy used in the introduction, the startup files are like messages DOS reads when checking in every day. They can contain information as to how you want DOS to perform, or you can include instructions telling DOS to start one of your programs. This book tells you how to use these files to start a menu system.

The first file is called AUTOEXEC.BAT, and is the DOS *automatic-execution batch file*, thus its name. Every time you start your computer, DOS will look for this file during the boot process. If found, DOS executes each of the commands in the file, one at a time. Remember, AUTOEXEC.BAT is used to set your system up every time you boot, so you'll want to include commands in it that set various features of your system. For the shell system you will be creating here, AUTOEXEC.BAT will contain commands that set the screen prompt to display the current directory you are in, a useful feature. In addition, a path is set to the DOS directory and to a new directory you'll call SHELL. Remember, setting a path to directories establishes a link between them and other directories. The file listing below contains line numbers with explanations for each in the following text. Keep in mind that you must reboot your system before any of the changes take place.

```
ECHO OFF              ──────────  1)
CLS              ──────────────  2)
DATE        ──────────────────  3)
PROMPT $P$G        ──────────  4)
PATH \;DOS;SHELL      ──────  5)
CD \SHELL          ──────────  6)
TYPE MENU.TXT       ─────────  7)
```

Listing 3-1. The commands in the AUTOEXEC.BAT file.

1) **ECHO OFF** prevents DOS from displaying comments and error messages on the screen during batch file executions. Most of the comments from DOS are friendly but its often better not to display them when novices are operating your system. Using ECHO OFF simply makes your screen look a lot less confusing.

2) **CLS** is the clear-screen command. You can use to clear the screen before displaying a menu or help screen.

3) **DATE** asks the user to enter the current date. You only need this command if your system does not have an internal battery backed-up clock.

4) **PROMPT PG** changes the DOS prompt to display the name of the directory you are in. For instance, if you were to move to the DOS directory, the prompt would change from C:\> to C:\DOS>, helping you keep track of the current directory.

5) **PATH \;\DOS;\SHELL** is the PATH command that sets up a link to the DOS and SHELL directories so commands in them can be executed from other directories.

6) **CD \SHELL** is the Change Directory command that moves you to the SHELL directory upon booting your system. You can think of the SHELL directory, which you'll create in a minute, as you would the waiting room of an office. This is the directory where most of your DOS related activities will take place.

7) **TYPE MENU.TXT** is used to display the main menu on the screen.

There is a chance that your system may already have an AUTOEXEC.BAT file. It could have been created by someone else or been left on the system by a previous user. If so, you will need to alter the file. The following command will help you determine what action to take:

```
C>EDLIN AUTOEXEC.BAT↵
```

If you are creating a new file, you will see "New file" above the EDLIN asterisk prompt, and you should refer to *Creating A New AUTOEXEC.BAT* below. If you are editing an existing file, you will see the message "End of input file," and should refer to *Editing an Existing AUTOEXEC.BAT* below.

DOS 3.3 and above:

A new command called **FASTOPEN** can be placed in your AUTOEXEC.BAT file to help speed DOS's ability to find files. This command simply stores the location of files you have recently accessed in case you need to access them again. The next time you need the file, DOS knows exactly where it is without having to lookup the location information in the disk directory. If you want to use this features, place the following command after the CLS command in the AUTOEXEC.BAT file listing shown above. NOTE: The 100 in the command is the number of files or directories that DOS should remember. You can increase this if you want. In the example, drive D is also specified for those who might have a second hard drive. If you don't have a D drive, leave out this portion. DOS 4 users: see also Appendix E.

`\DOS\FASTBACK  C:=100  D:=100`

Creating a New AUTOEXEC.BAT

You're here because your screen says "New file." At the EDLIN asterisk prompt, type **i** (insert) and enter the lines of the file as shown in boldface below. On line 8, press the F6 key (or Ctrl-Z) to end insertion and then type **e** (end edit) at the asterisk prompt to end editing and write the file to disk.

```
C>EDLIN AUTOEXEC.BAT
New file
*i↵
      1:  ECHO  OFF↵
      2:  CLS↵
      3:  DATE↵
      4:  PROMPT  $P$G↵
      5:  PATH  \;\DOS;\SHELL↵
      6:  CD  \SHELL↵
      7:  TYPE  MENU.TXT↵
      8:  <F6>
*e↵
C>
```

Editing an Existing AUTOEXEC.BAT

You're here because you already have an existing AUTOEXEC.BAT file and your screen says "End of input file." It may contain commands that execute memory resident programs like SideKick and ProKey, or even public domain utilities. You'll want to keep these commands intact while adding the new commands you will need for the shell system. Five commands need to be added at the beginning of the file and two at the end. To insert the first five commands, type 1i to begin inserting before the current first line. Note that existing lines will automatically shift down. Press Return after each line and press F6 (or Ctrl-Z) on the sixth line.

```
End of input file
*1i↵
    1:*ECHO OFF↵
    2: CLS↵
    3: DATE↵
    4: PROMPT $P$G↵
    5: PATH    \;\DOS;\SHELL↵
    6: <Ctrl-Break>↵
```

Now, display the file contents as you have it so far by typing L (list). Your file should now contain the five lines above plus any additional lines that were already in the file. Note the number of the last line in your listing; you will need to insert two lines after it. Type #i where # is the last line number + 1 and i is the insert command. Then type the two lines shown below, pressing F6 (or Ctrl-Z) to end insertion.

```
*#i↵
    # CD \SHELL↵
    # TYPE MENU.TXT↵
    # <F6>↵
*
```

Before writing the altered file to disk, check for commands that may have been duplicated by typing **L** to list. You can delete duplicated lines by typing the line number and **d** for delete. Once the file is complete, type **e** to end editing.

Initializing the New File

You can run the AUTOEXEC.BAT file by either rebooting your system or typing AUTOEXEC. Before doing so, however, you should create a SHELL directory branching from the ROOT and then move

the file MENU.TXT, currently in the ROOT directory to the new
SHELL directory. The following commands will accomplish this:

```
C>MD SHELL↵
C>COPY MENU.TXT SHELL↵
C>
```

If the syntax of the COPY command is unfamiliar to you, it will be
covered in more detail in the next chapter. Later, you'll change the
file MENU.TXT in the SHELL directory into a more elaborate menu
using EDLIN. For now, try rebooting your system or typing
AUTOEXEC to see how it works. If you did everything right, you
should see the menu displayed on the screen, along with a DOS
prompt that tells you the current directory, as shown below:

```
Good Morning, Mr. Phelps

Hard drive C is available

C:\SHELL>
```

The CONFIG.SYS File

Recall from earlier that CONFIG.SYS is the startup file where you
can store customization options for DOS. Commands placed in the
file will usually make settings that maintain themselves throughout
an entire computing session. Typically, commands in CONFIG.SYS
tell DOS how to use devices like printers, plotters and scanners,
optical drives, and mouse pointers. These commands are often referred to as **DEVICE DRIVERS**. For example, if you use the
Microsoft Mouse, you need the command DEVICE=MOUSE.SYS in
your configuration file. Connecting a scanner might require the
command DEVICE=SCANNER.SYS. As you can see, several commands can be placed in the file, each beginning with **DEVICE=**.

There are other commands that can be placed in CONFIG.SYS
besides the device drivers. One of the most important is the
BUFFERS command. Although buffers will be covered in more detail later, you can refer to the box to learn a little more about it.

The first command you'll place in CONFIG.SYS is DEVICE =
ANSI.SYS. This command will cause DOS to load a special keyboard
and screen program called ANSI.SYS. It is a special file supplied on
your DOS disk that tells DOS how to handle the keyboard and
screen. You'll be using this feature later when the keys on the

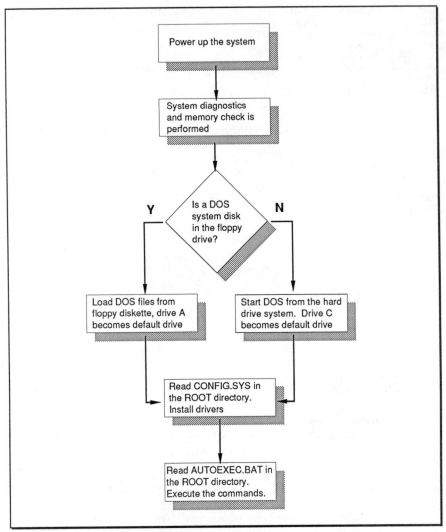

Figure 3-2. The startup procedure for DOS systems.

keyboard are reassigned. For instance, you can assign the DIR command to one of the function keys. The second command will be BUFFERS=25 as discussed earlier.

To create a new configuration file, use the EDLIN editor as you did when working with AUTOEXEC.BAT. Type the command shown on the next page. Note that backslash is placed before the filename so that it can be edited from any directory.

```
C:\>EDLIN \CONFIG.SYS↵
```

If you are editing a new file you will see the message "New file" and if you are editing an existing file you will see the message "End of input file". Add the following lines to the file by typing **i** (insert). The order of the commands in the file doesn't matter in most cases. Some third party programs that load from CONFIG.SYS must be the first command in the file- refer to your manual for details. Watch that you don't create duplicate commands if you are working on an existing file.

```
DEVICE  =  \DOS\ANSI.SYS
BUFFER  =  25
```

In the future, as you add new programs or external equipment, you may need to add new commands to your configuration file. This can easily be done with the EDLIN editor.

The BUFFERS Command:

When your computer needs to get at some data stored on the hard drive. it doesn't just get one character at a time. Instead, it grabs a block of about 512 characters known as a sector. This is transferred to memory for processing. If the file is larger than 512 bytes, several sectors are read into memory.

Now, let's say that you need the same block of information over again during the course of your computing session. Without buffers, DOS would have to go back out to the disk to get the block a second time. BUFFERS allows you to set aside a certain amount of internal memory where DOS can temporarily store blocks of previously read data. When you ask for the same data over again, DOS first checks in the memory reserve before going to disk. That's good for speed as well as extending the life of your hard drive. The more BUFFERS you have, the less DOS has to go to disk. BUFFERS are managed by the computer. If you haven't used a block of data in a while, DOS throws it out and loads in a more useful block.

For now, you'll set BUFFERS at 25, but, as you'll see in Chapter 13, you can boost this number depending on memory size, to increase the efficiency of the hard drive. Because buffers speed up your system by eliminating repetition, it would seem that the more you have the better. Buffers, however, take up memory; usually 512 bytes, so 25 buffers take up about 13K of memory. This can be a lot on a 256K system, however most systems these days come with 640K, so it doesn't make much of a dent. If you are using disk intensive programs like data bases you should consider more that 25 buffers.

Hierarchical Filing Structures

When IBM announced its first personal computer with a hard drive, the IBM XT, in 1983, it saw a need for organizing the large amount of information that could be stored on the drive. Along with the XT, IBM announced IBM PC DOS 2.0, which added a very important feature known as the **Hierarchical Filing System**. Recall the office building analogy used in the introduction to understand how hierarchical filing separates the large storage area of a hard drive into multiple storage areas called directories. In fact, you can think of a directory the same way you think of a diskette. In the days before hard drives, PC users would place each of their programs or data on separate diskettes. The diskettes themselves

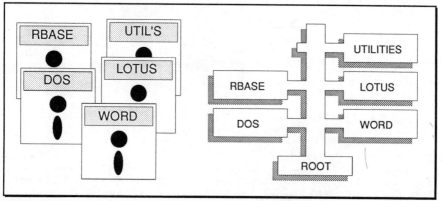

Figure 4-1. Organizing files into directories on hard drives is similar to the way original PC users had to organize their programs and data onto several diskettes.

helped keep the user organized by separating applications and data onto separate and distinct media. Now that hard drives are common, users can separate applications and data into directories that perform the same function as separate diskettes.

A Word About the Wording

You will notice in the various texts and reference binders you read that the DOS hierarchical filing system is called many different things. You'll see reference to "tree structured directories" and "directory filing systems" but keep in mind that these all refer to the same thing.

The first level of the directory structure is called the **ROOT** directory. Every hard drive has a ROOT directory since it is created when the drive is formatted. All other directories branch from the ROOT and because they branch from another directory, are often referred to as subdirectories. In this book, I refer to all directories that branch from the ROOT directory as the **ROOT-level directories**. Directories that branch from root-level directories are referred to as subdirectories. Technically, if a directory branches from another, it is a subdirectory. The ROOT-level directories are subdirectories of the ROOT directory. I tend to avoid this directory/ subdirectory name shuffling, however, to eliminate confusion, as

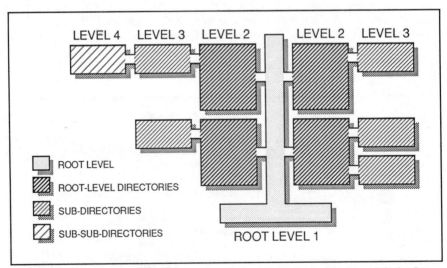

Figure 4-2. The ROOT level is the base that all other directories branch from. It is the first level. Branching from it are the ROOT-level directories and branching from them are subdirectories. Fourth level subdirectories, as shown above, are rarely used since they tend to cause confusion and slow the drive down.

119852

you can tell by the previous sentence. Since every directory has a name, I'll just use its name in upper case when making reference to it in the text, whether it is a directory or subdirectory. For example, the ROOT directory or the LOTUS directory.

Figure 4-2 should give you a good idea of the naming and reference conventions I'll use in this book. Keep in mind that any directory, whether a ROOT-level directory or a subdirectory, can have branching subdirectories. That means you could build a directory structure that is several levels deep. Take a look at Figure 4-2. The ROOT is the first level directory. The ROOT-level directories are the second level and any directories that branch from the ROOT-level directories are at a third level. You could create fourth and fifth level directories, but you should avoid this since it can create confusion and degrades drive performance.

How to Work with Directories

There are many reasons for adding directories to your hard drive. Often, you just need a place to archive excess files but in most cases, a directory is used to separate specific types of files from other types. Since directories can branch from other directories, you can create specialized directories for each of your applications. For instance, you could attach two subdirectories to a directory called WORD. WORD holds the program files for the Microsoft Word word processing program and each of the branching directories would hold specific types of files. One subdirectory might hold personal letters and the other might hold business correspondence. In another case, several people might be using one computer, so you could create a directory for each user.

There are several rules and general procedures you should keep in mind when working with tree structured directories:

- DOS always keeps track of a current directory for each drive on your system. For example, lets say you log into the WORD directory on your hard drive. Then you switch over to the floppy drive to look at some files on a diskette. If you decide to copy any of the diskette files to the hard drive, DOS will copy them into the WORD directory since that was the last place you logged on the hard drive.

- All subdirectories trace a path back to the ROOT directory; it is this path that makes up the full name of any file in a subdirectory. Let's say you attach a subdirectory to the WORD directory called PERSONAL. The PERSONAL directory is now known to DOS as \WORD\PERSONAL. When issuing commands on files in this directory from another, you need to specify the full path name.

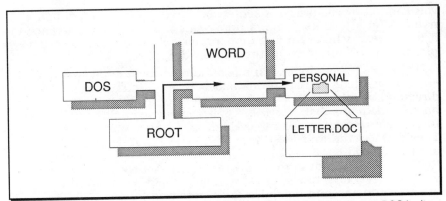

Figure 4-3. A file called LETTER.DOC in the PERSONAL directory is known to DOS by its full name: \WORD\PERSONAL\LETTER.DOC

- Directories are listed as <DIR> when you execute the DIR command. Don't mix these two up. The DOS command DIR is used to list files in a directory. <DIR> in the file listing designates a subdirectory.

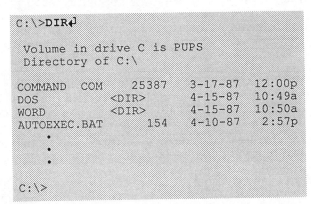

```
C:\>DIR↵

Volume in drive C is PUPS
Directory of C:\

COMMAND   COM     25387    3-17-87   12:00p
DOS             <DIR>      4-15-87   10:49a
WORD            <DIR>      4-15-87   10:50a
AUTOEXEC.BAT      154      4-10-87    2:57p
     .
     .
     .

C:\>
```

- DOS treats different directories as if they were separate diskettes. You copy files between directories the same way you copy files between diskettes. There are no file name conflicts between files of the same name in separate directories since each directory is autonomous from others.

- Directories cannot be removed until all files in them have been deleted and any subdirectories attached have been removed.

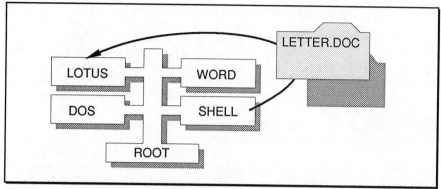

Figure 4-4. Files can be copied between directories. In this example, the command: COPY \SHELL\LETTER.DOC \LOTUS duplicated the LETTER.DOC file in the LOTUS directory.

Creating Directories

In the last chapter, you created the SHELL and DOS directories on your hard drive, so you already have some experience with the DOS commands used to create and move through directories. Figure 4-5 should represent the directory structure on your hard drive if you've been following the routines in this book. To create a directory, you can use the MKDIR command which stands for Make Directory. It can be abbreviated to MD as we'll be doing in this book.

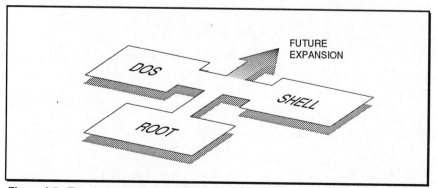

Figure 4-5. The above diagram should represent the way your directory structures looks if you've been following the examples in this book.

You can make a directory two ways. The first way is to move to the directory you want your new directory to branch from. If it's to branch from the ROOT, you'll need to go to the ROOT directory to create it. If it is to branch from the WORD directory, you'll need to move to WORD first. The second way to create directories is to simply stay in the directory you are in, but specify the full path the new directory will have in your MD (make directory) command.

Use the second method now to create a directory called TEST that branches from the ROOT directory. To get an idea of how directories can be created while you're in a completely separate directory, go to the SHELL directory using the **CD (Change Directory)** command. You'll be using the CD command often to move from one directory to another. Simply specify the directory you want to move to next to the command as is shown below.

```
C:\>CD SHELL↵
C:\SHELL>
```

You can see that the DOS prompt has changed to reflect the name of the directory you're now in. From SHELL, issue the command to create the ROOT-level directory TEST.

```
C:\SHELL>MD \TEST↵
C:\SHELL>
```

The important part of the MD command above is the backslash character before TEST. It tells DOS what directory TEST will branch from. If you had left it out, TEST would have been created as a branching subdirectory of the SHELL directory since you are in SHELL. You can list the ROOT level directories by typing:

```
C:\SHELL>DIR \↵

 Volume in drive C is STARSHIP-3
 Directory of  C:\

COMMAND  COM     23791   12-30-85   12:00p
DOS             <DIR>     1-19-87   11:00p
AUTOEXEC BAT        76    1-19-87   12:40p
CONFIG   SYS        55    1-19-87   12:45p
SHELL           <DIR>     1-19-87    1:00p
TEST            <DIR>     3-19-86   12:43a
     .
     .
     .
C:\SHELL>
```

The ROOT Directory Symbol:

The backslash character is used to represent the ROOT directory of your hard drive. All other directories branching from the ROOT have a specific name that you give them. The ROOT directory symbol can be used in commands. For example:

```
DIR \
CD \
```

The first command lists the files in the ROOT and the second moves you directly to the ROOT directory. When the backslash is used with filenames and paths, the first occurrence of the backslash represents the ROOT directory and indicates that the directory branches from the ROOT or the file resides in the ROOT. Don't confuse the backslash symbol representing the ROOT with the backslash character used to separate directories in pathnames. For example, the first backslash in the following filename indicates that the file branches from the ROOT. The remaining directories along the path to the file are separated by the backslash.

```
\DATA\MARCH\CLIENT.DAT
```

If you were in the DATA directory, the file would be called MARCH\CLIENT.DAT.

The listing shows directories with the label <DIR>. If you type a directory listing of your current directory (assuming you are still in SHELL, just type DIR), you will not see branching subdirectories, at least not yet. Note in the command above that you requested DOS to list a directory other than the one you were in by specifying the path of the directory to list. In this case, that path was simply ROOT (the backslash).

Moving Through Directories

There are two ways to move to other directories, the "step-by-step" method or the "direct" method. I'll cover both here so you can get an idea of the different ways to use the CD command. For the example, you'll move from the current directory SHELL to the new TEST directory. Moving between the two directories will involve passing through the ROOT directory since they branch separately from it.

Step-by-Step Move

The step-by-step move involves using two separate DOS commands. The first moves you back to the ROOT directory from SHELL and the second moves you up into the TEST directory. Type in the commands shown to see how they work, watch the DOS prompt change as you move to ROOT and then to TEST.

```
C:\SHELL>CD \↵
C:\>CD \TEST↵
C:\TEST>
```

Another way to perform the same task is shown below. This time, a special trick you can use with the CD command is taken advantage of. The double dots following CD in the first line tell DOS to "move back" one directory level. One directory level back from SHELL is the ROOT directory. The second line performs the same function as the second command above. This time, however, the backslash was left out since you don't really need to use it when the directory you want to move to is attached to the directory you're in. (Note: If you typed the command above, you won't be able to do the example below since you're already in TEST.)

```
C:\SHELL>CD ..↵
C:\>CD TEST↵
C:\TEST>
```

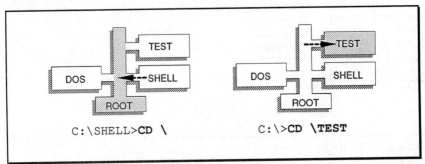

Figure 4-6. You can move between directories step-by-step through the ROOT directory.

The Direct Move

A much simpler way to make the same move using just one command is to specify the full path of the directory you want to move to. The example below uses the command **CD \SHELL** to move directly back to the SHELL directory from the TEST

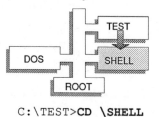

C:\TEST>**CD \SHELL**

directory assuming you are in that directory from the last example. Obviously, this method is preferable to the previous examples since you can get to where you want to go with one command. Occasionally, however, you may need to step through individual directories and the **CD ..** and **CD <directory name>** commands are the ones to use.

```
C:\TEST>CD \SHELL↵
C:\SHELL>
```

Using Batch Files to Move to Directories

You can make the process of moving to directories and starting your programs even easier by placing them in batch files. Then, by typing the name of the batch file, the command is instantly executed. Typically, you would do this if your CD command is a long string that you find too cumbersome to type often or if you have someone using your system that is not experienced. The batch file should have a simple one or two character filename to make it easy to type and execute. In addition, you should use a filename that is easy to remember.

For example, assume that you have a directory called PERSONAL that branches from the WORD directory. To get to the directory using normal DOS commands, you could type:

```
CD   \WORD\PERSONAL
```

Placing this command in a batch file called PER.BAT would allow you to perform the same task by simply typing PER. In the example below, I created this batch file using the COPY CON command. You can alter this example to fit your own needs, however. If you use WordPerfect, you can create a directory called WP and then substitute WP for WORD in the CD command below. You might also prefer a different name for the batch file, so just substitute the name of your choice in the COPY CON command. Remember that the F6 key places an end-of-file marker in the file. If you don't have an F6 key, press the Ctrl-Z key.

```
C:\SHELL>COPY CON PER.BAT↵
CD   \WORD\PERSONAL↵
<F6>↵
C:\SHELL>
```

Notice that the file was created while in the SHELL directory. The file will "live" in that directory, but you will be able to execute it from any other directory since the path set by the AUTOEXEC.BAT file created in the last chapter tells DOS to look in SHELL for batch files and command files.

Listing Directories

Just as you can create any subdirectory from anywhere on your system, you can also list any subdirectory from anywhere else, as long as you specify the full path to the directory you want to list. For example, the following command will list the \DOS directory while you're in the \SHELL directory:

```
C:\SHELL>DIR \DOS↵
```

The backslash placed before the directory name tells DOS to start looking for the directory from the ROOT level instead of the current directory.

A convenient command to list directories is to specify the wild-card characters *. in a DIR command. Since most directories are named with filenames and not extensions, this command works because it specifies any filename but no extension. The example below will list the directories that branch from the ROOT directory:

```
C:\SHELL>DIR \*.↵
```

Working With Files

Copying files between directories is easy if you remember how to specify the source and destination filename in the copy command. Remember that the DOS COPY command copies files to different diskettes, to files with different names (duplicating) and to other directories. The file copying process can be classified into 2 categories. The first involves the need to copy to or from the current directory and the second involves the need to copy between two directories other than the current directory.

Copy to and from the current directory

Since SHELL is the current directory, let's use the MENU.TXT file in it for the examples. First, make a duplicate of MENU.TXT in the TEST directory using the following command:

```
C:\SHELL>COPY MENU.TXT \TEST↵
         1 File(s) copied
C:\SHELL>
```

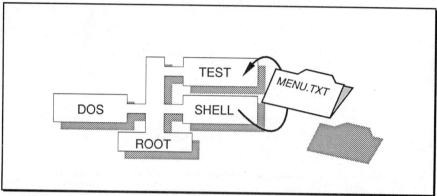

Figure 4-7. MENU.TXT is copied from the default directory SHELL to the TEST directory with the command COPY MENU.TXT \TEST.

The source file MENU.TXT is copied to the destination, which in this case is the TEST directory. The backslash before the destination name must be specified to indicate that TEST is a directory, not a file.

```
C:\SHELL>COPY MENU.TXT \TEST\MENU2.TXT↵
         1 File(s) copied
C:\SHELL>
```

This time, we have the same command and source file; the destination has changed, however. You know from the previous command that the TEST directory already has a file called MENU.TXT. Now, a second copy of the file exists with a different name. You can list the directory now by typing the following directory command:

```
C:\SHELL>DIR \TEST↵

 Volume in drive C has no label
 Directory of C:\TEST

.               <DIR>      4-15-87   12:30p
..              <DIR>      4-15-87   12:30p
MENU     TXT        57     4-15-87    1:20p
MENU2    TXT        57     4-15-87    1:21p
         4 File(s)   12369920 bytes free

C:\SHELL>
```

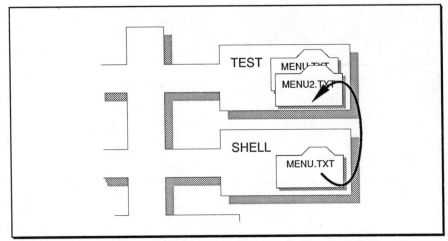

Figure 4-8. MENU.TXT is again copied to the TEST directory, but this time with a different name, using the command `COPY MENU.TXT \TEST\MENU2.TXT`. Note: SHELL is still the current directory so the path of the source file does not need to be specified.

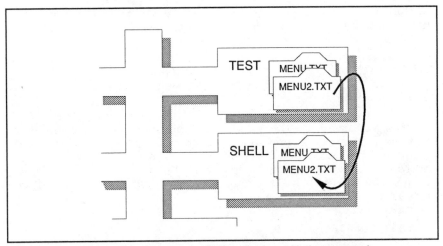

Figure 4-9. MENU2.TXT is copied to the SHELL directory with the command `COPY \TEST.MENU2.TXT`. The command only needs to specify the path and name of the source file. Since the destination is the current directory, it need not be specified.

Now, assume that you want to copy the file MENU2.TXT from TEST to your current directory, SHELL. The source filename should now be what the destination was in the last command since you need to specify where the source file is.

```
C:\SHELL>COPY \TEST\MENU2.TXT↵
          1 File(s) copied
C:\SHELL>
```

In this example, there was no need to specify a destination since it is the current directory and the file name is not being changed. The source file specifies the path to the TEST directory and the file to be copied in it.

Copying between two directories other than the current directory

For this next set of examples, you'll need to be in the ROOT directory so type the following:

```
C:\SHELL>CD \↵
C:\>
```

Occasionally, you'll need to copy files between two directories, neither of which are your current directory. Now that you're in the ROOT directory, try copying files between SHELL and TEST. In the example below, the file MENU2.TXT in the SHELL directory is copied to the TEST directory as MENU3.TXT. The complete path for both the source and the destination must be specified. As you can see by the length of this command, copying between directories can be tedious. Sometimes it is easier to move to either the source or destination directory before copying as described above since this will reduce the size of the command required to copy the files.

```
C:\>COPY \SHELL\MENU.TXT \TEST\MENU3.TXT↵
          1 File(s) copied

C:\>
```

Path Name Syntax

DOS keeps track of where things are on your system by remembering pathnames. A pathname is not much different from the directions you might give someone to get to your home; it tells DOS the exact location of a file or the directions to a directory. Because paths are used for both files and directories, some people find them confusing, but if you remember a few pathname features, you shouldn't have too much trouble.

Pathname Features:

The Path is the tag that DOS puts on all files to specify the directory they live in.

The first backslash encountered in a pathname always represents the ROOT directory. All other backslashes in the same command or filename are simply separators.

The last item in a pathname can be either a directory or a filename

---

Let's look at a few examples using the SHELL directory and the file MENU.TXT in SHELL. You don't need to type these, just look over the command syntax.

```
DIR  \
DIR  \SHELL
DIR  \SHELL\MENU.TXT
```

The first command asks for the directory listing of the ROOT directory, since the single backslash was specified. In the second command, the directory listing for the SHELL directory is requested. In this case, the backslash specifies that SHELL branches from the ROOT directory. In the third example, the file MENU.TXT in the SHELL directory is listed. This is a good example of how the backslash character is used first to specify that SHELL branches from the ROOT directory. The second use of the backslash simply separates the filename from the directory name SHELL.

All of the commands could be executed from any directory on the system since the full path for the desired action is specified in each.

Setting the Search Path

DOS attaches a path to every program or data file on your system, so that you must specify the path to get to that file when you want to use it, unless you are in the same directory. You can, however, specify a permanent **search path** that DOS will use when you request certain files, specifically DOS commands, programs and batch files. In the last chapter, you placed the command

PATH = \;\DOS;\SHELL in the AUTOEXEC.BAT startup batch file. This "search" path is what DOS will use every time you turn your system on and until you change it.

| SYNTAX |

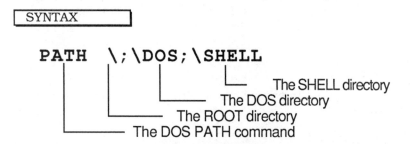

When you execute a command, DOS performs the following:

1. Fetches the command from the command line.
2. Check to see if it is an internal command. (Is it in memory?) If so, DOS checks for syntax errors and executes it if correct.
3. If the command is not internal, DOS looks on the disk drive in the following order, assuming the path shown above.

   A: DOS looks in the current directory for a command file matching the command.

   B: If not in the current directory, DOS references the path setting. In the setting above, DOS would first look in the ROOT (the backslash), then the DOS directory and then the SHELL directory. DOS stops searching when the command file is found or issues the message "Bad command or file not found."

You can add other directories to the PATH command in your AUTOEXEC.BAT file. For example, you could create a UTIL directory to hold public domain utilities. You would then add ";\UTIL" to the path as shown above using the EDLIN editor. You can even specify another drive as part of the path. When adding a new directory to the path, make sure to use a semicolon to separate each directory entry in the path.

One thing to remember is that DOS always searches the current directory first for a command or batch file before it searches through other directories. This feature can be used to advantage. For example, you can override commands in lower level directories like DOS and SHELL by creating batch files of the same name in the current directory. You could override the FORMAT.COM command by creating a FORMAT.BAT command that simply displays a message like "Sorry, you can't format from here." This will protect your system from accidental erasure if someone else is using it.

Displaying the Directory Structure

The DOS TREE command can be used to display the tree structure of your filing system. Try typing the following commands; I don't display the listings for lack of space.

```
C:\>TREE↵
```

To display the files in each directory, add the /F parameter to the command:

```
C:\>TREE /F↵
```

You can pipe the screen output into the MORE command to page the listing:

```
C:\>TREE /F | MORE↵
```

To print the listing, enter the following command. The printout can be the map of your system.

```
C:\>TREE /F > PRN↵
```

You can also use the CHKDSK command to display the directories and their files. The following command will list each subdirectory and the files they contain:

```
C:\>CHKDSK /V↵
```

Making a Subdirectory Appear as a Drive

You can trick DOS into thinking that one of your directories is a disk drive by using the SUBST command of DOS 3.1 and above. There are basically two reasons for doing this. First, some programs don't understand hierarchical filing structures although, these days, this is rare. Instead, they insist on reading and writing files to drive A or B only. With SUBST, you can rename one of your directories B and solve the problem. This situation rarely happens with modern software.

The second reason for using SUBST is to make long subdirectory path names easier to use. For example, \TEST\TEST2 could be renamed D or E. Then, when referring to a file in TEST2, like MENU.TXT, you can simply call it E:MENU.TXT. Don't substitute a path with a drive specifier that already exists, like A or C. This will lock out those drives until you remove the substitution. In addition, if you need to use letters above E, you will need to specify a LAST-DRIVE command in your CONFIG.SYS file. To increase your drive count, type:

LASTDRIVE = x

where **x** can be any drive letter up to Z.

The SUBST command takes the following form, where *d:* specifies the drive letter that you want to use in place of the subdirectory name, and *d:path* specifies the drive and path you want to nickname:

SUBST *d: d:path*

To call the TEST directory drive D, issue the following substitute command, and then issue the directory command to list your new drive D:

```
C:\>SUBST D: C:\TEST↵
C:\>DIR D:↵
    •
    •
    •
C:\>
```

The following command, with the /D option removes a substituted drive. The substituted drive to be removed is *d:*

SUBST *d:* /D

To see the current substitutions, type SUBST. Caution should be taken when using SUBST. The following commands should not be used as they rely on the normal subdirectory name, not the substituted name: ASSIGN, BACKUP, DISKCOMP, DISKCOPY, FDISK, FORMAT, JOIN, LABEL and RESTORE

Pathing Data Files

Just as you can call commands and batch files from other subdirectories by specifying their paths in the DOS PATH command, you can call data files and program overlays needed by your programs with a new command available in MS DOS 3.2 and PC DOS 3.3. APPEND locates data files outside of the current directory. The syntax of the APPEND command the first time it is loaded is:

`APPEND` `d:path[; [d:]path . . .]`

The path to be searched is specified in *d:path* with the semi-colon used to separate each additional path statements as required.

APPEND is an ideal command for users who would like to create a directory structure that stores program files in one subdirectory, and data or work files in another. This is ideal for systems that have several users. Each user can have their personal files stored in their own directories. All program files can be stored in single directories and accessed by those users.

If you enter a new APPEND command, the previous command is cancelled. You should take care the first time you run an application with APPEND. It is possible that your application will not write a file back out to the appended drive, but instead write it to the current drive. I would suggest that you experiment with the applications you'll be using before working with important files.

In the next chapter, I'll discuss a way of organizing your directory structure around your data files. The APPEND command can then be used to get at the data files from directories that hold program files.

Removing Directories

To remove a subdirectory you must first remove all files and branching subdirectories from it. In the examples above, you created the TEST directory. To remove it, enter the following commands:

```
C:\SHELL>DEL \TEST\*.*↵
C:\SHELL>RD \TEST↵
```

This removes all files in TEST and then removes the directory using the RD (Remove Directory) command. You should always be sure to backup to floppy any files that might be of value before deleting a directory.

Designing Your System

Now that you've worked with directory structures, you're ready to start thinking about the best way to design a structure for your own system. In the last chapter, you created the SHELL and DOS directories. You can leave these on your hard drive since they will be used to store various files created in the remaining chapters of this book. This chapter will help you determine the best directory structure to create for your particular needs, depending on the type of programs you use and the way you work.

There is one rule you should always keep in mind when designing your hard drive directory structure:

The way you work, not the programs you use, is the most important consideration when creating a directory structure for your hard drive.

The important point here is to not fall into the trap of designing your structure around the programs you use. Instead, consider the way you will be working with your computer. Many people work on what I will refer to as *projects*. Below is a list of various businesses and some projects they might work on. Each project consist of documents that have been created using several different types of applications, like a word processor, spreadsheet, graphics or accounting program.

- Construction firm: One of many construction projects.
- Legal Office: A single case.
- Accounting office: The accounting for one client or business.
- Your business: If you own more than one business, each would be considered a separate project or group of related work, appropriate for its own directory.

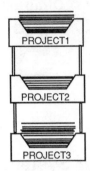

Since the files related to each project need to be kept together, it doesn't make sense to create the letters in the word processing directory and the spreadsheets in the spreadsheet directory. Instead, you could create a special directory to hold all files related to a particular project, whether the files are created by the word processor, spreadsheet or graphics program. Remember that you can work with programs from other directories by setting the correct DOS PATH. That means you can execute programs in other directories from your special projects directory.

When thinking about the way you work, you might relate it to the way you use the different rooms in your home. Typically, most houses are designed with a separate kitchen, dining room, recreation room and utility room. This is fine if you like to do one thing at a time, but if you're like me, you may want to exercise while listening to the stereo in your living room, or watch TV while eating. An alternative house design might place the kitchen, TV, workout equipment, stereo and living room couch in one big room, making everything conveniently accessible at the same time. A hard drive directory structure can be similarly designed to make all of its program accessible from a single directory.

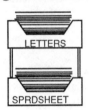

On the other hand, much of the work you do may be totally unrelated. In other words, your letter and document writing may have no relation to your use of a spreadsheet. In this case, you may simply prefer to write your letters in the word processing directory and create spreadsheets in the spreadsheet directory. This would be the simplest way to create your directory structure, but it causes problems when locating and backing up files, as you'll see in a minute.

After a while, you may notice that your word processing directory becomes cluttered with files. To help organize the directory, you could subdivide your word processing directory by creating separate subdirectories for business documents and personal documents. I will refer to directory structures designed around actual programs as **Application Oriented Directory Structures.** Those designed around your work habits into special project directories will be referred to as **Task Oriented Directory Structures.**

Design Scenarios

At this point, its a good idea to look at the number of ways people might go about installing applications and data directories on their hard drives and the advantages and disadvantages to each situations.

The Retail Store Manager

Bill manages a small retail store and uses his computer for simple letter writing and accounting. He rarely creates files in word processing or accounting that need to be grouped together in a special directory so he chooses to organize his hard drive into an applications oriented structure. Each application will be stored in a directory that branches from the ROOT directory, as can be seen in Figure 5-1. The files created by those applications are stored in the

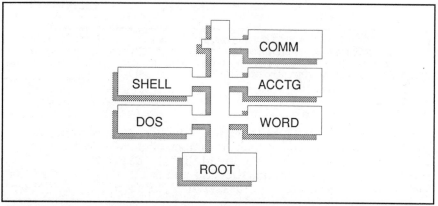

Figure 5-1. Bill, who manages a retail store uses the simplest of directory structures. The files he creates when working with each of his applications are stored in the directory for that application, instead of special data directories. This makes groups of files harder to organize and remove, but Bill assumes he won't be creating enough files for this to cause a problem.

the same directory. In addition, Bill must send his daily sales figures from the accounting program to the head office using a telephone communications program stored in the COMM directory. The file to be sent is created daily by the accounting program and Bill simply sends the file after completing his daily accounting task while still in the accounting directory. He can start the communications program from any directory since the COMM directory is specified in the PATH.

The Retail Store Owner

Jim owns several retail stores, one of which is managed by Bill, as described above. His computer is used to receive the incoming accounting files from each of his stores over the telephone lines. These are appended daily to his multiple-store accounting system. Jim also likes to use Lotus 1-2-3 to track sales figures in a spreadsheet format. The structure he has decided to use, shown in Figure 5-2, is very similar to that of Bill's system, with the addition of the subdirectories that branch from the LOTUS directory. This allows Jim to keep historical sales information for each store individually.

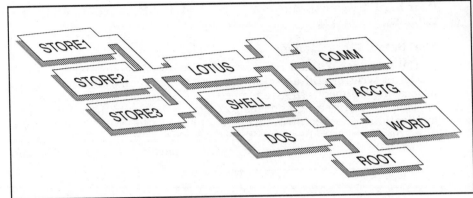

Figure 5-2. Jim, as the owner of 3 retail stores, uses Lotus 1-2-3 to track sales for each of his stores. The subdirectories branching from the LOTUS directory are used to store the worksheets for each. The data files for other applications are stored in the directories of those applications, such as the accounting directory.

The Typing Service

Mary owns a small typing service. She uses her computer to write letters and documents for a number of clients. When Mary first got her system home, she found that the dealer had set up a directory called DOS for the DOS files and another called WORD for her Microsoft Word program files. When she turned the computer

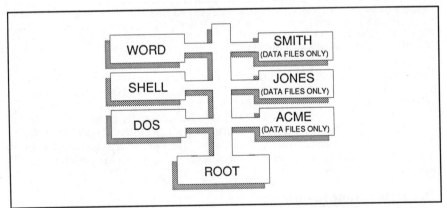

Figure 5-3. Mary's typing service uses a directory to work on and store files for each client.

on, the DOS prompt displayed a C prompt and a backslash, indicating that she was in the ROOT directory. Fortunately, the dealer had placed a PATH command in the AUTOEXEC.BAT file to tell DOS where to find the Microsoft Word program files.

Mary knew enough about directories and the PATH command to

know that she could run Word from any directory. In fact, if she started Word from her current directory, the ROOT, any files created would be stored in the ROOT unless she specified the exact directory to store the files from the program. She decided not to clutter the ROOT directory with a lot of files and considered moving to the WORD directory before starting her program, thus causing the program to store files in the WORD directory. After considering the fact that she would be working with several clients and would need to create files for each that should be kept separate from other clients, she decided to create the directory structure illustrated in Figure 5-3. Each client has their own directory and Word can be started from any of these directories because of the path setting. The program files for Word stay in the WORD directory and the files for each client are separate from others.

The Advertising Agency

John and Debbie use their computer for a number of tasks during a typical day. Their advertising agency works with new clients on a regular basis, but has two major accounts that are a constant source of work and income. The two major accounts have been assigned special directories (Figure 5-4) so that all files related to them can be grouped together. Other files of importance are stored in the directory of the application that creates them. Some of these files are actually forms that are used over and over again by both John and Debbie. A special TEMP directory has been created for work that is to be deleted on a regular basis. Simple notes and letters created with the word processor that do not need to be kept on the disk are written while the user is in the TEMP directory. At the end of each month, these files are cleared, thus helping to unclutter the disk. Using a TEMP directory in this way makes hard drive clean up a cinch.

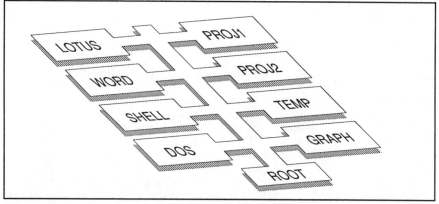

Figure 5-4. The directory structure for an advertising agency has two directories assigned to two special accounts. A TEMP directory is used to work on temporary files that are deleted from the system on a regular basis.

The Construction Company

Joe owns a small construction company that works on several projects at a time. New projects are continuously taken on as existing projects are completed. With each project, a number of files are created, including letters, proposals, estimates and tracking or accounting information. Joe has decided to use a task oriented directory structure (Figure 5-5) because he will need to add new directories as projects are accepted and remove old directories as projects are completed. Since whole groups of files need to be deleted occasionally, it is convenient to have these grouped into individual projects directories, making both backup and deletion of the files easy. This also makes it easy to backup the files to floppy disk for archive purposes before deletion. Joe simply copies the entire contents of the data directory to floppy disk. The applications programs are stored in their own individual directories and accessed from each of the project directories as needed.

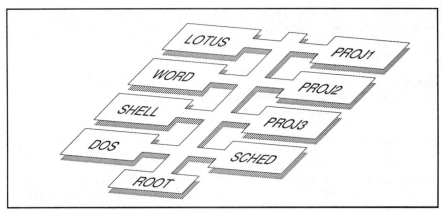

Figure 5-5. Joe's construction company uses a task oriented design. All work is done from one of the projects directories. Directories are added with new projects, and archived and deleted as projects are completed.

The Power User

Jack is a power user. He likes to collect programs, some of which he may never use, but he has them just in case he may run into a special need. Jack has managed to acquire several modem communications programs, graphics programs, word processors and spreadsheets, along with a number of games and educational programs for his kids. One of his sons likes to program using Pascal, but Jack likes to program with BASIC, so the LANGUAGE directory has several branching subdirectories. Almost half of his hard drive is filled with programs, But Jack is happy because his system is organized in a way that makes each application easy to get to and he never forgets what he has because each is displayed on a menu that he can choose from.

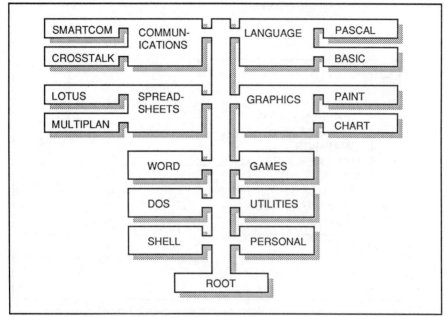

Figure 5-6. The power users directory structure. There are so many directories and subdirectories that the menus shown in Figure 5-7 are required to navigate through the structure.

Usually, when writing a letter or creating a graph, Jack works in the directory of the application. One directory called PERSONAL, however, is used to create documents that will be stored on the system permanently. That way, when he needs to refer back to a document created previously, he can look in the PERSONAL directory. Figure 5-6 displays the structure of Jack's directory. In addition, Figure 5-7 displays the main menu and some sample submenus that help Jack and his kids move around on the system. In the next few chapters, you'll see how menus are created.

The Multiple User System

Jill and Dave share an office and one computer. They both use a word processor and spreadsheet program, but each of them work on different tasks. There is a need for Jill to keep her files separate and distinct from Dave's. Figure 5-8 shows a directory structure that can help them do this. Branching from the ROOT directory are subdirectories for both Jill and Dave. This allows both to work with the programs, but in their own directories. Files will be kept separate and special batch files can be used to automatically place each user in their respective directories, depending on the application they choose.

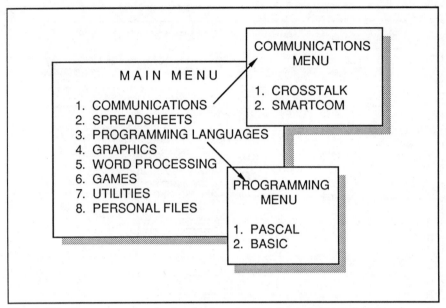

Figure 5-7. The menu system for the directory structure shown in Figure 5-6 has sub-menus for some of its selections. Menu development is covered in Chapter 6.

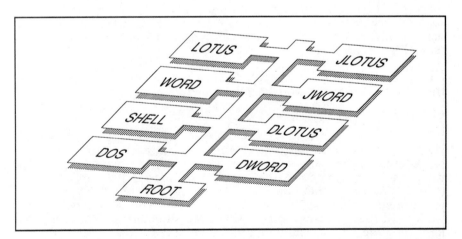

Figure 5-8. A multiple user directory structure. Each user has their own directory for each application they may use. A password system described in Chapter 8 can be used to place the user in the correct directory before starting an application so files they create are stored in their data directories and not those used by others.

Backup Considerations

Backing up your hard drive should be considered when designing a hard drive directory structure. Backup is discussed in detail
in Chapters 10 and 11, but I will briefly cover it here so you can see
the importance of planning your structure around a backup procedures. First, consider what needs to be backed up on your hard
drive. Since your applications programs are presumable tucked
away in a safe place on their original diskettes, you can always restore your programs from those if your hard drive goes down.
There's really no need to include the programs in your regular
backup routine since they would take up a lot of diskettes and time.
What you really need to back up are the data files and this is where
the task oriented directory structure is best. Since all of the data
files are stored in a single directory, backup becomes a simple
matter of backing up each of the data directories only. This
decreases the time and number of diskettes involved in a backup.

Because of the way the DOS BACKUP command works, it's also
better to have these special data directories branching from the
ROOT directory as shown in Figures 5-3, 5-5 and 5-7, rather than
from an applications directory, as shown in Figure 5-2. The hard-
est files to back up are those mixed with program files in applications directories, so structures like Figures 5-1, 5-2 and 5-6 are
not recommended when backup procedures are taken into
consideration. Figure 5-9 shows a directory structure designed especially for ease of backup. It is similar to the multiple user system
of Figure 5-8. With this structure, a single backup command can be
used to backup the DATA directory and each of the subdirectories
that branch from it. Once again, Chapters 10 and 11 cover this
subject in more detail.

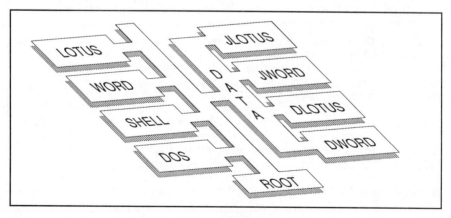

Figure 5-9. This directory structure, similar to Figure 5-8, is designed to make backups
easy. When backing up, the DATA directory is specified. The four subdirectories that branch
from it are then automatically backed up.

Making the Decision

The best thing you can do at this point is try to plan how you or other people will be using the hard file system. Careful planning now can save you from a lot of headaches later. If you are using just a few applications, you'll probably have little trouble is deciding on a structure and then using that structure once it's in place. If your directory structure will be large, however, you'll want to carefully plan everything from the directory names to the number of subdirectory levels. If you know that your system and needs will be expanding, be sure to take this into consideration as you put together the foundation for the future.

If your system will be large and hold a lot of files, try to keep things as simple as possible. The structure shown in Figure 5-6 is more complicated than most users will need. It contains third level subdirectories that tend to increase confusion and slow down file access. A typical structure for large systems consists of creating directories for each application that branch from the ROOT, avoiding third level directories. As discussed previously, you may want to store all of your data files in separate directories to make backup easier.

Security should be a consideration when designing a structure. This can be a real problem if several people use the same system. You should determine whether all users are experienced or whether they are novices. Then, plan your system to keep novice users locked into their own subdirectories. This is covered in Chapter 8. You may want to place private files in a subdirectory that can be locked out from other users through software password schemes, also covered in Chapter 8. Keep in mind that a complicated structure without menus and password systems will increase the chances that novice or unauthorized users could accidentally erase or copy over valuable files.

By far, the biggest decision involves whether more than one user will be using the system and whether you want to separate data files from program files. If you separate data files, do you want to subdivide them further into types, such as personal and business files? In making your decision, you should consider how long files will remain on the hard drive before you remove them. How "clean" can you keep your system and do you have the time to keep it that way? If not, a directory structures that uses directories specifically for data files and subdivides those into distinct groups will make it easier to clean up your hard drive on a regular basis. It also helps to reduce the chances of duplicate file names since the more data directories you have, the less files will be stored in each directory.

Keep in mind that some programs will not operate at all with data files stored in other directories. This will depend on the programs you are using. Old version of WordStar would only let you work with files in the program directory. DOS has several commands, however, that trick DOS into working with other drives or subdirectories. These are the ASSIGN, SUBST and APPEND commands. Caution should always be taken when using these commands, however, since they alter the normal performance of DOS.

Creating the Directory Structure

Once you have decided on a directory structure, you can install it on your hard disk. The first step is to create the entire directory structure before copying the software to the system. This helps the system run a little more efficiently by placing the directory information DOS needs to locate files closer to the outer tracks of your hard drive, rather than in the middle of a lot of program and data files. Chapter 13 discusses various topics on improving hard disk access in more detail.

As an example, I'll illustrate how the multiple user directory structure shown in Figure 5-9 is created. If you've decided to create a structure similar to this, you can follow along, substituting the names of the directories you've decided to use. First, make sure you're in the ROOT directory by typing:

```
C:\SHELL>CD \↵
```

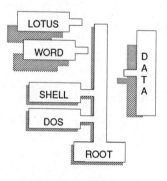

If you've been following along with the examples in the previous chapters, you already have a DOS and SHELL directory. To add the new LOTUS, WORD and DATA directories, execute the MD (Make Directory) commands below. The illustrations on this page and the next page show how the new directories are attached to the ROOT directory. Remember, you can substitute your own directory names in place of the ones shown here.

```
C:\>MD LOTUS↵
C:\>MD WORD↵
C:\>MD DATA↵
C:\>
```

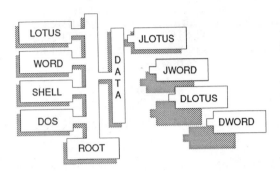

After these ROOT level directories are created, you can move up into the DATA directory and create the branching LOTUS and WORD directories for each user. Note that the DATA directory serves only as a branch point from the ROOT for the four user directories. It will not be used for file storage. Enter the following command to first move to the DATA directory and then create the four user subdirectories.

```
C:\>CD DATA↵
C:\DATA>MD JLOTUS↵
C:\DATA>MD JWORD↵
C:\DATA>MD DLOTUS↵
C:\DATA>MD DWORD↵
C:\DATA>
```

Installing Software

After you have created the tree structure, you can begin copying your program files to the hard drive or you can wait to complete the whole menu system by performing the steps in the next two chapters. Because of a problem in DOS called *file fragmentation*, you will want to copy all of your program files to the hard drive before you actually begin creating any data files. File fragmentation will be discussed in Chapter 13, but you should know that it affects the ability of your drive to read and write files efficiently. It's not that your drive gets older or wears down. The problem is a natural occurrence of trying to store variable sized files on a storage media that can be both written to and erased. The importance of getting *program* files on first is to reserve a permanent place for them on the drive so they do not affect the fragmentation problem.

Consider for a minute what happens when you erase a two page file from the hard drive. A "hole" is made available for a new file. Now consider what happens when you try to store a 4 page document to the hard drive. The first two pages are stored in the hole made available by the erased file and DOS fragments the file by placing the remaining two pages in the next available area somewhere else on the disk. Because DOS has to move the read/write heads to two different locations on the disk, write time and read time increase. Over time, more and more files are erased and more files are fragmented. The fragmentation problem increases slowly and you may not be aware of it until one day your drive operates so slow that you must take steps to alleviate the problem. Chapter 10 discusses how this is done. Basically, the hard drive is *completely backed up*. It is then formatted (erased) and the files are restored. When the files are restored, they are copied to the drive as contiguous files (files that can be read sequentially).

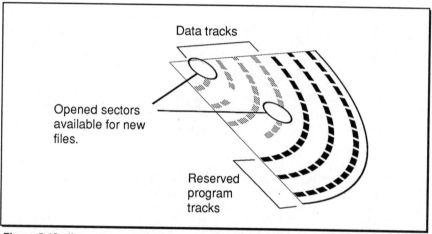

Figure 5-10. If you copy your permanent, non-alterable program, menu and batch files to the hard drive first, they will be placed in the outer tracks of the drive. The rest of the drive is then available for data files. This will isolate file fragmentation problems to the data area.

One way to help decrease the natural fragmentation of the drive is to place files that are never altered or erased together on a section of the disk that is separate from the area where data files are stored. This will confine files that fragment like data files to one area of the drive. Program files like your word processor or spreadsheet program fall into the category of "first-on" files. In other words, you should copy them to the hard drive before creating or copying any data files. The batch files and menus of your directory structure also fall into the first-on category, so you may want to continue reading the next two chapters before creating your first data files.

Maybe now you can see why it is important to build a task oriented directory structure that has special directories for data files. When you want to un-fragment your disk, all of your data files will be on a set of backup diskettes separate from program files. This will allow you to restore the data files after restoring all of the first-on files.

Pathing to Program Files

The next step is to set the PATH in your AUTOEXEC.BAT file to point to the directories that contain program files. You will then be able to run your programs from the data directories. You can use EDLIN to alter the files. Since AUTOEXEC.BAT is in the ROOT directory, its best to first move to that directory before editing. Type the following commands to get to the ROOT and edit the file:

```
C:\DATA>CD \↵
C:\>EDLIN AUTOEXEC.BAT↵
End of input file
*
```

For the example, you'll want to locate the line in the batch file that contains the PATH command, and change it to read as follows:

```
PATH = \;\DOS;\SHELL;\LOTUS;\WORD
```

First, type **L** (List) to list the file. Locate the line number with the PATH command and type that number at the EDLIN prompt. Type the command as shown above on the blank line under the existing command and press Return when done. This will replace the old command. You can refer back to Chapter 3 for a complete description of the PATH command. This new command makes the ROOT, DOS, SHELL, LOTUS and WORD directories available from other directories. Next, type **e** to end edit and write the changes to disk. When you reboot your system, the command will be executed and DOS will know where to look for the program files.

Now that DOS knows where the program files are located, you can move to the proper data directory and use the program. To move to the JWORD directory, you would type the following commands, the first moving you to the proper directory and the second executing the Microsoft Word program:

```
C:\>CD \DATA\JWORD↵
C:\DATA\JILLWORD>WORD↵
```

In the next few chapters, you'll see how to automate this process further. There is really no need to type the long CD command as shown above. Instead, you can create menus with selection numbers that make the whole process as easy as pressing two keys.

Menus and Help Screens

In the last chapter you created the directory structure for your programs and data files. In the next chapter, you'll be creating batch files that automate your activities on the hard drive. This intermediate chapter covers menus. Menus can describe in detail the programs that run on your system or the tasks that are performed. They can become the "front end" to your directory structure. In addition, they can display help information, reminders or instructions to both you or novice users who might be working at your system.

Note: Users of IBM PC DOS version 4 may prefer to use the DOSSHELL menu system instead of the techniques described here. Refer to Appendix E for more information.

Menus are the main component of "turnkey systems." Combined with the batch files discussed in the next chapter and built around your directory structure, the turnkey system can make your computer easier to use for both you and novice or temporary users. Several features and benefits are listed below:

- It's easy to start a task or program on a turnkey system. Batch files contain the normal start-up commands.
- A turnkey system is easy for novice users to work with. Your secretary or assistant doesn't need to know a lot of DOS commands or learn special instructions to work with your computer.

- Menu selections ensure that the same commands are executed every time. You won't find yourself entering data in the
  wrong file or directory because you typed in the wrong DOS
  command. The menu selection batch files perform the same
  task every time without a hitch.

Menus aren't really essential. Once you've designed and built a
directory structure that fits your present and future needs, you can
begin using your system without them. Menus, however, provide a
convenient way for you to make your system more accessible to
both you and other users. If you have a lot of applications, menus
can serve as handy reminders for those applications. In the next
chapter, you will create batch files that "launch" various applications. You can place the names of these batch files on your menus
as reminders.

Referring back to the directory structure in Figure 5-6, you can
see why menus would help the novice user find their way around
such a complicated directory structure. Often, making a choice on
one menu may cause a second menu to appear with more selections. This is one feature you can use to organize your programs
into groups, making them easier to use. Menus are also useful if you
don't like to work at the DOS level. Pressing one key to make a
menu selections is much easier than typing long DOS commands to
perform the same task.

You may be wondering just how making a selection on a menu
causes your computer to start an application or perform a particular
task. The most important aspect of creating any menu system is to
automate each selection on the menu with a batch file, covered in
the next chapter. If you recall from Chapter 2, a batch file is a set
of DOS commands that execute when you type the name of the
batch file on the command line. The trick to using batch files with
menus is to name each of your batch files after the selections on the
menu. For example 1.BAT is the batch file that contains the commands for selection 1 on a menu. After you decide what choices
you will have on your menu, you will number them in order and
then create the batch file for each.

Front End or Turnkey Menu Examples

There are several different types of menus you can create on
your system, but by far the most important and useful are the
menus you will create for your directory structure and applications
programs. In the next section, you will see how other types of
menus are used.

Your use of menus will depend on the directory structure you
have decided to create. Let's refer back to the examples in the

previous chapter to see what type of menus can be created. In the first example, Bill is the manager of a retail store who has a hard drive directory structure as shown in Figure 5-1. He has an accounting program, a word processing program and a communications programs that performs the single task of transferring his daily sales information to a home office computer. When he starts his system each day, the following menu appears:

```
MAIN MENU

1. ACCOUNTING
2. WORD PROCESSING
3. SEND DAILY SALES FIGURES
```

When Bill decides to write a letter, he simply presses the 2 key and Return. This starts his word processing program. Bill's boss uses a similar menu for his system, with the addition of the selections for working on each stores Lotus sales files. These are selections 4 through 6 on the menu for Jim's system shown below.

```
MAIN MENU

1. ACCOUNTING
2. WORD PROCESSING
3. RECEIVE DAILY SALES FILES
4. STORE 1 SALES FIGURES
5. STORE 2 SALES FIGURES
6. STORE 3 SALES FIGURES
```

The menu for Mary's Typing Service is shown next. The directory structure for this menu is illustrated in Figure 5-3. Notice how the menu is task oriented. When Mary wants to work with the files for Smith, she presses 1. In addition, Microsoft Word can be accessed from the menu when she wants to write personal letters or documents other than those for her special clients.

```
MARY'S TYPING SERVICE

1. SMITH ACCOUNTS
2. JONES ACCOUNTS
3. ACME ACCOUNTS
4. MICROSOFT WORD
```

Other Types of Menus

Not all menus are the same or are used for the same task. The menus described above are meant to be part of a "front end" system that helps you or other users navigate through your system. There are several other categories of menus, however, that you may want to consider placing on your system. These are utility menus, file menus, help menus, and instruction menus. Where they are stored, however, is important to their operation.

Most of the menus for a front end system designed around your directory structure are stored in the SHELL directory. The menus described next, however, are designed to be placed directly in the directory that they serve. Each category of menus has the same filename, no matter what directory they are stored in and they are all displayed to the screen by a common batch file that is stored in the SHELL directory. For example, a file called HELP.TXT can be placed in each directory on your system. You can then create a single batch file in the SHELL directory called HELP.BAT to display the help files in the current directory. In the next chapter, you'll be creating the batch files that display the special groups of menus discussed here.

File Menus

A file menu is similar to the utility menu described above, except that it is used to describe the data files created by various applications programs. You might want to keep track of the files created for a particular project. If these files are grouped into a special data directory all their own, then the file menu would also be placed in that directory. As new files are created, whether by a word processor, spreadsheets or graphics program, you can add their description to the file menu. The description might indicate the creation date, typist, destination of the printed file or just about any other important information you will need to track the progress of both the file and the complete project. A batch file called FILES.BAT (stored in the SHELL directory) can then be used to display these file menus when you are in the directory that holds them. This batch file is created in the next chapter.

Utility Menus

A utility menu can be created to list the names and functions of various programs or utilities you may add to your system. You may acquire quite a few of these small programs as you use your system and soon forget how to start them or what some of them may be used for. To help you remember, you can create a menu called UTILS.TXT that is displayed with a batch file called UTILS.BAT. The batch file, described in the next chapter displays the menu on the screen, one page at a time. Whenever you purchase new utilities, you can use the EDLIN editor to update the UTILS.TXT file with the new information. A sample utilities menu is shown below.

```
        P U B L I C    D O M A I N    U T I L I T I E S

BROWSE      Browse a disk directory
BUFF159     Increase type-ahead buffer to 159 keys
CLCK        Displays time in upper right
COVER       Create disk cover document
DISKRTN     Menu driven disk utilities
EQUIP       Displays system hardware configuration
FOGFIN      Evaluates the readability of a document
FREE        Displays remaining space on hard disk
INDEX       Disk indexing program
L           File listing program
```

Help Menus

Help menus can be beneficial to both you and novice users who might be using your system. A help menu can be used to display the syntax of commonly used DOS commands or can be used in each of your directories to describe how to use various commands in an application specific to your system or needs. A DOS syntax help menu is described later in this chapter. Because most help menus are displayed using a common batch file (HELP.BAT), they are named HELP.MNU for each directory where they are stored.

Instruction Menus

Instruction menus can be used to display specific instructions to a novice or temporary user. For example, you might create an instruction menu that describes how to enter information into your data base for a part time person who is assigned to data entry. This menu would appear on the screen temporarily, when they make a selection on the turnkey menu described earlier. The user can choose to read the menu, or bypass it to go directly into their task.

Creating Menus

The "look" of your menus is not really an important issue when organizing your system, as long as they are legible. There is, however, a very simple method to make all of your menus appear professional. I will cover this here since it doesn't add a lot of extra work to the process of creating the menu system. You may have noticed that most of the menus shown in the book are surrounded by a box or menu border. You can create the same borders around your on-screen menus by using special graphics characters that are built into the character set of most DOS computers. The graphics characters for building menus consists of L shaped brackets to make the corners of the borders, and bars for making the tops and sides of the borders. These characters are available in both single and double line styles on IBM systems and many other compatible computers. The double line styles can be seen in Figure 6-1.

By the way: The file creation and editing techniques you learn here can be used to create many different type of files. You can use the graphics characters to create the menu borders shown here, as well as notes, letters and graphics displays to fit other needs.

Building a menu with these characters can involve a procedure of typing them one at a time to slowly build the menu. You'll be making use of a special trick available from EDLIN to make the whole process a snap, however. In addition, once you create your first menu box, you'll be able to make copies of it for creating other menus later. In other words, this first menu box will be used as a master file from which all other menu borders will be created.

Figure 6-1 lists the graphics character set available on IBM and compatible computer systems. Next to each character is what is known as its ASCII code. ASCII (pronounced "as-key") is an acronym for a national organization that attempts to standardize computer hardware and software features between many different manufacturers. Every character you type into your computer is coded with a number and it is these numbers that are referred to as the ASCII code. A file stored in ASCII form may be read by many different type of computers. For now, all you need to know is that the graphics characters below must be typed in using the ASCII codes since they are not a character on the keys of your keyboard, like the letters A or J. Your DOS manual or BASIC manual may have a complete list of ASCII codes for DOS systems. For now, the codes shown in Figure 6-1 will be sufficient to create your menus.

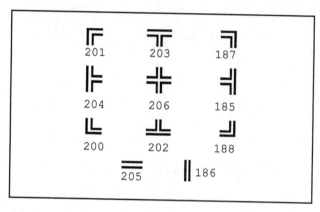

Figure 6-1. The graphics character set used to create menus and help screens on DOS computers. The numbers next to each character are the ASCII codes you type on the keyboard using a special key sequence to display them, as described in the text.

You can display any of these characters, even though they are not keys on the keyboard, by using a special key sequence. This involves holding down the **Alt** key while typing in the ASCII code on the numeric keypad. You cannot use the number keys along the top of the keyboard. When you let up on the Alt key, the character will be displayed. Try this now. At the DOS prompt, type *Alt-201*. Hold down the Alt key while typing 201 on the numeric keypad. Let up on the Alt key only after typing the three numbers. The left double-line corner bracket will be displayed. Next, type *Alt-205* several times. As you can see, the top border of a box is appearing. Typing *Alt-187* will display the right corner bracket.

Remember: When you see the alternate key sequence (Alt-201, for example), you should hold down the Alt key while typing 201 on the numeric keypad, not the numbers along the top of your keyboard.

Creating a border that would fill most of your screen using this one-character-at-a-time method is time consuming, so I will introduce you to a special trick using EDLIN that makes this process easier. The first thing to do is create a "dummy" border file using a character on the keyboard (like the asterisk) in place of the keys that requires an Alt-key sequence. Later, you can use EDLIN's search and replace feature to turn all of the asterisk characters into the appropriate graphics characters, as listed in Figure 6-1.

Figure 6-2 shows roughly what the dummy menu will look like when you type it on your screen. It's actually easier to enter the corner and sidebar graphics characters in the dummy menu since there are only one 1 or 2 or each. Later, in EDLIN, you'll be able to convert the asterisks to double line top bars using the EDLIN replace command. The EDLIN line duplication command can then be used to duplicate the middle line (the one with double line side bars) in order to increase the height of the box up to 22 lines.

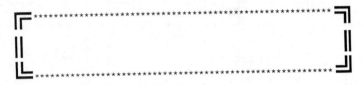

Figure 6-2. The initial "dummy" file used to create menu borders. This is what you will create on the screen before going into EDLIN.

To get started, you'll first need to be in the SHELL directory. Remember, SHELL is the directory that holds files used in your menu system. After getting into SHELL, you can type the following COPY command to begin creating the dummy menu on the screen:

```
C:\>CD \SHELL↵
C:\SHELL>COPY CON BORDER.MNU↵
```

When you press Return, the cursor will jump down to the next blank line. Press Return twice to insert two blank lines, then type in 10 spaces with the space bar and press Alt-201. The upper left corner character will appear.

```
C:\>CD SHELL↵
C:\SHELL>COPY CON BORDER.MNU↵
    ↵
    ↵
---------►  ╔
```
Type 10 spaces here.   ╲ *Type Alt-201 to display this character.*

Next, type in 58 asterisk characters across the screen and at the end, type Alt-187 to display the right corner bracket. At this point, the top of the menu border is done and you can press Return.

Type 58 asterisks

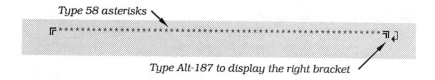

Type Alt-187 to display the right bracket

On the next line, type over 10 spaces with the space bar. Then, type Alt-186 to display the left side-bar bracket. Press the space bar 58 times until directly under the right corner bracket created on the first line and press Alt-186 again to get the right side-bar. This is the line you can duplicate to increase the height of the menu.

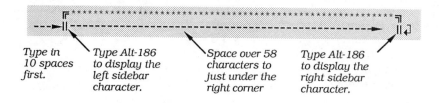

*Type in
10 spaces
first.*

*Type Alt-186
to display the
left sidebar
character.*

*Space over 58
characters to
just under the
right corner*

*Type Alt-186
to display the
right sidebar
character.*

To make the bottom menu border, space over 10 blank spaces, type Alt-200 (the lower left corner), type 58 asterisk characters, then type Alt-188 for the right corner bracket.

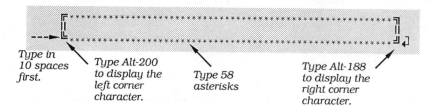

*Type in
10 spaces
first.*

*Type Alt-200
to display the
left corner
character.*

*Type 58
asterisks*

*Type Alt-188
to display the
right corner
character.*

On the next line, press the F6 key (or Ctrl-Z) and the Return key to write the file to disk.

The next step is to use EDLIN to alter the dummy menu, completing the borders around it with the correct graphics characters. Get into EDLIN to edit the file by typing the command below. Once in EDLIN, you will see the message "End of input file" and the EDLIN asterisk prompt. Type L to list the file.

```
C:\SHELL>EDLIN BORDER.MNU ↵
End of input file
*L ↵
    1:*
    2:
    3: ╓***************************************************╖
    4: ║                                                   ║
    5: ╙***************************************************╜
*
```

The first thing to do is replace the asterisk characters with the top-border graphics character (#205) using the EDLIN replace command. When using replace, you must first specify the range of lines for the replacements. Immediately after the line numbers, type R for Replace. Immediately after that, type the character to be replaced (the asterisk), followed by F6 (or Ctrl-Z) and the new character (type Alt-205):

```
*1,5,R*<F6><Alt-205> ↵
```

EDLIN goes through an interesting display as it replaces each asterisk with the specified graphics character. Now all you have to do is expand the height of the box. This is easily done with the EDLIN Copy command. The next command duplicates line 4 ten times by copying it into lines 5 through 15, which it automatically creates as part of the process:

```
*4,4,5,15C ↵
```

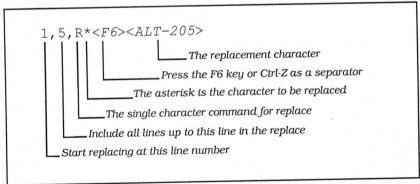

```
  1,5,R*<F6><ALT-205>
  │  │ ││ │  │     └─── The replacement character
  │  │ ││ │  └─────── Press the F6 key or Ctrl-Z as a separator
  │  │ ││ └───────── The asterisk is the character to be replaced
  │  │ │└─────────── The single character command for replace
  │  │ └──────────── Include all lines up to this line in the replace
  │  └────────────── Start replacing at this line number
```

Figure 6-3. The EDLIN Replace command, used to change the asterisks in the dummy menu to the correct graphics characters.

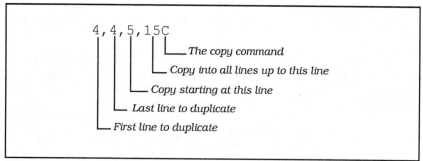

Figure 6-4. The EDLIN Copy command, used to duplicate the side border line, thus increasing the height of the menu frame.

Type **e** to end edit and write the file to disk. When the DOS prompt reappears, you can view your new file by first clearing the screen and using the DOS TYPE command to display the file:

```
C:\SHELL>CLS↵
C:\SHELL>TYPE BORDER.MNU↵
```

If you did everything correctly, you should have a professional looking menu border displayed on your screen. It can be used as a standard menu frame to create other menus, help screens, directory title screens and so on. When you need a border for a menu, its easy to make a copy of BORDER.MNU using the DOS COPY command. Make a copy now for later use by typing the next command.

```
C:\SHELL>COPY BORDER.MNU MENU.TXT↵
```

By the way, if you are wondering why COPY CON was used to create an initial file and then EDLIN was used to edit it, you should note that EDLIN tends to word wrap all lines over 70 characters wide, which leads to a confusing display. COPY CON lets you create the initial copy of the menu directly on a full, blank screen. This helps you judge the position and centering of each line better than if working in EDLIN. If you ever need to create a different type of menu border other than the one made here, or if you need to use the graphics characters to design another type of on-screen graphics, you can follow the same procedures documented here.

Menu Titles

A blank menu isn't of much use. You'll need to add the text for each of your menu selections, once you have decided what your menu choices will be. To add titles and selections to the menu, start EDLIN once again by typing the command:

```
C:\SHELL>EDLIN MENU.TXT↵
```

At the EDLIN prompt, type 6. This will display the sixth line of the menu file for editing, which is 3 lines down from the top border. Note that two lines are displayed. The top line shows the existing line; the bottom line is where you will make changes to the line. The graphics character for the left side of the menu border is displayed 10 spaces from the beginning of the line. Before you begin editing, you'll need to become a little more familiar with the way EDLIN works.

EDLIN Line Editing Features

- To edit a line, type its line number on the EDLIN asterisk prompt.
- Two lines will be displayed. The top line is the line as it currently is. The bottom line is used to make changes.
- The top line acts as a *template* for editing. You can copy characters from it to the lower line, or type new character, insert additional characters, or delete characters.
- Pressing either the F1 key or the right arrow will copy letters from the top line to the bottom line.
- If you want to type a different character in place of one in the upper template, simply type it to copy over the old character. You can use the Insert key to add additional characters, and then resume copying from the template where you left off. You can also use the Del key to remove characters from the upper template.
- Once you've made the appropriate changes, you can press the F3 key to copy any remaining characters in the upper template out to the end of the line.
- Press the Return key to make the changes or press Ctrl-Break to start over or cancel the changes.

In order to make changes to line 6 of MENU.TXT, you'll first need to copy characters from the upper template past the graphics character for the menu border using the F1 key or right arrow key. Then type the menu title, centering as close a possible. Last, you press the F3 key to copy the remainder of the template to the lower line. The remainder of the template includes the right menu border character. Here are the steps in detail:

1. Type 6 at the EDLIN prompt.
2. Press the F1 or right arrow key 32 times. Notice that the right menu border is copied down in position 10.
3. Type "M A I N M E N U" at position 20.
4. Press the F3 key to copy the remainder of the line out, which includes the right menu border. Press the Return key to accept the changes.

Its easy to calculate where to begin typing a title that you want to center in a menu. There are a total of 80 characters across on a normal screen. Ten of these are used on the left and right side of the menu to help center it on the screen. An additional 2 are used by the left and right border characters. That leaves 58 spaces available inside the menu itself. The title is made up of 16 characters, which leaves 42. Dividing this number in half for spacing on the left and right of the title gives 21 characters. So the title begins 21 characters from the right of the left menu border, or 32 characters from the extreme left of the screen, adding back the 10 spaces and the graphics character.

Adding Menu Selections

At this point, you can add other lines of text to your menu depending on what your system needs are. Referring to the last chapter, you can add selections for each application you have, like Lotus 1-2-3 and Microsoft Word, or you can add selections for groups of software, like Business Software and Personal Software. Remember that each selection on the menu should be preceded by either a number or letter, or even a word. These selection choices will be the names of batch files that automate your menu, as discussed in the next chapter. Before completing the rest of your menu, you may want to read through Chapter 7 for more information.

Submenus

Your main menu can have selections that call other menus. Where you place these other menus is the topic of this section. Assume that your main menu has a selection called UTILITIES. This selection executes a batch file that displays a menu called UTILS.TXT in the UTILITY directory. Now assume that you have a selection called BUSINESS SOFTWARE on the main menu. This

batch files displays a file called MENU.TXT. Since this is the name
of the main menu in the SHELL directory, the menu for the business software selection will need to be stored in another directory,
say BUSINESS. The main menu batch file for BUSINESS
SOFTWARE would then transfer the user to the BUSINESS directory and display the MENU.TXT file there. Figure 5-6 shows a directory structure that might use submenus. There are four directories
that serve special applications, such as communications or spreadsheets. These directories have several branching subdirectories
that hold related software packages. The main menu and submenus
are shown in Figure 5-6. Each submenu would be stored in the appropriate directory.

Automating Your System

You are here because you've built the directory system and created the menus to make it easier to use. The last step is the most important: automating your menu system with batch files. Recall from Chapter 2 that a batch file is a collection of DOS commands that are executed when you type the batch file name on the DOS command line. The file AUTOEXEC.BAT you created in the ROOT directory is a special batch file that is automatically executed by DOS when you start your system. It is the only batch file that does this. All other batch files must be executed by the user. You can, however, execute AUTOEXEC.BAT just as you would any other batch file by typing its name on the DOS command line.

With batch files, you don't need to remember long commands, and excessive typing and mistakes are eliminated. Consider the two commands you would type in order to start the Lotus 1-2-3 spreadsheet program stored in a directory called LOTUS:

```
CD \LOTUS↵
LOTUS↵
```

The first command changes to the LOTUS directory, assuming it branches from the ROOT directory. The next command starts Lotus 1-2-3. That's a total of 16 keystrokes. In addition, when you exit Lotus, you would need to type another command to move back down to the ROOT or some other directory. It doesn't seem like a lot of typing until you consider that all of these keystrokes can be placed in a batch file that can be executed with as few as 2 keystrokes if you placed the command in a batch file called L.BAT. (You would type "L" and press Return).

Batch files of this type are so useful that you can create and use them even if you are creating the menuing system. After going over the batch file rules, you'll get a chance to create two useful batch files for "launching" programs.

Batch File Rules

The rules for creating batch files are few and simple. First, a batch file always has an extension of BAT. This is how DOS knows it is a batch file. You can use EDLIN or COPY CON to create batch files. A word processor like Microsoft Word or WordPerfect can also be used to create the files, but make sure you save it as an *unformatted* text file. That means the file is saved using alphanumeric characters without special formatting for bold, underline and other features that word processors tend to add.

Remember: The AUTOEXEC.BAT file is designated by DOS as the automatic startup file. DOS looks for this file when you start your system and runs the commands in it. You can however, type "AUTOEXEC" and run it at any time, just like other batch files.

When choosing a filename for your batch file, make sure not to use the name of a DOS command. DOS always attempts to execute DOS commands before batch files. If your batch file has a similar name, it will never get executed since DOS will keep attempting to execute the DOS command instead. DOS will look for batch files in other directories if you specify the directory in your PATH command.

To execute any batch file, simply type its name on the DOS command line. You don't need to type the "BAT" extension. Each line in the file is interpreted, one at a time, as if you were at the keyboard typing in DOS commands. Therefore, each line in your batch file must be a valid DOS command. In most cases, only one command can be placed on a line.

Batch files have their own small set of subcommands you can use to enhance the performance of your batch files. Typically, only a few are used on a regular basis. The most used commands are listed below:

- **CLS**: Clears the screen. Its a good idea to use this command before displaying a menu.
- **ECHO OFF**: Placing this command on a batch file line will allow your batch file to run "invisibly." Normally, commands executed in a batch file cause screen clutter. ECHO OFF keeps the screen clear.

- **GOTO**: You can cause a batch file to execute commands over again or jump to another part of the batch file depending on the users input by using the GOTO command.
- **IF**: You can cause your batch file to execute certain commands only IF a condition is true. For example, you can cause a file to be erased, only if the user has made a backup. This is an advanced command not covered in this chapter.
- **PAUSE**: Causes your batch file to temporarily stop, until the user presses a key. This gives the user a chance to insert diskettes or perform some other task before continuing.

Batch File Types

Batch files can be grouped into several types that differ according to how they are used by your system. These types are described briefly below and in more detail in the remaining part of this chapter.

- **Application Batch Files**. Used to start a particular program, these batch files usually take on the name of that program. They may or may not be associated with a menu system. The two commands at the beginning of this chapter used to start Lotus are typical commands you might find in an application batch file. The main purpose is to move a user to a directory and start a program with as few keystrokes as possible.

- **Menu Selection Batch Files**. Menu selection batch files come in two types:
  - *Numbered Batch Files*: Written for menus that use numbers. A menu with three selections would need batch files 1.BAT, 2.BAT and 3.BAT.
  - *Mnemonic Batch Files*: Similar to numbered batch files except that the filename is designed to be easier to remember. This makes it easy to execute the batch file if the menu is not on the screen. For example, the batch file name to execute a phone list management routine could be P.BAT for Phone or T.BAT for Telephone.

- **Directory Sensitive Batch Files**. These are often standardized batch files used to display common menus throughout your system. Typically, there is one copy of the batch file in the SHELL directory, rather than multiple copies in each directory. Some examples of this type of file are:
  - HELP.BAT: Displays a help file for the current directory.
  - MENU.BAT: Display the menu for the current directory.
  - MM.BAT: Moves the user to the SHELL directory and dis-

plays the Main Menu.

- DOS.BAT: Displays a menu of DOS command syntax.
- UTILS.BAT: Displays a menu of utility programs.
- FILES.BAT: Displays the files menu.

- **DOS Command Batch Files.** These batch files simply contain DOS commands that are either too long to type manually or too complicated to remember. Any DOS command that you type on a regular basis can be placed in a batch file and executed with as little as two keystrokes.

Application Batch Files

The application batch file is used to make access to your programs easier. Using names that are similar to the programs they start, you can usually remember them without building a menu system. The examples in this section are excellent examples of how you can make access to your programs or applications a snap. I'll be using the directory structure shown in Figure 5-9 for the examples. Its structure will fit a wide variety of needs so you can alter the files I create here to fit your own needs. Before creating the files, there is one topic that needs to be covered:

Changing Directories from Inside Your Program

An important thing to find out about any of your programs is whether they allow you to specify which directory you want to use for file storage and retrieval *once you're in the program*. Early on in the life of DOS and many of the programs written for it, you had to first go to the directory you wanted to use for storing your files and then start the program from there. Often this meant that the program also had to be in the same directory so both program files and data files became mixed. As programs were written to take advantage of DOS's hierarchical filing system, features were added that let you specify which directory to use once you got into the program. Today, you can operate both ways. You can either get into the directory you want first or specify it once in your program. The decision as to which way you want to do it is largely based on the number of keystrokes and which is easier to remember.

Method One:

1. Move to the data directory
2. Start the program (the path must point to the program directory).

Method Two:

1. Start the program (you can be in any directory, as long as the path points to the program directory).
2. From inside the program, select the directory you want to use for file storage or retrieval.

The first method requires a batch file for each data directory and probably a menu to help the user remember which batch file to use for each directory. The second method requires only one batch file. The problem with it is that the user may forget to log onto the proper data directory, thus saving files in the wrong place. Also, the command to switch directories from within a program may be long. I prefer the first method, even though it does take more disk space. With the price of hard drives dropping, and capacities going up, I doubt if this will be a problem to anyone.

Writing Application Batch Files

Application batch files can be written for any program you own, whether you are using menu or not. In fact, you may create menus for novice users and application batch files for yourself. Since these batch files often use the name of the application they launch, they are easy to remember so you may not need a menu. If you would like to automate your system the easiest way and move on, you can create these simple batch files and skip the menu system until later.

For the examples, I will use the directory structure shown in Figure 5-9. This structure has both program directories and data directories, so you'll be creating batch files that launch programs directly or move the user to a data directory and then launch the program, as covered in the previous section.

The first batch file is used to start Lotus 1-2-3 directly. The user can then select a directory once in the program (method 2 above). Type in the batch file, calling it LOTUS.BAT. The first command ensures that you are in the SHELL directory when creating these batch files.

```
C:\>CD \SHELL↵
C:\SHELL>COPY CON LOTUS.BAT↵
ECHO OFF↵
CLS↵
CD \LOTUS↵
LOTUS↵
CD \↵
CLS↵
DIR *.↵
<F6>↵
C:\SHELL>
```

In this first batch file, I will explain each command, several of which are unusual or different from previously created batch files.

ECHO OFF	————— 1)
CLS	————— 2)
CD \LOTUS	————— 3)
LOTUS	————— 4)
**CD **	————— 5)
CLS	————— 6)
DIR *.	————— 7)

Listing 7-1. Batch file commands for LOTUS.BAT.

1) **ECHO OFF**: This is the standard batch file subcommand to turn the display of commands off while the batch file executes. It eliminates confusing screen.

2) **CLS**: The clear screen command. You should use this command in conjunction with ECHO OFF.

3) **CD \LOTUS**: Switch to the LOTUS directory. By specifying the backslash, you can execute the batch file from any directory. Without it, DOS will attempt to find a LOTUS directory branching from your current directory.

4) **LOTUS**: This is the command to start the Lotus program. Commands to start other programs can be substituted if you are altering this example to fit your own needs.

5) **CD **: This command executes *after exiting* Lotus. It transfers the user to the ROOT directory. This example assumes that a menu system is not in use. If that is the case, substitute CD \SHELL in this line.

7) **DIR ***. This command displays the directories that branch from ROOT directory. It is essentially a lazy-man's menu system since the listing displays the directories as if they were a menu. If you are using a menu system, substitute this line with TYPE MENU.TXT.

The batch file JW.BAT listed below is used to start Microsoft Word from the JWORD data directory as shown in Figure 5-9. This batch file would only be used by Jill when she logs onto the system. If Dave wants to run Word, he might create and use a batch file called DW.BAT. In the batch file below, the Change Directory command transfers Jill to the JWORD directory that branches from the DATA directory. Word is started (assuming that the path points to the WORD directory) in the fourth command. The rest of the commands are similar to the previous batch file except that the user is transferred to the SHELL directory after exiting WORD.

```
C:\SHELL>COPY CON JW.BAT↵
ECHO OFF↵
CLS↵
CD \DATA\JWORD↵
WORD↵
CD \SHELL↵
CLS↵
TYPE MENU.TXT↵
<F6>↵
C:\SHELL>
```

Batch commands for many other programs would follow a similar format. The batch files can be stored in the SHELL directory. In the examples above, simple, two character batch file names were used. You may want to refer ahead to *Using Mnemonics in Selection Codes* to determine what your batch file naming strategy should be.

Menu Selection Batch Files

This is the section you've been waiting for if you created any of the menus in the last chapter. You'll see how to create the batch files that automate the selections on the menu. One thing to be aware of is where the batch files for your menu selection are stored. In most cases, this will be the same directory as the menu itself. Consider, however, what happens in a multi-menu system like that shown in Figure 5-6. The menus for this system are shown in Figure 5-7. Notice that the main menu contains selections 1 through 8. That means that 8 batch files, 1.BAT though 8.BAT will be stored in the SHELL directory along with the main menu file MENU.TXT. Now look at the submenus for communications and programming. They both have menu selections of 1.BAT and 2.BAT, just as the main menu does. There are several points to be made about this situation:

- Both the communications and programming directory have their own version of 1.BAT and 2.BAT. When you are in one of these directories and type 1 or 2, the batch file in that directory is executed, not the one in the SHELL directory. DOS will always execute batch files in the current directory before looking down the path.

- The PATH commands directs DOS to find batch files in the SHELL directory, but you can override them by placing a batch file with a similar name in your current directory.

- In DOS, there can be only 1 filename per directory. That means the SHELL directory can only hold the selection batch files for the main menu, unless you decide to use a different selection scheme, like the alphabet, or a combination, like A1 or A2. Submenus need to be stored in another directory, along with the batch files that automate them.

- The DOS path as assigned by your AUTOEXEC.BAT file points to the SHELL directory. You can execute selections on the main menu from other directories without necessarily displaying the main menu on the screen.

Let's follow the chain of events in a menu system with submenus, like that of Figure 5-6 and 5-7. When you boot the system, the AUTOEXEC.BAT file moves you to the SHELL directory and displays the Main Menu. Pressing 1 will execute the batch file 1.BAT in the SHELL directory. This batch file moves you to the COMM (communications) directory and displays the menu there. Pressing 1 will execute the batch file 1.BAT in the COMM directory, which starts the Crosstalk program.

Using Mnemonics in Selection Codes

So far, I've been talking about using numbers as selection codes on your menu. You're not just limited to numbers, however. You can use letters of the alphabet that are mnemonically linked to the selection for a very good reason. Your menu selection batch files will execute whether you have the menu up or not. So, the letter L can be used for the Lotus menu selection. This makes it easy to remember the selection code for Lotus whether the menu is displayed or not. If a multiple menu system is to be created, like that of Figure 5-6 and 5-7, it becomes easy to display any menu on the system by typing the name of the selection from the main menu that normally displays it.

For example, assume that you've just finished a task in the Programming directory. Also assume that the selection code for the Communications menu is C. To get to this directory (COMM) and display its menu, all you would have to do is type C. There is no need to go through the main menu. This, of course assumes that there are no batch files in the programming directory with the filename of C.BAT to override the one in the SHELL directory. Also, the change directory (CD) command in the C.BAT batch file must use the ROOT backslash symbol to specify that the directory to change to branches from the ROOT, since you might execute the command from another directory. The command would be **CD \COMM.**

```
         MAIN  MENU

   C - COMMUNICATIONS
   S - SPREADSHEET PROGRAMS
   P - PROGRAMMING LANGUAGES
   W - WORD PROCESSING
   G - GAMES
   U - UTILITIES
```

Figure 7-1. Menus don't have to use numbers. You can use letters of the alphabet as mnemonics to help you remember how to start a menu selection, even when the menu is not displayed.

As an example of how to build the batch files for a menu system, I'll use the the directory structure used by the advertising agency in Figure 5-4. You will find its general structure useful for a number of different applications. The projects directories can be used to hold files for special clients, jobs, contracts or just about any set of files that you need to keep together. You can create as many of these as you want and name them according to your needs. The TEMP directory is used to create files that are temporary and may be cleared off at the end of each week or month.

Single Menu Example

There are two type of menu systems you can build for this structure. The first uses one menu and assumes that you will select the directory you want to work in from your program. The main menu is shown in Figure 7-2. The menu selection codes are mnemonically linked to the selections so you don't have to go through the menu if you remember the mnemonics. The menu is still displayed every time the system is started, however.

```
JOE'S CONSTRUCTION

L  -  LOTUS 1-2-3
W  -  MICROSOFT WORD
G  -  GRAPHICS PROGRAM
```

Figure 7-2. Main menu for the directory structure like that of Figure 5-4.

The example below shows how each of the batch files are created, assuming the user is in the SHELL directory.

```
C:\SHELL>COPY CON L.BAT↵
CD \LOTUS↵
LOTUS↵
<F6>↵
C:\SHELL>
```

```
C:\SHELL>COPY CON W.BAT↵
CD \WORD↵
WORD↵
<F6>↵
C:\SHELL>
```

```
C:\SHELL>COPY CON G.BAT↵
CD \GRAPH↵
GRAPH↵
<F6>↵
C:\SHELL>
```

Note that the CD command in each file specifies the backslash before the actual directory name. This specifies a directory that branches from the ROOT directory.

Multiple Menu Example

The next example uses a main menu and several submenus designed around the task oriented nature of the directory structure. The main menu and its submenus are shown in Figure 7-3. This method is actually better for directory structures larger and more complicated than that of Figure 5-4, but I use the small directory here for practical purposes. A multi-menu system has the disadvantage of being harder to build. You have to create several menus and lots of little batch files that take up room on the hard drive. This type of system is ideal, however, as a turnkey system for the novice user, or a power user like Jack in Chapter 5.

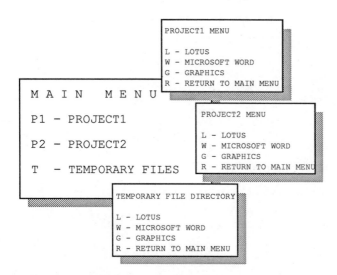

Figure 7-3. A multi-menu system example.

The main menu defines how the system is used. The user selects the task to work on. The submenu for that task appears and the user can select which application to use, either Lotus, Word or the graphics program. Once in the program, all files created for a particular project are then stored in the appropriate directory, whether they are spreadsheets, documents or graphs. If the user is creating temporary files not related to any project, the T (Temporary) selection can be made on the main menu and the normal system programs are made available on the submenus. Note that each submenu has an option of returning to the main menu.

The batch files for this menu system are mnemonic and each of the submenus use the same batch files which are stored in SHELL. (The alternative to this scheme would be to create separate batch files for each of the submenus and store them in the directory of the submenu.) In this example, each submenu has common selections so their batch files can be shared. To create the system, type in the batch files for the main menu below. Remember, you can substitute the batch file and program names that fit your needs. Make sure you are in the SHELL directory before starting.

```
C:\SHELL>COPY CON P1.BAT↵
ECHO OFF↵
CLS↵
CD PROJ1↵
TYPE MENU.TXT↵
<F6>↵
C:\SHELL>
```

```
C:\SHELL>COPY CON P2.BAT↵
ECHO OFF↵
CLS↵
CD PROJ2↵
TYPE MENU.TXT↵
<F6>↵
C:\SHELL>
```

```
C:\SHELL>COPY CON T.BAT↵
ECHO OFF↵
CLS↵
CD TEMP↵
TYPE MENU.TXT↵
<F6>↵
C:\SHELL>
```

Note the use of the batch file subcommands ECHO OFF and CLS. These are used by the main menu batch files to clear the screen before the submenus are displayed.

The following examples create the batch files that automate the three submenus. You can stay in the SHELL directory to create them. Each batch file contains commands to return the user to the SHELL directory and display the main menu once they have exited from the program called in the first line of the batch file, except for R.BAT, which simply returns the user to the main menu. The command CD \SHELL returns the user to the SHELL directory and the last command, TYPE MENU.TXT, displays the main menu once again.

```
C:\SHELL>COPY CON L.BAT↵
LOTUS
ECHO OFF↵
CLS↵
CD \SHELL↵
TYPE MENU.TXT↵
<F6>↵
C:\SHELL>
```

```
C:\SHELL>COPY CON W.BAT↵
WORD
ECHO OFF↵
CLS↵
CD \SHELL↵
TYPE MENU.TXT↵
<F6>↵
C:\SHELL>
```

```
C:\SHELL>COPY CON G.BAT↵
GRAPH
ECHO OFF↵
CLS↵
CD \SHELL↵
TYPE MENU.TXT↵
<F6>↵
C:\SHELL>
```

```
C:\SHELL>COPY CON R.BAT↵
ECHO OFF↵
CLS↵
CD \SHELL↵
TYPE MENU.TXT↵
<F6>↵
C:\SHELL>
```

Directory Sensitive Batch Files

Some batch files are used throughout the entire system, no matter what directory you may be in. They are stored in the SHELL directory, where the path command ensures that DOS will find them. You can create these batch files for a number of uses. The first one to build is MENU.BAT. This batch file is used to display the menu for the current directory you are in when you type "MENU." Make sure you are in the SHELL directory and enter the following commands:

```
C:\SHELL>COPY CON MENU.BAT↵
ECHO OFF↵
CLS↵
TYPE MENU.TXT↵
<F6>↵
C:\SHELL>
```

The next batch file, MM.BAT, can be used to return you to the SHELL directory and display the main menu from any directory by typing "MM":

```
C:\SHELL>COPY CON MM.BAT↵
ECHO OFF↵
CLS↵
CD \SHELL↵
TYPE MENU.TXT↵
<F6>↵
C:\SHELL>
```

If you create help files in your directories, the following HELP.BAT batch file can be used to display the help files of the directory you are in when you type "HELP." Note that a HELP.TXT file will need to be created in the appropriate directories.

```
C:\SHELL>COPY CON HELP.BAT↵
ECHO OFF↵
CLS↵
TYPE MENU.TXT↵
<F6>↵
C:\SHELL>
```

You can create a menu that lists the syntax of DOS commands you use often and then display that menu at any time. An example menu is shown in Figure 7-4. The batch file to display this menu, called DOS.BAT, is listed below. The DOS command MORE is used to page the file to the screen if it is larger than one screen. In addition, you will want to store the DOS command listing in the SHELL directory as a file called DOS.TXT.

If you want to create UTILS.BAT (displays the utility menu) or FILES.BAT simply substitute UTILS or FILES where you see DOS in the batch file below.

```
C:\SHELL>COPY CON DOS.BAT↵
ECHO OFF↵
CLS↵
MORE < \SHELL\DOS.TXT↵
<F6>↵
C:\SHELL>
```

```
DOS command syntax

BACKUP d:[path][filename[.ext]]  d:[/S][/M][a][d:mm-dd-yy]
CHKDSK [d:][filename[.ext]]   [d:]path][filename[.ext]]
DIR [d:][path][filename][.ext][/P][/W]
ERASE or DEL [d:][path[filename[.ext]]
FIND [/V][/C][/N] string [[d:][path]filename[.ext]...]
FORMAT [d:][/S][/1][/8][/V][/B]
PRINT [[d:][filename[.ext]]][/T][/C][/P]...]
RECOVER [d:][path]filename[.ext]  or: RECOVER [d:]
RENAME    [d:][path]filename[.ext]  filename[.ext]
RESTORE [d:]  [d:][path]filename[.ext]][/S][/P]
SET [name = [parameter]]
SORT [/R][/+n]
TREE [d:][/F]
TYPE [d:][path]filename[.ext]
```

Figure 7-4. An example of a DOS command help menu.

DOS Command Batch Files

Another use for batch files is to automate some of the DOS commands that are too cumbersome to type or too hard to remember. These might be commands to backup your hard drive, which you can place as a selection on your main menu, or they might be commands to move to a special directory. In the example below, a set of DOS commands is combined to create a utility called DIRDATE.BAT. This batch file will sort the current directory by date and then page it to the screen. Remember, the vertical bar is above the backslash key on most keyboards.

```
C:\SHELL>COPY CON DIRDATE.BAT↵
DIR | SORT /+24 | MORE↵
<F6>↵
C:\SHELL>
```

Now that you have almost completed you menu system, you may want to consider backing up the directory structure and all of its related files. You can refer to Chapters 10 and 11 for this information. If the system goes down, you will be able to recreate the structure and all of the menu and batch files by restoring the back-up set. After backing up the directory structure, you can copy your software to the hard drive, if you haven't already done so.

8

Maintaining and Protecting Your System

Now that you have finished creating most of your directory structure and menu system you need to start thinking about protecting your work. The first thing to do is develop a backup strategy, so you may want to refer to Chapters 10 and 11 right away. Backing up your hard drive is essential. You have spent days, weeks and maybe even years building up your system and the data on it. Yet it only takes a second to lose that data. This could happen from a simple electrical surge that destroys your means of using the hard drive, or it could happen through theft of your system. Protecting your data from real loss is part of the subject of this chapter.

The System Manager

If your system is being used by more than one person, it's a good idea to assign the task of maintenance to a *system manager*. The job of the system manager is to maintain the integrity of the computer and its storage devices. As a single user you may fall into this position by default. Responsibilities of a system manager include the following:

- Backup of files or the complete hard drive at regular intervals. (Chapters 10 and 11)
- Archive and removal of old files. (Chapters 10 and 11)
- Installation of new software, including the creation of new directories. (Chapters 5 through 7)
- Setting up users on multiple-user systems. (Chapter 5)

- Update and maintenance of a turnkey system when new users are assigned to the computer. (Chapter 7)
- Optimizing the hard drive at regular intervals either using the backup command or third party software utilities. (Chapter 13)
- Evaluation of software that other users intend to install on the system. Will it cause the system to crash? Does it take up too much disk space or memory. Will it tie up the system from more productive work.
- Scheduling of users time on the system.
- Analysis of hardware problems, such as disk errors. (Chapter 8)
- Selecting new hardware, expanding the system and its storage potential. (Chapters 12 and 14)
- Establishment of general procedures as required.

Lock Important Files

Before you go any further there are several important tasks you need to perform. The menu and batch files you created in the previous chapters are susceptible to accidental erasure and you should take measures now to protect them. Some of the best computer users have lost files by copying over or deleting them. A common mistake occurs when a set of files from one disk is copied to another, and one of the files has the same name as a file you wanted to keep on the destination disk, or the file that copies over an existing file is an old version. Sometimes an inexperienced user will accidentally erase one of your valuable files. There is a way to protect against this by using the DOS-3 command ATTRIB (attribute).

ATTRIB allows you to set the read/write attribute of a file to a read-only status protecting the file from accidental erasure or alteration. If a file's attribute has been set to read only and an attempt is made to erase the file, the message "Access denied" is displayed. If an attempt is made to alter the file with an editor such as EDLIN, the message "File is read-only" is displayed.

The ATTRIB command takes the following form:

```
ATTRIB [+/-R]  [d:][path][file name]
```

where +R sets the attribute to read-only and -R resets the attribute to both read and write. You can use wildcard characters in the filename position to make a whole directory of files either read-only or read-write.

The first thing to do is change the attributes of each of the menu and batch files to read-only. Type in the commands listed below to protect the menu and batch files in SHELL and the startup files in the ROOT directory.

```
C:\>ATTRIB  +R   \SHELL\*.*↵
C:\>ATTRIB  +R   \AUTOEXEC.BAT↵
C:\>ATTRIB  +R   \CONFIG.SYS↵
C:\>
```

The first command protects the menu and batch files in the SHELL directory using wildcard characters to specify all files. The second command protects AUTOEXEC.BAT and the third CONFIG.SYS, both in the ROOT directory. If you ever need to alter any of these files, you will need to set the file attribute to the read-write status. To do so, type the command exactly as above except replace the +R with -R. After altering the files you would then reissue the ATTRIB command to return the files to read-only status.

In addition to protecting your menu and batch files, you should back them up, a subject covered extensively in Chapters 10. You can backup your complete system before installing the software so you will have a copy of the structure for easy reinstallation.

Solving Drive and File Problems

Hard drives suffer from two types of damage. The first has to do with improperly stored files and the second has to do with actual physical damage to the surface of platters in the drive. There are ways that you can monitor and fix problems of this sort using both DOS commands and programs available off the shelf.

Improperly Stored Files

Say you're saving a file to disk and the power goes down. What does DOS do with the part of the file already written to disk? Or, what happens when an unsuspecting employee ends a session at the computer by turning the switch off without first exiting the program in use. Sometimes, the computer will simply lock up while working with a file. All of these situations can write incomplete or unusable data to a disk. Because DOS never finished writing the complete file, portions of the disk may still be marked as "in-use" even though the information in them is incomplete and often useless. Technically, DOS refers to these areas as "lost clusters."

If you have a suspicion that a file may have been saved improperly, try to load it again or look for its name in a directory listing. If you see the file in the directory listing, check its file size. If it has a size of 0, then the file is saved improperly and may not be fully recoverable. Sometimes, the file will have a filename extension of $$$ or TMP. When DOS saves a file to disk, the characters or data are stored in blocks of 512 characters or bytes each. You may only be able to recover the number of blocks that DOS managed to write to disk before the interruption. You can use the DOS CHKDSK (Check Disk) command to look for lost clusters and possibly recover them.

To check for lost clusters, enter the following command:

```
C:\>CHKDSK /F↵
```

The /F parameter in the command specifies that you would like DOS to correct errors in either the directory or File Allocation Table or FAT (the FAT, covered in detail in Chapter 12, is where DOS keeps track of files). If lost clusters are found, CHKDSK asks if you would like to recover the data in them. If you say yes, CHKDSK converts the clusters into files that are given the name *FILEnnnn.CHK*, where nnnn is a sequential number starting at 0000. The files are placed in the ROOT directory so that you can look at them with your word processor or editor. If they contain useful information, you can rename them, otherwise you can simply erase them.

Problems with Media

Another problem you could have with your system has to do with hardware. The magnetic media that holds the electronic information representing your files can actually wear or go bad over time. These areas are often confined to various sectors rather than the whole hard drive at once. Files stored in those areas may become unreadable suddenly, or may begin to show sign of their inability to hold data properly. Almost all hard drives have some bad sectors straight out of the factory, but the formatting procedures used when setting up the drive usually catches these sectors and marks them as unusable. This does nothing, however, for sectors that go bad through use. It is usually after you have already lost data that you find out about the bad sectors. You will then need to restore from your backup set- if you have one.

With DOS, there is only one way to tag sectors that are bad. You must first backup the entire disk and then reformat using the procedures described in Chapter 2. DOS will then attempt to find the bad sectors. DOS, however, does not have the ability to detect sectors that have the *potential* for going bad. There are two programs you can use for this. The *Norton Utilities Disk Test* program, for example, will find bad sectors and de-allocate them without having to reformat the drive. If you have data in the sectors, there may be nothing you can do to save it.

A better solution would be to monitor sectors on a daily basis to determine if and when they will go bad. *Disk Technician* by Prime Solutions automatically keeps track of all sectors on your disk and de-allocates them from storage when they loose their potential to store data. The program is an automated artificial intelligence (AI) software system that prevents, detects, repairs and recovers hard disk data loss. Every bit on your hard drive, whether written to or not is tested using special repair algorithms. If there is data in the area being tested, it is temporarily stored in system memory until Disk Technician completely tests the storage area. When an error is revealed, the program repairs it by writing out a complete new track using Disk Technician's own factory low-level format. The track is then thoroughly re-tested and if good, the data is written back to disk. Data in non-repairable areas are automatically relocated to good areas of the disk. The bad areas are then marked as unusable.

An interesting aspect of Disk Technician is that a complete log of your hard drive is kept on a floppy disk. The test is run for a few minutes at the beginning of each day and the results are stored on the diskette. Through this log, Disk Technician is able to "know" in advance when a sector may go bad, based on the number of "near errors" it has logged in the past. The program also comes with an automatic head parking program called *SafePark*. SafePark will move the head of your hard drive to an assigned parking area every 7 to 15 seconds (user definable). If the power should go down or the system is subjected to unexpected vibrations, the heads will most likely be in the safe parking zone where they will not crash onto valuable data areas. The automatic parking feature during actual operation is a must for your hard drive.

Moving a Hard Drive System

If you plan to move your hard drive computer system, you'll need to "park" the heads unless it has an automatic parking feature. Hard drives can withstand some amount of shock, but its best not to take chances when moving your system around. If the system is bumped to hard, there is a chance that the read/write head can "crash" down onto the disk surface, causing damage and lost data.

You will need to refer to the owners manual of your system or hard drive to determine whether your drive is self-parking. If not, run the park program, usually called SHIPDISK, PARK or SHUTDOWN. This program may be stored on the DOS disk of your system or on the Diagnostics diskette in the user manual. Older drives may need to have a screw tightened on the drive itself before transportation. That means you'll need to open the system to get at the screw.

When you run the program, the drive light will flicker for a second or two. A message then appears, telling you to shut the system off. When you start the system up after moving, the heads will automatically free themselves. There is no need to run an "un-park" program.

Protection From Theft and Accidents

Using a hard drive has its drawbacks. Because so many files can be stored in one place, your system is more prone to accidents and theft. For example, you or another user could accidentally type in a command that destroys a file or groups of files. On the other hand, a thief could walk out with your system as well as the backups in the file drawer. They may be after the computer itself or may be after the data. If the thief is caught and you get your system back, the data may be trashed beyond recovery. Industrial spies may either steal your data without you ever knowing about it, or they may take the entire system with them for unlimited access. There are several steps you can take to protect yourself.

Protecting Your Hardware

The most obvious thing you can do to protect your hardware is to lock it down. If someone steals your CPU, the hard drive and all of your data go with it. There are various chains, clamps and covers you can use to protect your system. Locking your CPU to a desk will make it harder to steal, but keep in mind that these devices may not always protect what's inside your machine. Locking the keyboard will not prevent someone from opening the computer cover and removing the hard drive or even the boards. It is not uncommon for people to remove memory and expansions boards from systems at work and place them in their home systems. Many of the newer systems like the IBM AT and Personal System/2 machines are supplied with keys to lock down the cover.

Protecting Your Software

After locking down your system, you should consider how to protect the data on it. If it is in a high traffic area or if you are working on highly sensitive data for either the government or the private sector, you may need to consider advanced security measures like file encryption or special boards that lock out unauthorized users. On the other hand, you may only be concerned with keeping inexperienced users or disgruntled employees out.

Inexperienced or curious users can be a major problem on systems that are shared in an office or at an industrial site. You will want to protect files from accidental erasure and even protect the entire hard drive from accidental formatting. One way to protect your hard drive from accidental formatting is to completely remove the FORMAT.COM command from the drive. Formatting of floppy diskettes for data backups would then be performed on another system or by the system manager only.

The ATTRIB command used at the beginning of this chapter is the best way to prevent accidental erasure, but this command does not protect against a mass format. ATTRIB will prevent users from creating files with the same name as existing files, erasing the original.

Protecting files from unauthorized access can be a big problem. You could simply lock your system down, but this can be broken if the person desiring access has enough time and the right tools to get in. Only file encryption techniques can protect your data from this type of access. Keeping casual users out and making sure that "honest" people stay honest is often as simple as placing a locking cover over the keyboard or even taking the keyboard with you. Once again, the level of security you need should be considered. Obviously, if you take the keyboard, someone can simply attach another one.

Removable hard drive media is another option. There are various hard drives on the market like Iomega's Bernoulli Box that lets you remove the hard drive platter containing your data and take it with you. This is far more effective than copying your files to tape or diskette and then erasing them on the hard drive. You've probably heard of programs that help you recover erased files. These programs are possible because DOS doesn't actually erase all of the data in a file, it just removes the name from your directory listing. The next time you save a file, the new data is written over the old. In the mean time data is still on the hard drive in a recoverable state. Anyone with a file recovery program can restore the original files contents to readable condition.

One of the best ways to lock up your system and its files is through the use of special file encryption board that must be physically installed inside your computer. Critical files can then be scrambled according to various encryption techniques. Passwords and other access codes are then required to restore the file to its original state. The passwords are kept on the board in battery backed-up memory. In addition, many of these boards come with lock and key systems that prevent removal of the boards and access to the inside of the machines. Unscrambling the files can only be done on the system and board that scrambled them, or with another board that is set to the same encryption coding scheme. This allows you to send files on diskette or modem to other persons authorized to read your files.

DOS Password System

There are a number of techniques you can use to keep unauthorized users out of your system. One that I particularly like can be done completely with DOS. The routine blanks the screen on you computer until the user types in a correct password. The password typed in by the user is actually the name of a batch file that takes over the functions of the AUTOEXEC.BAT startup batch file. A new AUTOEXEC.BAT file is used only to run the password system.

One thing to keep in mind is that this password scheme is not completely full-proof. Its function can best be described as a system lockout that keeps honest people honest or inexperienced users confused. An experienced user who really wants to break past the password scheme can probably figure it out quickly. One way to do this is bypass the AUTOEXEC.BAT file that starts the password system by either pressing Ctrl-Break as the system starts or simply starting the system with a DOS disk in the floppy drive and then logging over to drive C. I must reiterate, however, that the scheme is not meant to protect your system from thieves. It can be thought of as a "don't touch" sign for your computer.

Creating the password system involves four steps:

1. Determine what the password for your system will be.
2. Rename your AUTOEXEC.BAT file to the password.
3. Create a new AUTOEXEC.BAT file that contains the routine to blank the screen and ask the user to enter their password.
4. Add a line to your password file that restores the screen after the user types the correct password.

First, rename AUTOEXEC.BAT by typing the following command, using your password in place of *<password>* below.

```
C:\>RENAME  \AUTOEXEC.BAT   \<password>.BAT↵
```

Now, create a new AUTOEXEC.BAT file by typing the commands below. You will probably not be familiar with the fourth line of the batch file since I have not covered it yet. This is the command that blanks the screen and is available due to the fact that you included the ANSI.SYS device driver in your CONFIG.SYS file. ANSI.SYS allows you to manipulate your screen in various ways, such as changing the foreground or background colors on a color monitor. In this case, it is used to blank the screen. The DOS PROMPT command allows you to execute ANSI.SYS options, as will be discussed in the next chapter. For now, simply type in the command to get the password system up and running.

```
C:\>COPY CON \AUTOEXEC.BAT↵
ECHO OFF↵
CLS↵
ECHO ENTER PASSWORD↵
PROMPT $e[8m↵
<F6>↵
C:\>
```

Next, you need to fix up the old AUTOEXEC.BAT file that you renamed with your password, adding the command that restores the
screen. Once again, this command relies on the ANSI.SYS driver
loaded at boot time from CONFIG.SYS. For now, simply make the
changes by typing the following commands:

```
C:\>EDLIN \<password>.BAT↵
End of input file
*
```

Type **1i** to insert a line of text before the first line of the file.
Then enter the lines listed below, making sure to press Return and
F6 (or Ctrl-Break) to exit the insert mode. Note: the character
before the m is a zero.

```
*1i
    1:*PROMPT $e[0m
    2: <F6>
*e
*
```

Type **e** (end editing) to write the file to disk. To see how this
system works, type AUTOEXEC at the DOS prompt. The screen
should go blank. You can type in your password (the name of your
password batch file); nothing will be displayed as you type but DOS
keeps track of each keystroke as normal. When you press Return,
your batch file executes, restoring the screen, setting the normal
prompt and path, and then displaying the menu.

Any time you want to change your password, simply rename your
password batch file using the DOS RENAME command:

RENAME   <oldpassword>.BAT   <newpassword.BAT>

Tips, Tricks and Techniques

This chapter isn't for everybody, but many of you will appreciate some of the things discussed here. It is for those who have the time or desire to learn a few things about DOS out of the ordinary. Some of the routines here can be better served by third party software, if you want to spend the money. The first topic, for instance, can be done much better with keyboard assignment software like RoseSoft's Prokey or Borland's SuperKey, but I would be doing you a disservice by not mentioning the features available from DOS that do the same thing.

Assigning Commands to Keys

If you've found yourself typing a DOS command over and over again and would like to assign the whole thing to a single key, this section is for you. For example, the command to use the EDLIN editor can be placed on the Alt-F1 key or a command to list a directory, paged and sorted in order by date can be placed on the Ctrl-F10 key. You can also place commands to execute your batch files, like the one that displays the current or main menu. Any key on your keyboard can be reassigned, but for this discussion, only the function keys or "F" keys are used. It is possible to change the layout of your complete keyboard, say to the DVORAK layout, if you want.

The fact that you can reassign the keys on you keyboard is due to the ANSI.SYS command you placed in CONFIG.SYS in Chapter 3. If you did not do this, you'll have to refer back in order to add the command before continuing. There is not enough room in this book to discuss the complete process and the structure of the ANSI commands, however, you can refer to the *IBM DOS Technical Reference Manual* for more information. For now, all you need to know are a few basics to create some useful key assignments you can use to make your menuing system easier to use and your work with DOS simpler.

1. The DOS PROMPT command can be used to issue ANSI keyboard commands.
2. If you want the keyboard changes to be permanent, you can place them in your AUTOEXEC.BAT file so they will be made every time you boot.
3. Any DOS command can be assigned to a key.
4. The names of batch files can be assigned to a single key so that several commands can be executed with a single keystroke.
5. It is best to use the Alt-F keys and Ctrl-F keys.
6. The key assignments only work while in DOS. Your programs may have their own key assignments.

Note: This feature may not work on some keyboards since the internal mapping of the keys may be different or it does not support the option. Also, some versions of MS DOS may not support this feature.

Let's try assigning the DOS directory command (DIR) to the Alt-F1 key so you can get an idea of how key assignments work. Note that the /W (wide listing) option is specified and the character following the left square bracket is a zero, not the letter o. Type the following command:

```
C:\>PROMPT $e[0;104;"DIR /P";13p↵
```

Now, press the Alt-F1 key to execute the command. Notice that you didn't even have to press the Return key. There will be times when you want a key to place text on the DOS command line that you can further edit. For example, you can assign the string "EDLIN" to a key. When you press that key the word EDLIN will be typed by DOS; then you can press the filename and press Return. To assign EDLIN to the Alt-F2 key, type:

```
C:\>PROMPT $e[0;105;"EDLIN ";p↵
```

Looking at the changes between this example and the last, notice that the number 104 changed to 105. These are the location numbers of the keys Alt-F1 and Alt-F2. The text inside the quotation marks is the "string" you want to assign to the key. The last change is the use of p instead of 13p. This specifies that you do not want a carriage return, where as 13p indicates a carriage return. Note that using p on some machines or DOS versions may not work and will cause garbage to be displayed on the screen.

All you need to know to assign a string to any key is its key number, shown in Table 9-1, the string to assign, and whether you want a carriage return or not. Everything else is typed exactly as above. The command syntax is shown in Figure 9-1.

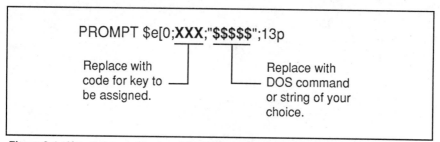

Figure 9-1. Key assignment syntax. The key number **XXX** can be found in Table 9-1. The string $$$$$ can be any DOS command, batch file name or even a string of text. The **13p** can be replaced with **p** if you don't want a carriage return executed after the string. (Note: Some machines or versions of DOS do not support the **p** option.)

Function Keys	1	2	3	4	5	6	7	8	9	10
	59	60	61	62	63	64	65	66	67	68
Shift-Function Keys	1	2	3	4	5	6	7	8	9	10
	84	85	86	87	88	89	90	91	92	93
Ctrl-Function Keys	1	2	3	4	5	6	7	8	9	10
	94	95	96	97	98	99	100	101	102	103
Alt-Function Keys	1	2	3	4	5	6	7	8	9	10
	104	105	106	107	108	109	110	111	112	113

Table 9-1. DOS function key location codes. The keys label is on the top; the code is directly underneath.

If you developed the menu system described in the previous chapters, you created batch files that display menus and help screens. You can assign these batch files to the function keys, making them even more convenient. Here's an example of keys and commands you might want to assign. Notice that some of the assignments are batch file names and others are DOS commands.

```
Alt-F1:      SYNTAX
Alt-F2:      HELP
Alt-F3:      MENU
Alt-F4:      MM
Alt-F5:      EDLIN
Alt-F6:      TYPE
Alt-F7:      CLS
Alt-F8:      DIR /P
Alt-F9:      DIR /W
Alt-F10:     DIR | SORT /+24 | MORE
```

Placing the following commands in your AUTOEXEC.BAT file will assign the keys as listed above every time you boot your system. Edit AUTOEXEC.BAT using EDLIN by typing the following. (Note: If you created the password system in Chapter 8, substitute your password batch file for AUTOEXEC.BAT.)

```
C:\>EDLIN \AUTOEXEC.BAT↵
End of input file
*
```

Type L (list) to determine the line number of the existing PROMPT command in your batch file. You will want to insert the following commands before that number. Type **#i** where **#** is the line number before your existing PROMPT command and **i** is the insert command.

```
PROMPT  $e[0;104;"SYNTAX";13p↵
PROMPT  $e[0;105;"HELP";13p↵
PROMPT  $e[0;106;"MENU";13p↵
PROMPT  $e[0;107;"MM";13p↵
PROMPT  $e[0;108;"EDLIN  "p↵
PROMPT  $e[0;109;"TYPE"p↵
PROMPT  $e[0;110;"CLS";13p↵
PROMPT  $e[0;111;"DIR  /P";13p↵
PROMPT  $e[0;112;"DIR  /W";13p↵
PROMPT  $e[0;113;"DIR  |  SORT  /+24  |  MORE";13p↵
```

Note that some of the commands have the 13p carriage return option at the end. These are the commands that execute immediately. The last key assignment is a special DOS command that sorts the directory listing by date and displays the listing one page at a time using the MORE command. Remember that the character after the left square bracket is a zero.

Logging User Time on a System

It may be important for you to keep track of the amount of time spent on your system for security, tax, rental or payroll purposes. This can be done by adding a few lines to your AUTOEXEC.BAT file, or, if you are using the password system discussed in Chapter 8, to your password batch file. The time tracking routine requires that you either set the date and time on your system manually every time you boot, or rely on a battery backed up date and time setting. If you system does not set the date and time automatically, you'll need to include the DATE and TIME command in your AUTOEXEC.BAT or password file so DOS will ask for them.

The commands you'll need to add to your file are listed below. The first command causes DOS to first display the date set by the clock or typed in by the user. The double-arrow you see in the command is a special DOS feature called redirection that lets you redirect messages that would normally appear on the screen into a file or to a printer. In the case of this log-on routine, the date and time of each of your computing sessions is appended to the existing TIME.LOG file in the SHELL directory. This file grows in size as you use your system.

```
DATE  >>  \SHELL\TIME.LOG  <  \SHELL\CR
ECHO  LOG-ON  TIME:  >>  \SHELL\TIME.LOG  <  \SHELL\CR
TIME  >>  \SHELL\TIME.LOG  <  \SHELL\CR
```

The second command is used to place the string "LOG-ON TIME:" in the file to improve its appearance when displayed, as you'll see in a minute. The third line append the time to the file.

Note the \SHELL\CR option at the end of each line. This executes a carriage return so that you or another user won't need to stand by to press it. The file contains a single carriage return and nothing else. You can create it in the SHELL directory by typing:

```
C:\>COPY  CON  \SHELL\CR↵
↵
<F6>
C:\>
```

To add the log on lines to your AUTOEXEC.BAT or password batch file, use the EDLIN line editor as you have done previously. Your batch file should be similar to the listing below after inserting the lines described above. If your system sets the date and time automatically, you can leave out the DATE and TIME commands, but if they are required, be sure to insert the three log-on commands above after DATE and TIME.

```
ECHO  OFF
CLS
DATE
TIME
DATE  >>  \SHELL\TIME.LOG  <  \SHELL\CR
ECHO  LOG-ON  TIME:  >>  \SHELL\TIME.LOG  <  \SHELL\CR
TIME  >>  \SHELL\TIME.LOG  <  \SHELL\CR
PROMPT  $P$G
PATH  \;\DOS;\SHELL
CD  \SHELL
TYPE  MENU.TXT
```

The **QUIT.BAT** batch file listed below is essential to the log system. It appends the *log-off* time plus a dashed line used to separate the log-on and off times of each session in the TIME.LOG file.

```
C:\>COPY  CON  \SHELL\QUIT.BAT↵
ECHO  LOG-OFF  TIME:  >>  \SHELL\TIME.LOG  <  \SHELL\CR↵
TIME  >>  \SHELL\TIME.LOG  <  \SHELL\CR↵
ECHO  ----  >>\SHELL\TIME.LOG  <  \SHELL\CR↵
<F6>↵
C:\>
```

You can list the user log at any time by typing the command shown below. **MORE** is a DOS command that pages files to the screen. Each log-on session is separated by the dashed line. When your file becomes old or too large, simply delete it, rename it, or use EDLIN to remove old lines. If you delete the log file, the routine above will simply create a new one.

```
C:\>MORE  <  \SHELL\TIME.LOG↵
Current date is Fri 1-18-86
LOG-ON TIME:
Current time is 1:29:05.73
LOG-OFF TIME:
Current time is 3:15:13.79
-------------------------------
Current date is Sat 1-19-86
LOG-ON TIME:
Current time is 10:12:05.87
LOG-OFF TIME:
Current time is 10:43:06.31
-------------------------------
Current date is Sun 1-20-86
LOG-ON TIME:
Current time is 1:02:31.30
LOG-OFF TIME:
Current time is 3:23:18.73
-------------------------------
```

You can keep a separate log for each user on a multiple user system by making changes to the password batch file described in the last chapter. First, add the following line to the password file:

`SET USER = %0`

The %0 (percent sign zero) is a special batch file feature that represent the name of the batch file. The global variable USER will be set equal to the users password, since that is the name of the batch file. In the log commands and the QUIT.BAT file described above, replace all instances of TIME.LOG with %USER%.LOG. This will cause all time log information to be stored in a file with the users password as the filename. You can then view each file to see when they were on the system.

Finding Files on Hard Drives

Say you've been working with your system for a while and have forgotten where you stored a particular file. The batch file below can help you locate any file in any directory on your system. It uses the DOS CHKDSK and FIND command. CHKDSK, typed with a /V option can be made to list all files in all directories. This list is "piped" into the FIND command, where the particular file you are looking for is located in the list and displayed to the screen. Since the listing produced by CHKDSK includes the complete pathname of each file, you can quickly determine the directory location of the file. Type in the commands shown below to create the batch file, called LOCATE.BAT:

```
C:\>COPY CON \SHELL\LOCATE.BAT↵
CHKDSK /V | FIND %1
<F6>↵
C:\>
```

Each part of the command in the batch file needs to be explained. First CHKDSK /V is the Check Disk command with the /V option that requests a list of files in all directories. This list is then "piped" to the FIND command by using the DOS pipe symbol |, which is usually located above the backslash character on most DOS keyboards. The FIND command then searches for the filename you specify when you execute the batch file. The filename you type on the command line is inserted in place of the %1 characters, which is referred to as a batch file *replaceable parameter*.

Let's say you want to find the location of all of your MENU.TXT files. Type the following command, noting that the name of the file you want listed is specified on the command line after the name of the batch file:

```
C:\>LOCATE MENU.TXT↵
    •
    •
    •
C:\>
```

Setting Up a Memory Drive

A memory drive, often referred to as a RAM drive is actually a block of your systems memory that acts like a disk drive. You can copy files to it from other drives and operate from it, just as you would a normal drive. The concept of a memory drive is often confusing to many people but consider this: your computer can operate faster if everything it needs is in memory, rather than on the hard drive. If your program must constantly go out to the disk to get additional information, why not load all of that information in memory before you even begin? Your application would then run several times faster. A memory drive is not to be confused with the BUFFERS command or a disk cache program. A memory drive acts like a disk drive, but in memory. Buffers and disk cache programs manage blocks of data moving to and from a hard drive.

The big drawback is that since everything is stored in memory, you will loose it if the power should go down. Also, nothing can stay stored in a RAM drive when your system is off so you will need to reload the memory drive every time you start you system. You can safely use memory drives and take advantage of their speed if you follow one rule: don't work with data files in memory drives unless you constantly save the file to a physical storage device. Here's an example of how a memory drive might be installed and loaded if you own Microsoft Word:

A command called VDISK.SYS included with DOS 3 is used to install a 360K memory drive called drive D every time a system boots. The command to install the drive is in the CONFIG.SYS file. When Word is selected from the main menu, a batch file first copies the Word program files to the memory drive. The batch file then makes one of the hard drive data directories the current drive. Last, the Word program is called from the memory drive. In this scenario, only the program files are loaded to the memory drive. The data files are still called from the hard drive. When you save your files, they are permanently saved on physical drive C, not electronic drive D, so there is no chance of lost data.

Most applications programs come with instructions on how they are best used with memory drives. The Microsoft Word manual list the specific files to be copied to the memory drive. Occasionally, you may need the speed of a memory drive to sort a data file like a mailing list or to scroll through a large document. Copying the data files to the memory drive will make the task quicker, just make sure to copy the altered file back to your physical hard drive before shutting off your system. If you have long batch files, you can copy them to a memory drive, making them run at lightning speed.

To install a memory drive, you will need to add the VDISK.SYS command to your CONFIG.SYS startup file. There are several optional parameters you can use to install the drive, but for lack of space, I do not cover them here since you will usually not need to be concerned with them anyway. The command below, when added to the CONFIG.SYS file, installs a 360K memory drive:

```
DEVICE = \DOS\VDISK.SYS 360
```

Note that the path \DOS was specified so DOS can find the VDISK.SYS driver file in the DOS directory. Also, the memory disk becomes drive D if the last drive on the system is drive C. You can specify other drive sizes in place of the 360 shown above. If you are one of the fortunate people to have extended memory above 640K and have DOS 3, you can tell DOS to install the drive in extended memory, leaving all 640K of regular memory available to your application. The /E:7 option specifies installation in extended memory. The following command installs a 180K memory disk in extended memory:

```
DEVICE = \DOS\VDISK.SYS 180 /E:7
```

Batch file commands to install Microsoft Word into a memory drive are shown below. Notice the source and destination syntax of the COPY commands and how Word is called from memory drive D. These commands would be inserted into your menu selection batch file used to start Word.

```
COPY  C:\WORD\MW.PGM  D:
COPY  C:\WORD\MW.INI  D:
COPY  C:\WORD\WORD.COM  D:
CD \DATA
D:WORD
```

Starting with Different Configurations

The AUTOEXEC.BAT and CONFIG.SYS files created in Chapter 3 will work for most of your applications, but occasionally you may want to start your computer with a different set of commands. You may decide to use a memory disk, but only when working with your data base. When working with a spreadsheet, a memory disk in not necessary since it takes up too much memory. You might also want to set a different buffers setting.

Since the commands in CONFIG.SYS only take affect when your system boots, you would normally need to rewrite the file to start with a different configuration. Instead, you can have a second configuration file that can be renamed when you want to put it to use. Assume that you have created an alternate configuration file and automatic execution file, calling them CONFIG.ALT and AUTOEXEC.ALT respectively. These batch files contain an alternate set of commands for booting your system. The following batch files will rename the existing configuration and automatic execution files, calling them CONFIG.TMP and AUTOEXEC.TMP. Then it renames the alternate files with the appropriate name so that you can reboot your system with the new set installed:

```
C:\>COPY CON ALTBOOT.BAT↵
RENAME  \AUTOEXEC.BAT  \AUTOEXEC.TMP↵
RENAME  \CONFIG.SYS  \CONFIG.TMP↵
RENAME  \AUTOEXEC.ALT  \AUTOEXEC.BAT↵
RENAME  \CONFIG.ALT  \CONFIG.SYS↵
C:\>
```

The next batch file resets the original files back so you can reboot under the normal start-up batch file commands:

```
C:\>COPY CON \SHELL\RESET.BAT↵
RENAME  \AUTOEXEC.BAT  \AUTOEXEC.ALT↵
RENAME  \CONFIG.SYS  \CONFIG.ALT↵
RENAME  \AUTOEXEC.TMP  \AUTOEXEC.BAT↵
RENAME  \CONFIG.TMP  \CONFIG.SYS↵
C:\>
```

Special Interest Topics

Protecting Your Data, Part One:

Developing Strategies

Blessed are the pessimists
for they have made backups

- Anonymous

Consider for a minute the number of hours and amount of money you have put into getting your hard drive system up and running. Besides purchasing the equipment and software, and then installing it, you probably have a lot of time invested in data entry. What would you do if your hard drive suddenly stopped working today? What if someone stole your computer or it was destroyed in a fire?

There is no doubt that you should back up your system. How you do this depends on your needs and budget. You can easily back up your hard drive to diskettes using DOS commands. Another method is to purchase a streaming tape backup system that will back up your entire hard drive to a digital cassette tape. This chapter and the next will cover various backup topics and help you make a decision as to what is best for you. Most of the backup methods described here and in the next chapter allow quite a bit of flexibility in the backup procedures. You can back up individual directories, back up by dated files or back up only files that have been modified since a previous backup.

If you decide to save money by not purchasing additional hardware, you can use the DOS BACKUP command as an acceptable alternative to help you administer your backup strategies. The command has several options. You can back up the entire hard disk, single files, single directories, files that have changed since the last backup, or files with dates later than the last backup. The DOS RESTORE command is used to copy the backed up files back to a new hard drive. Hopefully, you will never have to use RESTORE for this reason!

In addition to BACKUP, there are two other DOS commands you can use to protect your data, COPY and XCOPY (DOS 3.2 and above). The strategy for using these commands, however, is a bit different than that of BACKUP. We will look at ways you can use these commands either in conjunction with the BACKUP command or individually.

All of the routines discussed here assume that all programs and data files can be backed up and restored properly. You may have a problem with copy protected software. Most copy protected programs that have been backed up with BACKUP are usually not useable in a restored form. The normal procedure is to uninstall the copy protected software before performing your backup, then reinstalling after the backup. Check with the manufacturer to see what procedure they recommend and what their replacement policy is if you loose your copy due to a hard drive problem.

Part of any backup strategy is what you do with your diskettes or backup tapes once you copy the files to them. You could simply put them in a drawer where they will be available for the next backup session, or in case you need them for a restore operation. You would then need to be concerned with what happens in a fire. Obviously, the backup set isn't going to make it if kept in a drawer. You could try placing them in a fireproof safe, but keep in mind that diskettes are susceptible to both heat and smoke, which might penetrate to the diskettes, depending on the quality of the safe. Part of the backup strategy discussed here involves carrying a second backup set to a different location on a regular basis.

Another problem occurs when your backup set is degraded as you write a new backup set to it. In this scenario, a power outage occurs as the backup set is being written to with the newer backup information. Now the backup set has some old and some new files and at least one file that is not readable at all; the one you were writing to when the power went down. A rare situation? Maybe not.

There is a need for a backup method that maintains at least one good backup set while another set of disks is being updated. You should also store at least one set in a location other than the system. The backup rotation method as illustrated in Figure 10-1 accomplishes this. Here's how it works. You will always keep two complete sets of backup diskettes. One set receives the backup files and is taken to a remote location or locked in a safe. A second backup set is made at the same time as the first initial backup. Two complete backup sets now co-exist.

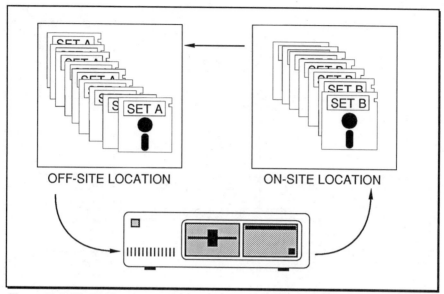

Figure 10-1. The backup rotation method. Two sets of diskettes are kept at different locations and rotated to the hard drive system. One set always has the latest data.

You do not have to back up twice each time, only the first time to establish the two sets. An interval is established for this master backup, say once per week or once per month, depending on how often the data changes. During this interval, an intermediate set of diskettes is appended to the set. The intermediate set contains all files that were altered or added in between the master backup intervals. Assume that you will perform the master backup at the end of each week as shown in Figure 10-2. During the week, an intermediate disk is created for each day and all files altered or added on that day are backed up. In the event of a RESTORE, the latest master backup set is copied to the new replacement drive first, followed by the intermediate backup diskettes that were created on each day following the most recent master backup.

Obviously, the closer together the major backup intervals, the less intermediate diskettes you will need to create between the major backup intervals. Figure 10-2 illustrates the rotation method with master backups being made on Friday and intermediate sets being made each day of the week. The first two master sets are created on the first Monday. Set A is delivered to the off-site location. On Friday, a new master set is made on set B and the intermediate diskettes are no longer any good since the new master set contains all new or altered files. This set is delivered to the off-site location and set A is brought back on-site on Monday. During the next week, intermediate sets of diskettes are made for

MON	TUES	WED	THUR	FRI
INITIAL MAJOR BACKUP Set A to remote site Set B on-site		INTERMEDIATE BACKUPS		Create new master set on B. Deliver off-site
MON	TUES	WED	THUR	FRI
Return set A to on-site location.		INTERMEDIATE BACKUPS		Create new master set on A. Deliver to off-site location.
MON	TUES	WED	THUR	FRI
Return set B to on-site location.		INTERMEDIATE BACKUPS		Create new master set on B. Deliver off-site

Continue switching sets from week to week.

Figure 10-2. The calendar depicts how two disk sets are rotated between the computer and an off-site location. Initially, a complete backup is made to both sets, one of which goes off-site. During the week, intermediate backups are made of any files that have been added or changed. The backup interval can be days or months instead of weeks.

each day. On Friday, a new master set is created on disk set A and it is delivered to the remote site. You can see that each master set of diskettes is good for two weeks before it receives a new backup set.

An important aspect of backups is to keep track of exactly when the last backup was performed and what work was done on the system since that backup. In the event of a restore, all work performed after the latest backup will need to be redone. Assume that you own a retail store that tracks its inventory with a PC. Each days sales are entered into the system, and as new products arrive, they must be received into the inventory. Purchase orders are also tracked by the system. If a daily backup procedure is performed *after* normal sales entry, receiving and purchasing procedures, you will always know exactly where you left off and what work will need to be redone in the event of a crash. Part of your strategy, then, is to follow a strict procedure, performing normal data entry functions with backups at an appropriate break-off point.

The Archive Bit

Almost all of the backup procedures covered here and in the next chapter have options that rely on a special feature of all DOS files called the archive bit. Along with every file name, DOS stores the date of its creation, the time, the size and several attributes or flags that can be altered with the ATTRIB command. You've already seen how to change the read/write attribute of a file to protect it from accidental erasure in Chapter 8. The attribute of interest here is the *archive bit*.

Think of the archive bit as a flag. When the flag is up and waving, the file wants to be backed up. After backup, the bit may be set to off by the program or command performing the backup. The importance of the archive bit becomes clear when you see how it works with the BACKUP command. Looking at the previous example, all files are backed up on Monday. When they are backed up, the archive flag is set to off on all files backed up. If any files are either altered or created after the backup, their archive flag is set back on. These files will then be included in the next backup when new or modified files are requested.

Using the BACKUP Command

Backing up your hard drive can be a tedious task but it is the price you pay for the luxury of owning a hard drive. Fortunately, the BACKUP command is one way to make this task easier. BACKUP will copy all of your files to a set of diskettes. The time this process takes depends on how fast your system can copy from the hard drive to the floppy and the number of files your floppy diskettes will hold. Owners of IBM AT type machines with 1.2MB floppy diskettes are at a definite advantage. One diskette will hold a little over a megabyte of disk files. IBM Personal System/2 owners can back up to 1.44Mb 3.5" diskettes.

You will need to establish a backup strategy like the one discussed earlier before you begin to use BACKUP. Part of this strategy is to determine how many diskettes you will need to back up the amount of information stored on your disk. You *must* format all of your diskettes before you proceed with BACKUP. Failure to have enough diskettes will force you to abort the procedure so you can format more. The worst part is that you have to start all over. Not a fun task if you're backing up to 20 or 30 diskettes. Version 3.3 of IBM PC DOS has alleviated this problem, as I'll discuss later.

You can use the CHKDSK command to determine how many diskettes you will need for the backup. The display produced by CHKDSK shows the total disk space and available disk space in bytes. Subtract the bytes available from the the total disk space to arrive at the total bytes to be backed up. Divide this number by the byte size of your diskettes, either 360,000, 1,200,000, or 1,440,000, depending on the type of drive you have. This will produce a number close to the number of diskettes you will need. Format this amount, plus one or two extras to be on the safe side.

BACKUP has several optional parameters you can use, depending on the type of backup you decide to do. Remember, options are specified on the command line with the command. The options are:

/A **Append**. This option will add the files you are backing up to those files already on the destination diskette. It can be used for intermediate backups. Assume you performed a major backup on Monday. During the rest of the week, one or more diskettes are used to back up individual files that have been added or changed. Specifying the /A parameter lets you append new files to the same diskette during the week.

/M **Modified Files**. Backs up files that have the archive switch set on (backs the file up when the "back-me-up" flag is flying). This option would be used in the scenario just described. It looks for files that have changed and adds them to the intermediate backup disk.

/S **Subdirectories**. Include all branching subdirectories. Used when backing up the entire drive or a single directory and its branching subdirectories like the DATA directory of Figure 5-9. Three data subdirectories branch from a ROOT level directory called DATA. You can back up all three subdirectories by specifying the DATA directory and using the /S parameter. To back up all three subdirectories with a single command you would type:

```
C:\>BACKUP C:\DATA A: /S↵
```

/D:date **Date**. Back up files that have been added or changed since the specified date. The date is entered as follows, depending on the part of the world you live and set by the COUNTRY command in the CONFIG.SYS file:

mm-dd-yy　North America
dd-mm-yy　Europe
yy-mm-dd　Other

This option requires that all files be dated properly.

Backup Tips and Techniques

There are several things to keep in mind when backing up with the BACKUP command:

- Remember, data files are the most important to back up. Place them in their own directories as discussed in Chapter 5 and illustrated in Figure 5-9. Presumably, you have a good copy of each of your programs on their original diskettes so there is no need to back them up on a regular basis.

- If programs are included in your backup scheme, you may need to uninstall copy protected versions before backing up. Check your operator's manual or contact the software company.

- BACKUP is not the same as COPY. COPY creates files that can be used as is on the target disk. BACKUP, on the other hand, creates files that contain control data only RESTORE can interpret. Therefore, RESTORE must always be used to copy a BACKUP file back to a disk before it can be used by other programs.

- All files on the target floppy diskette are destroyed unless you specify the /A option.

- Setting VERIFY on before you start the backup will make the process take longer, but ensure the integrity of your backup set. Simply type VERIFY ON at the DOS prompt before beginning.

- In order to always have good backups, you must back up on a regular basis, preferably at scheduled times. You may want to assign the backup procedure to a person on your staff.

- Once BACKUP starts, it is fairly automatic. You will be prompted for each new diskette until the process is complete.

- Label each diskette with consecutive numbers starting at 1. If you have to restore the set, you will be prompted for each diskette in order. Make sure to write on the labels before you place them on the disk, or use a soft tip marker.

- BACKUP sets the archive bit off (lowers the "back-me-up flag") automatically. If a file is altered or added after a backup session, the archive bit is set back on (the flag is raised).

- There is a problem with BACKUP on version 3.0 of DOS. After the backup is complete, list the first diskette. If the file BACKUPID.@@@ has a file size of 0, the backup was unsuccessful and you will need to do it again.

- DOS version 2.0 and 2.1 BACKUP will back up to floppy only. With all versions of DOS 3, you can now back up to another hard drive. With hard drives dropping in price, many users may want to consider purchasing a second drive just to use for backup.

- Be prepared to replace your disk sets at certain intervals. Diskettes wear out, depending on use. If you back up to a disk set on a weekly basis, you should consider replacing the set after a year. Mark its replacement date on the disk label.

DOS 3.3 Backup Command Changes

The BACKUP command under DOS 3.3 has some new enhancements that make the upgrade worthwhile if you use the command in your backup procedures. First, DOS 3.3 BACKUP lumps a large number of files into a single file on each backup disk. This saves space since individual files often take up more space than they need. It also decreases the backup time. A small control file used during restores is also placed on the disk.

BACKUP 3.3 won't restore older DOS hidden files over newer files, a problem with the old version when you backed up and restored in order to place a newer DOS on the disk. It will back up diskettes as you need them instead of making you calculate how many would be required before starting. Several options have been added to handle backups by time, as well as date, and it is now possible to create a log of your backup activities, including the full path and filename of each file backed up.

The new optional parameters are listed below:

/T to back up files that have been modified on or after the specified time of the date specified with the /D option. The time format set by the country code is used.

/F to format diskettes as needed. FORMAT should be accessible through the path setting

/L to create a log file. The file created is called BACKUP.LOG, and is stored in the ROOT directory.

Steps to Performing a Backup

Master Backup Procedures

When you have all of your backup disks ready, you can proceed with the master backup. Place the first disk in the disk drive and type the following command:

```
BACKUP C:\ A: /S⏎
```

This command specifies that BACKUP is to start at the ROOT directory (C:\) and is to copy all subdirectories (/S). Don't forget to specify the starting directory position when making a master backup. This should be either the ROOT directory or the name of the starting data directory as pictured in Figure 5-9, otherwise you may leave out entire subdirectories.

Intermediate Backup Procedures

The intermediate backup, as discussed earlier, is performed between the master backup intervals. How often you perform intermediate backups is determined by your individual use of the system. If you are making master backups at the end of each week, intermediate backups can be performed at the end of each day. Basically, there are two ways you can do this.

Backing Up by Date

The BACKUP date (/D) option allows you to select a starting date where intermediate backups are to begin. The date you select is typically the day after your last master backup. Each day, the intermediate backup procedure using the date will copy all files created or altered since the master backup to a set of diskettes, erasing the existing files on the disk. These existing files are no longer needed since the most recent files are being copied. You do not need to use the /A (Append) parameter when using the date parameter in backups.

Since dated intermediate backups copy over the files from the previous day, you can maintain two sets of intermediate diskettes and switch off each day. This will maintain at least one good set of files as well as those on the master backup set. Performing dated backups does have drawbacks, however. The backup procedure tends to take longer each day since all files created or altered since the master backup are copied. Dated backups are best when the interval between master backups is short, say a week. This will prevent altered and new files from building up extensively.

To make an intermediate backup of the hard drive using the /D date option, you can use the following command, substituting the proper month, day and year for *mm-dd-yy*:

```
BACKUP  C:\  A:  /S/D:mm-dd-yy↵
```

Note that your date format may be different depending on the part of the world you live. See the option formats described earlier. This command also specifies that the backup starts at the ROOT directory (C:\). Specify the directory you want to start at in this position and be sure to use the \S option to back up any subdirectories.

Restoring files that have been backed up using the dated method is a snap. You first restore your master set, then restore the intermediate copies which contain only one version of each file that has changed since the master backup. This ease of restore becomes apparent when compared to the /M backup option, covered next.

Backing Up Modified Files

The BACKUP parameter /M specifies that all files that have been added or modified since the last major backup be copied to the intermediate backup diskettes. This option copies all files that have their archive bit set on. In order to integrate this option into your backup strategy, you must also use the /A append option, except when making the first intermediate backup after the master backup.

The main thing to keep in mind when using the /M option is that every file that has been added or modified since the major backup is kept intact and is copied during a restore. Using the weekly backup example of Figure 10-2, you would make your master backup either Friday evening or Monday morning. On Monday evening, you would make the first intermediate backup. You can consider the intermediate diskettes of the previous week outdated since you just performed a major backup, so the first intermediate backup will not require the use of the /A append option:

```
BACKUP    C:\  A:  /S/M↵
```

On Tuesday evening, the second intermediate backup is made. The files from the previous day are not copied over. There may be modified files from Monday that had their backup flag (archive bit) turned off. If you copy over Monday's disk, you will lose these files.

Tuesday, you must perform a modified append (/M/A) backup. The command is:

```
BACKUP    C:\    A:   /S/M/A↵
```

Each day the intermediate backup set becomes larger and larger, because all versions of new or modified files are retained. During a restore, each diskette in the backup set is restored in order; newer files copy over older versions during the restore.

The BACKUP /M/A procedure is faster than the dated procedure because each day you only need to back up files that change instead of all files since the last major backup. Restoring, however, is a lengthy procedure, because you must copy every version of every file that changed between the major backups. The number of diskettes you will need increases with the time between major backup interval.

It is not recommended that duplicate sets of incremental files be maintained when using the /M/A option. Since all versions of modified files are kept, it is possible that you might copy an older file over a new one when performing a restore.

Backing Up Subdirectories

If you decide to store all of your data files in individual directories, you will need to specify the directories in your backup command. The two examples on the next page illustrate how you can back up a single directory or a directory and its branching subdirectories.

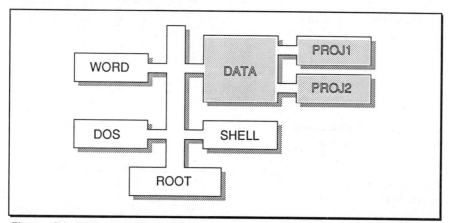

Figure 10-3. When the DATA directory is backed up using the BACKUP /S parameter, all subdirectories are automatically included. Backups are easy when all files that need to be backed up are grouped into directories that branch from a single directory as shown above.

In the next example, a directory called DATA is backed up using the /S (Subdirectories) parameter so that subdirectories branching from DATA will also be backed up. See Figure 10-3. This is the command you want to use if you set up a task oriented directory structure as discussed in Chapter 5.

```
BACKUP   C:\DATA   A:  /S↵
```

In the example below, a ROOT level directory called TEST is backed up to diskettes on drive A. The command backs up all files in TEST but does not back up any branching subdirectories.

```
BACKUP   C:\TEST   A:↵
```

Backing Up Individual Files

To back up individual files, simply specify the name of the file in the BACKUP command.

```
BACKUP   C:\WORD\MYFILE.DOC   A:
```

One of the biggest advantages of BACKUP besides its use in backing up a hard disk is its ability to back up a file that is larger than the size of the diskettes you have access to. For example, you cannot make a single backup of a file that is 400K in size if you have 360K disk drives and are using the COPY command. DOS will issue an error message telling you that there is not enough room on the diskette. The BACKUP command will bail you out of this situation. It has the capability of crossing the file over to a second diskette and prompts you to enter this diskette when the first is full.

Using RESTORE

I personally hope that you never have to use this command for its intended purpose. RESTORE, however, can be used beneficially when integrated into an optimizing routine as will be covered in Chapter 13. Believe it or not, hard drives are like tires— they wear with age. Some drives will outlast other by years, due to better plating techniques or superior components. Eventually, you will need your backup set. There is no way around it unless you intend to switch drives or move to optical disk before your drive fizzles.

The RESTORE command is simpler to use than BACKUP. There is no planning required— you should have done all of that when establishing your backup strategies. The RESTORE command uses two options similar to BACKUP command options. The /S option restores subdirectories and the /P option prompts you before it restores a file.

DOS 3.3 Restore Options

/A restores files modified on or after the date specified.
/B restores files modified on or before the date specified.
/M restores files modified or deleted since they were backed up.
/N restores files that no longer exist on the target.
   Note: /B, /A and /N should not be used together.
/L restores files modified at or later than the given time.
/E restores files modified at or earlier than the given time.

If you are restoring your entire backup set because your original hard drive went down or you are optimizing your drive (covered later), you must locate the latest master set of diskettes and restore them to the drive first. Place the first disk in the floppy drive and type the following command:

```
RESTORE  A:  C:\  /S↵
```

This command tells DOS to begin restoring at the ROOT directory and restore all subdirectories. DOS will create the required subdirectories as it restores those files previously stored in subdirectories. If you would like to monitor and select files to be restored, include the /P (Pause) option in the command following the /S option.

Restore allows you to restore an individual file. The structure of the command to perform this is somewhat odd at first glance. Unlike COPY, which requires you to specify the source file to be copied to the target, BACKUP requires that you specify the target name that the restored file will hold once it is restored from the backup set. If you remember this, you will never need to refer to a reference manual when you can't get RESTORE to do what you want. For example, to restore the file \WORD\MYFILE.DOC from the backup set to the hard drive, you would type:

```
RESTORE  A:  C:\WORD\MYFILE.DOC↵
```

To restore an entire directory, simply specify the destination directory as part of the backup command. To copy all subdirectories branching from the directory, use the /S parameter:

```
RESTORE A: C:\UTILITY /S↵
```

If there are certain files that you do not want copied or if there are newer versions of files on your destination drive than on the backup set, specify the /P pause option so you can select the files you want to restore:

```
RESTORE A: C:\UTILITY /S/P↵
```

Optimizing with RESTORE

I have mentioned that you can optimize your hard drive using the BACKUP and RESTORE commands. Basically, the complete hard drive is backed up, then erased, and all of the files are then restored. When restored, the files are placed contiguously on the drive. In other words, the files are not broken into several parts all over the disk. They are stored in sequential sectors so that the read/write heads can operate most efficiently.

There is one extra step you can take to make your drive perform better. Recall that some files like your program files are never altered and never change in size, so there is no chance that they will ever fragment on the disk. It is best to place these type of files on the drive first where they will occupy permanent sectors on the disk. Once all of your program files and others that do not change in size are placed, the rest of the disk is available for your data files. This will limit files that fragment to one general area.

If you built your directory structure using data directories, it will be easy for you to optimize your disk in this manner. After backing up the disk and formatting to erase the old fragmented files, you can begin restoring. Simply restore all of your programs and any other files that will not be altered to the disk first. After they have been copied and assigned their permanent positions on the hard drive, you can then restore the data files.

If you are not using data directories, but instead, store all of your files in directories with your programs, you'll have a little more work to do. One way to achieve this optimization is to redesign your directory structure into a design using data directories before you perform a backup. Create a new directory structure and copy your data files to specific data directories. Back up the drive, format it and then restore first your program files, then the data files as discussed in the last paragraph.

Another way to optimize your disk if you don't have your data files separated from your program files is to first erase the program files in each of the directories on the hard drive, then back up the entire drive, which now holds only data files. This procedure assumes that you have all your programs intact on their original disks so that you can restore from them. To rebuild your hard drive after it has been formatted, you would first create the directory structure, then copy the program files to each directory, then copy your data files from the backup set. The directory structure you create should match the directories where each file is stored on the backup set. Obviously, this procedure is cumbersome and points to the fact that using a data directory oriented structure is superior when backup and restore procedures are considered.

Backup Strategies Using COPY

You have no doubt used the COPY command to copy files from one directory to another, to copy files from your floppy disk to your hard drive, and to copy files from your hard drive to a floppy disk. You can build a backup strategy using this command instead of BACKUP if you make a regular practice of backing up all of your files after you create them.

For example, assume that you have just typed in a long report using your word processor. To back up the report file, you can save it to the hard drive, and then save it again to a floppy disk while still in the program. This can easily be done in programs like Microsoft Word. If your word processor does not allow you to specify a drive for file storage, you can simply exit the program and use the COPY command to make a copy of the file from the hard disk to the floppy disk.

Using this method, you might have a complete set of backup diskettes for each type of data file, just like you would have a separate hard drive directory for each type of file. You can even use wild card characters in your COPY command to copy an entire directory to a floppy disk. For example, the following commands copy all files in the WORD\PERSONAL files directory to drive A. It is recommended that VERIFY be turned ON before copying important backup files. DOS will then double check the file to make sure it is exactly like the original.

```
VERIFY ON↵
COPY \WORD\PERSONAL\*.*    A:↵
```

Since program files are intact on their original diskettes, this method works as long as you regularly copy your new or modified files to the proper diskettes. The only thing you would lose in the event of a hard drive crash is the hard drive directory structure and menu system you may have created while reading this book. This set of files can also be copied to a diskette for later restoration, if necessary.

The COPY strategy can become cumbersome if the number of files to be backed up grows. You will need a more automatic routine. An option would be to create backup batch files that contain the commands for backing up your selected files. Another option is to place all data files in subdirectories, then copy the entire subdirectory to a floppy disk. You will need to make sure the files will fit on the disk before copying.

The XCOPY Strategy (DOS 3.2 and above)

XCOPY is a hybrid command that is a cross between the DOS COPY command and the DOS BACKUP command. It is not recommended that you use both XCOPY and BACKUP as part of your backup strategy. Choose either one method or the other because both commands alter the archive bit that tells DOS whether a file has already been backed up or not. If both commands are used, DOS will become confused and important files may not be backed up properly.

Unlike BACKUP, the files that XCOPY creates on the backup set can be used directly, without having to RESTORE them. This is the biggest advantage of XCOPY. If your hard drive goes down and you do not have access to another hard drive, even temporarily, you can still get at the files on the backup disks.

The XCOPY command uses the same format as the COPY command. A source and destination must be specified unless you are working in the directory or disk that is the source or destination. XCOPY will assume that you want to copy all files unless you specify the exact file or group of files to be copied. There are a number of optional parameters available with XCOPY that give you a lot of control. These parameters are listed below.

/A   **Modified files, keep archive bit.** This option tells DOS to only back up files that have not been previously backed up. New files or files that have been altered fall into this category. This command is very similar to /M below, except that the "archive bit" is not altered. The archive bit is the flag that informs DOS of the files backup status. Using /A with XCOPY will allow you to back up the same file again using the BACKUP command, if you must use both BACKUP and XCOPY at the same time.

/D   **Date**. Copies files whose date is the same or later than the date specified. The date is set according to the country code used in the computer and is entered as follows, depending on the part of the world you live and the setting of the COUNTRY command in the CONFIG.SYS file:

> mm-dd-yy North America
> dd-mm-yy Europe
> yy-mm-dd Other

This option requires that all files be dated properly. If your system does not have a built in clock, you must set DATE before starting your computing session. You can place the DATE command in your AUTOEXEC.BAT file.

/E   **Subdirectory creation option**. This option is extremely useful in that it creates a subdirectory on the target diskette that corresponds to the existing subdirectory on the hard drive, whether they will contain files or not.

/M   **Modified files, change archive bit**. This option tells DOS to back up only files that are new or have been altered, just like the XCOPY /A option above. The important difference, however, is that /M will alter the archive bit for the file, informing DOS that it has been backed up. This is the option to use if you are not using the BACKUP command as part of your backup procedure.

/P   **Prompt option**. This option simply tells DOS to show you each file name before it is copied. You have a chance to reject files that you don't want copied. This is used more for standard copy routines than it is when backing up. The /P option makes the XCOPY command a very useful tool for selectively copying files to various drives or directories.

/S   **Subdirectories**. This option is the most useful if you are using XCOPY for backup purposes. It will copy all specified files in the subdirectories attached to the directory you specify. If you specify the ROOT directory, the entire hard drive will be copied. If the floppy disk becomes full, XCOPY will display the message "DISK FULL" and return to DOS. This is not a problem if you specify the /M option, which sets the archive bit for those files copied. Simply execute the same XCOPY command again. All files remaining from the first XCOPY will be copied to the second disk. You can repeat this process until all files have been backed up. One caution: If a file is too large to fit on a disk, XCOPY will not split it across two diskettes as BACKUP will.

/V   **Verify option**. This option will make DOS verify all files that have been copied to make sure they are exactly like the originals. It is a good idea to use this option when backing up important files. The only drawback is that the copy will take longer due to the double check.

/W   **Wait option**. This option simply instructs DOS to wait for you to insert diskettes into the drive before continuing. The main use for this option is if you place XCOPY in a batch file that will be run by another person. The message "Press any key to begin copying file(s)" would appear on the screen before the process begins.

XCOPY has several advantages and disadvantages when compared to the BACKUP command as a means of backing up your data. The files on the backup sets created by XCOPY are readable and can be used without having to go through a restore procedure. This is useful if you need to get at the files or want to make them accessible to another user. XCOPY, however, has problems with large files and cannot copy them over diskette boundaries. It will attempt to copy a large file to a disk, but if there is not enough room, you will get a disk full message. You can simply run the command again with a new disk, assuming that the previous disk was partially used by other files, but if the file is larger than the entire size of the disk, you will not be able to back it up. BACKUP is the only command that can copy a file larger than a disk size.

The XCOPY command will not copy hidden files. In this respect, it is just like the COPY command. Since XCOPY takes advantage of your systems memory, it tends to be faster than BACKUP or COPY. As many files as will fit in memory are read before they are copied to the target disk.

XCOPY can be used to copy a group of files from one drive to another as with COPY but you can use the /P pause switch to choose which files to copy. XCOPY is also useful for making duplicates of diskettes that contain subdirectories, as it copies the entire disk. The files are copied one by one in contiguous form from the source to the target. This is different from the DISKCOPY command which makes an exact duplicate of a disk, including its file fragmentation.

Protecting Your Data, Part Two:

Other Software and Hardware

If you think the DOS backup facilities covered in the last chapter are cumbersome, there are, fortunately, alternatives. Backing up a hard drive is not one of the most pleasant chores you should perform, so anything that makes it more convenient or faster should be considered. This chapter will cover two alternatives: third party backup software and tape drive backups. First, I'll cover the software approach.

Backup Software

The need for a better mousetrap is certainly the case when considering the DOS BACKUP command. The number of third party backup alternatives attests to this. There are several reasons why you would consider using such a program. The first reason is that they are fast. The DOS BACKUP command can take over half an hour just to back up a 10MB hard drive. In addition, you will need up to 30 floppy diskettes. If you have to restore the backup set, count on another half hour of restore time. To slow things even further, its a good idea to set VERIFY on to check files during both backup and restore. Owners of new computers like the 80286 based IBM AT have the advantage of faster file transfers from hard drive to floppy diskettes, but the number of diskettes decreases due to the use of 1.2MB floppy diskettes.

The speed a particular program performs backup is probably one of the most important features to consider when purchasing a program. Speed, however, should not be the only consideration. Programs that are easy to use *will* be used and this makes them more desirable than programs that are fast but hard to use. Speed is achieved by compressing data and playing tricks with DOS. One program keeps the floppy disk running at all times. You are requested to swap disks in the drive even through the light is on and the drive is spinning.

Backup alternatives are not only faster than DOS's backup facilities, but also provide a better user interface. Many of the programs provide easy to use menus and windows that help you select the type of backup you want to perform and the files you want to back up. This is probably the most important feature. If a backup procedure is hard to perform, it may be neglected. Some programs offer Lotus 1-2-3 type scroll bar menus. Others present information in pop-up windows that don't clutter the screen with confusing information.

Another important feature of alternative backup programs is that most will minimize the number of diskettes you need to perform the backup. This is achieved through various data compression strategies that shrink your files before placing them on the backup set. Keep in mind, however, that files in this state are not usable until they have been restored by the backup utility. A good backup utility will also estimate the number of diskettes you will need before you begin, and the time required for backup as well as percent complete as you proceed. Almost all of the programs I have seen allow you to format a disk in the middle of the backup, unlike the the DOS BACKUP command (pre-DOS 3.3). You won't have problems if you didn't format enough diskettes before you started. One program actually formats diskettes as it copies, reducing the backup time considerably.

Additional features of these backup utilities include the production of various reports that list all files backed up and a summary of all backups ever performed. Although most of the programs available offer fairly good menuing systems, after a while, you may grow tired of them. With some programs, you can save various sets of backup parameters in configuration files for future use, thus bypassing the menu. Other programs allow you to do this through batch files. This feature becomes important if you intend to have an unskilled person performing backups. You can tailor the process to your own needs and make it simple by including lots of messages.

Many programs provide an extensive "include/exclude" features. This feature allows you to scroll through a list of all files on your hard drive, selecting those that should and should not be backed up. With some programs, however, you must use wildcard parameters as you would in DOS to include and exclude files. This can become tricky but is a little more automatic that scrolling through a complete list of files.

To help you compare features of the various programs on the market, I have included a brief description of two programs I have used.

DS Backup by Design Software

This program offers almost every feature you can think of, including two backup modes. Its menus are a little confusing at first, but once you get used to them, you will find this program a breeze to use. Once you set the various parameters on the menu, you can save them in a configuration file for future use. Thus, you can bypass the menu system, making it easy for inexperienced user to back up your system.

As I mentioned, the program offers two backup modes. The first produces readable files on the target diskettes so you can still get at your data if your hard drive goes down. The second option produces compressed files on the target, but offers a faster backup. You can back up to any logical DOS device, including another hard drive.

DS Backup allows you to restore files to subdirectories other than the one of original origin. This is handy if you want to reorganize your drive under different directory names. The number of diskettes you will need is displayed in the menu window and if you change the file selection, a new number is calculated.

FastBack by Fifth Generation Systems

This program has a picture of a cheetah on the front cover— and for very good reasons. FastBack is the fastest backup program I am familiar with as of this writing. This is the program that won't even stop the drive during disk swaps while it is backing up. Since the program uses Direct Memory Access (DMA) to increase its speed, it even checks the hardware circuitry of your computer before it begins. FastBack claims it will back up a 10MB hard drive to standard floppies in less than 8 minutes.

All of the standard options are available with FastBack except backup by date. You can copy specific files, subdirectories, modified files or the entire disk by command line specification. There is no menu. One advantage to the FastBack command line is that you can specify more than one file name. This allows you to back up several files or sets of files with different names. You can include your predefined FastBack command lines in batch files with plenty of messages for novice users.

When FastBack is executed, it immediately begins reading files from the hard disk. As each file is read, its path and name are displayed in the lower left portion of the screen. Prompts for disk changes are displayed in the upper left section of the screen. Each disk fills faster than you would normally think, so you need to watch the prompts. If your system has two drives, FastBack will alternate between the drives. This allows you to remove and insert diskettes in one drive while the other is being written.

FastBack labels each disk magnetically, so it is not necessary to label the diskettes. During a restore, warnings appear if you place a disk in the drive that is out of sequence. FastBack also uses its own formatting routine that has special error correction codes. It will format diskettes according to its own rules, even if you have pre-formatted a set of diskettes. Whereas DOS takes 65 seconds to format a 360K diskette, FastBack will format and fill it with data in only 40 seconds!

Hardware Alternatives: Tape Drives

If you are fed up with floppy disk based backup, you may want to consider either the purchase of a tape backup system or a second hard drive for backup use. The digital tape storage medium is the answer that many microcomputer users have been looking for. Tape storage is fast, reliable and easy to use in most cases. The ease of use comes from the ability to store an entire hard drive on a single tape the size of either a standard audio cassette tape or a VCR tape. Compare this to backing up to over 30 diskettes. Another plus is that once you start the backup procedure, you don't have to stick around. The software takes care of everything. You don't have to stand by and swap diskettes as the backup progresses.

Take a minute to add up all of the time you have invested in your system to come up with a good reason to buy a tape drive now. Then add up all of the time you or your assistants are spending backing up to diskette and the trouble you would have to go through to restore that data to a new drive. The $500 to $1000 price of a tape backup system seems small when all factors are considered.

The microcomputer tape backup industry is filled with standards that many companies have adopted. In fact, some standards were adopted by groups of companies. Standards, as it turns out, are meaningless in the tape industry. About the only standard that has caught on defines how data is written to a tape but does not define how it is read. Therefore, it is rare that you can expect to take a tape from one type of tape drive and read it on another. On the other hand, tape drive technology has come a long way. Manufacturers are able to store more and more information onto tape with each new model, it seems. Tapes are also getting smaller. You can now carry a complete backup of a 40MB hard drive home with you in your shirt pocket.

Tape Types

The majority of tape drive units on the market today use a 1/4 inch tape that was introduced by the 3M company in the early 1970's. Typical data cartridges come in tape lengths of 300, 450 and 600 feet. This length corresponds to storage capacities of 30, 45 and 60 megabytes. Two tape standards, known as DC300 and DC600 use quarter-inch tape in cartridges a little smaller than videocassettes. There size is approximately 4" by 6" by 5/8". The DC300 holds up to 30MB of information and the DC600 holds up to 60MB.

A tape cartridge that has become popular due to its compact size is the DC1000 minicartridge. This tape cartridge measures 2" by 3" by 1/2" and fits nicely in a shirt pocket. The DC1000 uses an 1/8" tape width and will record up to 10MB of information. Backup systems using this tape to back up drives larger than 10MB usually have software to cross over to a second tape. A newer tape, the DC2000, is the same size as the DC1000 but uses 1/4" tape and can store from 20MB to 40MB of information, depending on the number of tracks used. As more and more drives become available for minicomputers in the 20MB to 40MB capacity range, this tape cartridge will, no doubt, become increasingly popular.

The tape cartridges themselves are usually made from clear plastic so you can see the inner workings. Because of the high speeds the tape can reach, there are few areas of drag. Rotating spindles are used throughout to guide the tapes. An aluminum plate is fixed to the bottom of the cartridges for strength and each cartridge comes with its own case.

In addition to the tape cartridges described above, several major audio cassette manufacturers like Maxell, TEAC and Memorex have come out with digital cassettes that essentially use the same case as the audio cassette available in music stores. These tapes can operate at high speeds and store up to 20MB of information. Because they appear less sturdy than tape cartridges, tape cassettes have not caught on as well. They do offer a much quieter operation and perform most of the same tasks as the digital cartridge.

Tape Formats

One of the most common formats for storing files on digital tape cartridges has been established by a committee comprised of tape and drive manufacturers. The Quarter-Inch Compatibility (QIC) Committee is attempting to set standards not only for tape formats, but also for interconnection and interfaces. Several large companies such as Burroughs and NCR are now working with the standards established by the QIC committee. In addition, drives are available from a large number of manufacturers, including Tecmar, Genoa, Sysgen, Sigma, Alloy and others that follow the QIC specifications.

When writing data to a tape, the current QIC-24 standard will write to nine tracks in a bidirectional pattern. In other words, the first track is recorded all the way to the end of the tape. The second track is then recorded as the tape is wound in the opposite direction. The third track is recorded from front to back and successive tracks are written in this back and forth pattern until the tape is full. This pattern helps reduce the time it takes to both write and read data by eliminating tape rewinds. The QIC standards also specify that separate read and write heads be used to verify the data written to tape. As files are written by the first head, the second head reads them back to verify that they are the same as the version on the hard drive. An error checking scheme similar to that implemented on floppy disk drives has been established by the QIC committee.

Each backup session, according to QIC, is copied into a section of tape known as a volume. At the beginning of each volume is a directory listing of the files it contains. Each new backup volume begins where the last left off, so you can store multiple backup session to a single tape. Accessing a file in any one of these volumes, however, can be time consuming since the tape must wind in to the beginning of each volume to read the directory information for that volume.

An alternative to the QIC standard has been developed by Tallgrass. It allows directory-oriented random access to individual files on the tape. This standard is known as PC/T, an acronym for Personal Computer Tape. Under this format, error correction is improved, thus improving the quality of your backups. Duplicates of your data are written to several blocks on the tape— one block is written in a sort of reverse-order to improve the verification.

Tallgrass believes that this more elaborate error checking and file storage scheme is required on tape backup units because of the likelihood that particles of loose oxide could scramble a file. PC/T error correction is able to catch errors that might occur during a tape read, not just a write as is the case with the QIC standard. The duplicate files stored on the tape can be used to verify a tape read, something that cannot be done with a QIC tape.

One of the biggest single advantages of PC/T over QIC is that your backup tapes can be accessed as if they were a separate hard drive if your hard drive goes down. This is possible because PC/T stores information about all if its file volumes in a directory-like heading at the beginning of the tape. You can even append files, add new files and delete files from a backup set. By the way, PC/T and QIC tapes are not compatible.

Backup Methods Using Tape

There are two backup methods available with most tape drive systems. Both methods have advantages. The "mirror image" method is the fastest. The tape backup software starts at the very first cylinder of your hard drive and begins copying, byte after byte, to the tape. The software does not care that a file may be stored in a fragmented condition on the hard drive. It simply takes the sectors as they come with no regard for their contiguity. The final copy placed on the tape is an exact sequential image of the hard drive. If you restore the tape to the hard drive, you will end up with the same fragmented file structure you had before. Mirror image backup systems are becoming less common because they do not account for bad sectors on hard drives. If your hard drive or the one you are restoring to has bad sectors, the mirror image backup or restore will completely ignore them, causing loss of data. I do not recommend mirror image backup systems for this reason, unless the software has a way to correct it.

The "file-by-file" backup method will copy each file on the drive to the tape one-by-one. If a file is fragmented into several sectors on the hard drive, the tape software forces DOS to read each sector before writing the file to tape. Since the files that end up on tape are in a completely contiguous form, you can restore the tape to unfragment your hard drive. Problems with file fragmentation are covered in detail in the previous chapter.

Backing up using the mirror image method is the quickest. Getting to a single file on a mirror imaged tape is practically impossible if the file stored was fragmented on the original disk. The tape software does not keep track of how and where on the tape the file fragments may be stored. The file-by-file backup method, although slower, offers several advantages. First, it's easy to get to the files on tape if you need to restore just one or two. Tape then becomes a means of archiving files, not just backing up to prevent file loss. The second advantage to file-by-file backup is that you can restore the tape to a freshly formatted disk to unfragment your disk.

Tape Drive Types and Connections

There are a number of selection criteria in choosing a tape drive. One of the most important is whether you should purchase an internal or external tape backup. Internal drives tend to be less expensive since you use the computer's power supply and housing, but you must make sure that your computer can handle the extra power required by the drive. This is not a problem on AT class machines, but you should check with the manufacturer before installing an internal drive in a PC type machines.

One of the major considerations in purchasing an external tape backup is that you can actually move it to different machines to back up their hard drives. This becomes an important feature in an office environment where several hard drive systems are in use. Most external drive manufacturers sell extra controller cards for about $150 to $200. You will need to place one of these controllers in each machines you intend to back up.

Don't forget that internal tape drives will require not only an installation bay, but will also require a card slot. If you are running short of available slots, you can look at floppy interface tape drives. These drives use the bus connector that is included on the floppy drive controller card of most PC's (not available on AT type machines). When using a floppy connected tape backup, you will need to format the tapes, just as you would format floppy diskettes. In addition, you are limited to the 32MB storage limit set by DOS. This usually does not create a problem, however. The inexpensive drives offer a convenient way to back up several hard drive computers in an office environment.

Capacity of a drive is also a selection criteria. You should try to match the tape drive capacity with your hard drive capacity, but in most cases this is not a problem since the tape software will allow you to switch to a second or third tape if your backup drive is smaller than the hard drive. Tape drives units should be useful pieces of equipment for years to come, so it may be wise to purchase a drive of higher capacity to accommodate higher hard drive capacities. As hard drive prices fall, 30MB and 60MB drives are becoming more and more common.

The following checklist will hopefully make your tape backup selection easier.

- **Automatic operation**. Does the drive perform its operations by itself once you set things in motion?

- **Backup type**. Does the drive support both mirror image and file-by-file backups?

- **Capacity**. Does the drive match the capacity of your hard drive? If not, does the software allow you to overlap tapes?

- **Ease of restoring files**. How easy is it to restore a single file from the backup tape? Can single files be recovered from a mirror image backup tape?

- **Interface type**. Is the interface QIC, PC/T or other? You will need to determine which is best for your needs.

- **Backup options**. Does the backup software support the various backup options like backup dated files, modified files, subdirectories, etc?

- **Power Supply**. Does the unit rely on your computers power supply, and if so, can your computer handle it? This will depend on other boards or equipment you have installed.

- **Power Usage**. How much power will the unit require if it uses the computers power supply?

- **Price per megabyte**. Dividing the units price by the backup capacity will help you compare one drive against its competitors.

- **Price of extra interface boards**. If you plan to carry external backup units to other hard drive computers, you should check on extra interface board prices.

- **Size**. Does the drive fit into your system or on your desk?

- **Type of medium**. DC-2000 tapes are small, inexpensive and of high capacity. What tape type do you want to use?

Using a Second Hard Drive

One simple solution to backing up your hard drive is to simply get another one. Under DOS 3.0, 3.1 and 3.2, you can use the BACKUP and RESTORE commands to back up to another hard drive. The hard drive you are backing up to should be the same size or larger than the source drive. One advantage of this method is that the backup becomes almost completely hands off. You don't have to stand by to swap diskettes or tapes. You can also use commands like XCOPY and COPY to back up instead of the BACKUP command. This makes all of the files on the hard drive useable. In fact, this method is preferred.

You can build a backup batch file that includes all of the necessary COPY or XCOPY commands to backup specific files in specific directories or you can simply use the XCOPY command to backup the entire drive to the target. When finished, the target drive is completely useable. Your backup strategy could include switching between use of either drive on a regular basis. For example, the first week, you would use drive C. At the end of the week, you back up drive C to drive D. Drive D is then used during the next week, at the end of which you would back up to C and reverse the process. This distributes the hard drive wear and tear between the two drives. Keep in mind that this backup method does not allow you to store a backup set off-site, safe from fires or theft.

Hard Drive Concepts

Programs and data have a way of filling available memory.
- Anonymous

This chapter will introduce you to the concepts and technology that go into the development and operation of hard drives. This discussion will help you understand topics I'll cover in the next chapter, such as how to maximize the space and efficiency of your hard drive during day-to-day operations. In addition, if you are making a purchasing decision, this discussion will help you understand hard drive specifications.

The personal computer can use several types of storage devices, including the cassette tape. When the Personal Computer was first announced by IBM, one version came without disk drives. Instead, a port for a cassette tape recorder could be used to save and retrieve programs and data to and from tape. Naturally, very few of these were sold. One of the main reasons for using a computer is to access and manipulate information. That information must be easy to get to and this is something that cassette tape does not allow.

Most of the original PC owners purchased the floppy drive systems that were available at that time. In those days, floppy drives were single sided and held 180K of information, equivalent to about 60 pages of information. The double sided disk followed shortly, with a storage capacity of 360K. Users, however, were still screaming for more disk space and the need for hard disk storage in the PC environment was becoming obvious. Some manufacturers came out with hard drives, but modifications to the Disk Operating System were required to run them.

In 1983, IBM finally opened the PC arena to the use of hard

drives by announcing its IBM XT hard drive personal computer and, more importantly, IBM PC DOS version 2.0, which supported the use of hard drives without modification. Today, hard drives have become almost synonymous with personal computers and with falling prices, are within the grasp of most users. But, there is still confusion as to the use, operation and advantages of hard drives, and how to make the proper selection. The purpose of this chapter is to help clarify much of this confusion.

What is a Hard Drive?

The term "hard drive" is used throughout this book to describe a form of electro-mechanical magnetic mass storage device that may often be referred to as a "fixed disk", "hard file", "Winchester disk drive" and "non-removable drive." All of these terms refer to the same thing. These devices are able to store millions of bytes (a byte can be compared to a single character) of information in a closed and sealed environment that remains fixed (in most cases) in your computer. The details of the construction and operation of this device are covered here.

Figure 12-1. Seagate ST225 25MB half-height 5.25" hard drive, featuring two discs, four read/write heads and a track density of 580 tracks-per-inch. Photo courtesy Seagate.

You have probably seen or used floppy diskettes. The floppy disk is an information storage media that is flexible, removable and portable. When slipped into a floppy disk drive, data can be recorded on the round disk enclosed within the square plastic cover. The disk can then be removed for storage or can be used in another computer. In many ways, the recording of information on a floppy diskette is similar to recording information on stereo cassette tapes or video tapes. The flexible mylar disk is coated with a magnetic material that is electronically altered according to magnetic fluctuations in a recording head. These recorded fluctuations are later "read" when the information on the media must be retrieved. You can use the analogy of a blind person running their finger across a sheet of braille to get an idea of how these electronic fluctuations appear to the read/write head.

The way text and data is stored to a magnetic computer disk is actually simpler than the way music or voice is stored to magnetic tape. In fact, the method can be traced back to the old telegraph wires of the 19th century. In those days, a single wire and a device for turning a signal on or off was all that was available for communications. The well known Morse code was used to send text messages through the lines. Alpha characters were coded into dots and dashes with the letter A, for instance, being coded as a dot and dash. Information stored on disk is coded in a similar way, except that the dots and dashes become magnetic positive and negative patterns that are read by the computer as 1's and 0's (binary) or "on/off" patterns. Each character of the alphabet has its own special code of 1's and 0's. This coding scheme is known as binary.

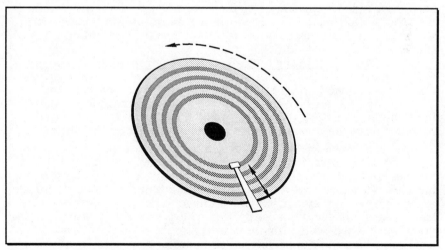

Figure 12-2. The read/write heads of a hard drive move back and forth over the spinning platters in order to access the tracks, exaggerated here for clarity.

Computer disks also differ from audio recording tape in that information is recorded while the disk is spinning at up to 360 revolutions per minute for a floppy disk or 3600 rpm for a hard disk. The read/write head moves back and forth in a straight line as the disk spins underneath. This allows for quick retrieval of information from any portion of the disk in as little as one revolution. This process is often referred to as a random access process. Audio tape, on the other hand, must be advanced or re-round to access a particular section, a sequential process.

Data can be read almost instantly by moving the heads to the track of data and waiting for the spinning platter to bring the proper sector in that track below the head, as shown in Figure 12-2.

Floppy diskettes can store approximately 60 to 120 pages of text using 360K floppy diskettes or up to 400 pages using high capacity 1.2MB floppy diskettes. The newest Personal System/2 computer systems from IBM will support up to 1.44MB of information on a single 3.5" disk and the Fuji Photo Film company is talking about the standardization of 2MB and higher on 3.5" diskettes. This may seem adequate, but often, programs such as a word processor, data base or spreadsheet will take up quite a bit of disk space, not leaving much room for data. A second drive can solve this problem to some extent, allowing you to run the program from one drive and store data on the other. But, floppy diskettes are slow, and force you to shuffle between diskettes for different programs or different sets of data. The hard drive helps solve all of these problems.

The concept of writing and reading data is the same with hard drives as it is with floppy drives. Hard drives, however, represent a significant increase in performance and durability. First of all, the hard drive spins many times faster than a floppy disk, decreasing the read/write time. In addition, much more information can be stored on the disk. Both of these enhancements are possible because of the use of rigid disks or platters (as opposed to floppy disks) and by maintaining a clean, sealed environment. Because the disk or platter is rigid, it can spin much faster and more information can be packed on its surface. The read/write heads are so close to the disk surface that a particle of dust can be five to ten times the size of the gap between them. In fact, the head actually becomes airborne above the disk surface by utilizing the airflow from the spinning disk.

You would think that hard drives are the most delicate of instruments. On the contrary, hard drives today are resistant to a high level of shock. Obviously, a hit with a hammer while the heads are seeking data may cause some damage to the disk surface and a loss of data, but for the most part, hard drives are very sturdy. Some hard drives can withstand an 8 foot drop without damage, assuming that the outer electronics boards are protected from cracking. Drives used in most portable computers are shock mounted to further prevent any data loss from head crashes. In addition, data integrity tends to be greater in sealed units which are not exposed to contaminating elements.

Newer drives use a specially plated thin coating of magnetic material that is hardened against "crashes" of the read/write head. This new "thin film" is a factor to look for when selecting hard drives. In addition to being able to withstand head crashes better than traditional coatings, thin film drives are capable of packing more data into the same area as a conventionally coated drive, as you'll see.

One of the biggest advantages of hard drives is their ability to store large amounts of programs and data in one place. All of your programs can be available for use at one time and it is much easier to share data files between programs. Hard drives are also 10 to 20 times faster than floppy drives, so they are much more convenient and enjoyable to use. Large files are loaded almost instantly, and disk intensive programs like mailing list managers and data bases perform extensive sorts and searches much faster.

The Disk Operating System

As the name implies, your Disk Operating System, or DOS, is designed to control the hard drive, as well as the floppy drives and various other parts of the system. Originally, before the use of disk drives, an OS, or Operating System, was used to make the computer easier to use. The OS contained predefined routines for working with keyboards, monitors and memory. A *disk operating system* contains all of these instructions, plus the routines for working with diskettes or hard drive storage units.

Before PC DOS or MS DOS can make use of a hard drive, however, formatting must be performed to map out the physical locations on the disk where files are stored. These locations are known as *tracks* and *sectors* and are basically defined by the size and type of your drive. A single track is the logical path that the read/write head makes as the disk spins beneath it. Each track is subdivided into sectors, which are the smallest unit or subdivision that DOS will use when storing or retrieving files. Typically, each sector will hold 512 bytes (characters) of information. Formatting locates and assigns addresses to the tracks and sectors of your drive, according to the drive type you tell DOS you are using.

The read/write head of the hard drive makes incremental jumps as it moves from the outside of the disk to the inside, or vise-versa. Each jump of the head brings it to a new track. This track extends all the way around the disk, forming a circle. Since most hard drives have disk platters that are coated on both sides, a track is also located on the other side where a second head is used to read it. The combination of these two tracks in the same physical location on either side of the disk is know as a *cylinder*, as shown in Figure 12-3.

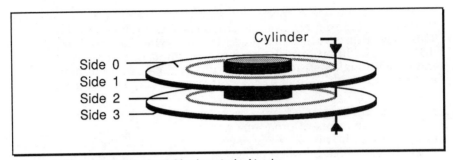

Figure 12-3. A cylinder of a hard drive is a stack of tracks.

Figure 12-4 illustrates the divisions on a platter of a hard drive. Extremely high capacity hard drives will use several platters, each side of the platter having its own read/write head. When platters are stacked, each cylinder extends through all of the available platters as shown in Figure 12-3. The heads of a typical 20MB hard drive will step through over 615 tracks or cylinders.

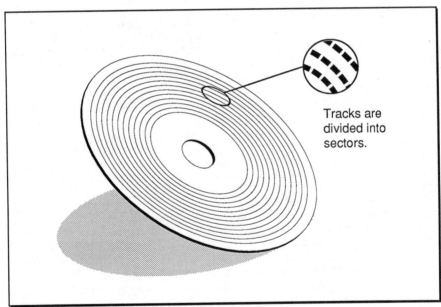

Figure 12-4. The sectors and tracks of a hard drive platter, exaggerated for clarity.

Since each track on a disk can store over 8000 characters, or about 3 pages of information, it is further divided into smaller units called sectors. A typical PC hard drive divides a track into 17 sectors, each able to hold 512 bytes or characters of data. DOS reads and writes to the disk in blocks of data, each block being 512 bytes long. When DOS stores a file, it uses either 4 or 8 sectors at a time in what is known as a *cluster*. DOS 2 stores files in clusters of 8 sectors each. DOS 3 uses 4 sectors per cluster unless the hard drive is 10MB or less, in which case 8 sectors are used. These are the smallest amounts of space that DOS will work with when storing files and has to do with a design trade-off based on hardware-software interfacing. A cluster of 4 sectors is equal to 4K of disk space. That means that even the smallest file (1 character) will take up 4K of disk space! (Be careful not to create a bunch of small, unneeded files and clean off old files as they become outdated.)

Data that is written to a sector of a hard drive is coded into binary data— the 1's and 0's or on-off states described earlier. The character A, for instance, is known to DOS as ASCII code 65. At the microprocessor level of your computer the letter A becomes 01000001. This machine level number is what is then copied to the magnetic media of the hard drive as positive or negative pulse changes as shown in Figure 12-5. (Technically, even this binary information is coded further to compress more data on the drive.)

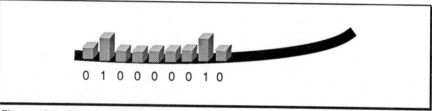

0 1 0 0 0 0 0 1 0

Figure 12-5. The binary coding 010000010 that represents the letter A is recorded to the disk as a series of magnetic fluctuations here represented as high and low spots on the track. In reality, this binary code is further compressed when stored on the drive. The disk controller card in your system handles the data conversions.

In order to operate efficiently, DOS and the hard drive typically follow one rule. All sectors in the available tracks of a cylinder spinning under the read/write heads are filled before the heads physically step to the next track (cylinder) in. This means that a file requiring more than 17 sectors will be partially written on another track, either on the flip side of the current platter, the first side of the next platter, or the next track in.

Assume that you are saving a large data base file of 20,000K size. Since 512 bytes can be stored in one sector, DOS will require about 40 sectors. The file will fit on a little over 2 tracks. Assume again that the hard drive is 20MB and has two platter. The file is written to the top track, then to the track directly opposite on the same platter, and finally, to the top track on the next platter. The important point here is that the heads themselves have not moved, just the spinning platter, decreasing access time.

When the last sector in a cylinder (remember, a cylinder is a stack of tracks, depending on the number of platters a drive has) is filled, DOS finally moves the heads into the next track and resumes writing at the top most track if necessary. DOS keeps writing files in this manner, filling sectors from the outer rim to the inner hub of the hard drive platters.

Files are not always stored one after the other on a disk until the disk is full. Actually, this only happens when the drive is new and you are loading software for the first time. Each new file is placed directly behind the previously stored file. As you use your drive, however, you will inevitably erase files, leaving blank "holes" that DOS will try to fill with new files. This may not seem to be a problem until you consider that a new file may be bigger than the previous file that occupied the space. In that case, DOS will need to find more free space somewhere else on the disk, in which case the file becomes "fragmented." If several blank holes are available on a disk in separate locations, DOS will fragment the file into several parts to fill the holes and then place the remainder of the file in the available space remaining on the disk. File fragmentation becomes worse the more you use your drive and erase files. This problem area and how to avoid it will be covered in Chapter 13.

DOS must keep track of where each file is placed on the disk, especially if the file becomes fragmented and is scattered into separate and multiple sectors. DOS does not go searching through each sector when you ask for a file. Instead, it maintains a table of contents like the one in this book to help it locate files or fragments of files. This table of contents is actually broken into two parts, the *Directory Information Table* and the *File Allocation Table*, also known as the FAT.

Recall the directory listing produced when you type the DIR command. This listing gets its date, time, file size and other information from the directory information table. In addition, the directory information table has a pointer to an entry in the file allocation table. You can think of the FAT as a grid of slots, each holding an information card. Each slot has an address that the directory information table can point to and the card in each slot is used to keep track of the sectors where a file is stored. The FAT is so important that DOS actually maintains two sets on the disk in case one becomes bad. The FAT does not actually keep track of every sector, but instead, several sectors are grouped into clusters as was discussed previously. A cluster is the smallest unit of sectors that DOS will work with and the FAT keeps track of the sectors for each file.

Hard Drive Specifications

From here on, I discuss topics that are somewhat technical, but interesting. If you are evaluating hard drives for your machines, the topics covered here can help you understand the technical jargon and specifications that manufacturers use in their brochures. This section will also help you purchase the right drive if you plan to order through the mail.

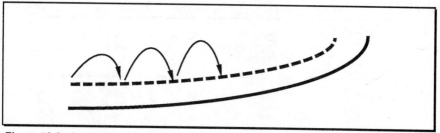

Figure 12-6. *Interleave.* A hard drive will skip over sectors if the the computer cannot move the data as fast as the hard drive can send it. The skipped over sectors are read when the platter makes another revolution.

It's interesting to note that on some versions of DOS used with slower 8088 and 8086 based systems that data is not actually written (or read) to disk from one sector to the next in sequential order as I may have led you to believe. Instead, DOS skips over sectors according to a predetermined "interleave factor" before it writes again. DOS eventually fills each sector in a skip-over fashion before jumping to the track on the other side of the platter as shown in Figure 12-6.

The reason DOS does this has to do with the processing speed of most 8088 based computers. Imagine the read/write heads positioned over a track on a platter spinning at 3600 rpm's. DOS gives the instruction to write data to a sector. As it finishes filling one sector, the next sector on the spinning platter is moving towards the read/write head. At his point, DOS must take a moment to "process" the next block of data before writing it. By the time it does this, however, the next sector, or possibly even the next, are already swinging under or past the head.

The interleave factor helps old PC's overcome this read/write problem. It is used to tell DOS how many sectors to skip before reading or writing again. In other words "write a sector, then skip three (or less) while getting more data, then write the next sector." The number of sectors depends on the processing speed of the computer, so faster machines will need a smaller interleave factor or none at all. In fact, programs are available to alter the interleave factor on newer, faster machines that might still be set at the old PC interleave factor.

Storage Capacities

You can easily determine the storage capacity of a hard drive if you know the bytes-per-sector, the number of sectors per track, the number of track-sides (or heads) and the number of cylinders. Table 12-1 is a list of common IBM hard drives. The table assumes that there are 17 sectors per track holding 512 bytes each.

	TYPE	CYLINDERS	HEADS	CAP (mb)
OLD XT	0	306	2	5.3
	1	375	8	26.1
	2	306	6	15.9
	3	306	4	10.6
NEW XT	0	306	4	10.6
	1	615	4	21.4
	2	306	8	21.2
	3	612	4	21.3
AT	1	306	4	10.6
	2	615	4	21.4
	3	615	6	32.1
	4	940	8	65.4
	5	940	6	49.0
	6	615	4	21.4
	7	462	8	32.1
	8	733	5	31.9
	9	900	15	117.5
	10	820	3	21.4
	11	855	5	37.2
	12	855	7	52.0
	13	306	8	21.3
	14	733	7	44.6

Table 12-1. IBM hard drive types and specifications.

Assuming that all hard drives used in DOS type machines have a rotational speed of 3600 rpm's, there is a fixed rate at which data transfers from the hard drive to the computer. This can be determined with the following simple math:

3600rpm = 60/3600 = 0.016 seconds

SO:

(17 sectors X 512 bytes)/0.016 = 522,239 bytes/second

This is the optimum rate that data is transferred from one track, assuming that all sectors are read sequentially and that the hard drive is operating at 3600 rpm. Due to the interleave factor, however, this figure will vary since data is rarely read sequentially from sector to sector. There are other factors that come into play, making just about every drive on the market appear faster or slower to you and your system. These factors will be discussed in the next few chapters and have to do with the technology used in the read/write heads as well as the contiguity of the files stored on the drive.

Keep in mind that, under DOS (version 2.0 to 3.2), the maximum capacity of a hard drive that can be addressed by DOS is 32MB. Drives with higher capacities will need to be partitioned with special software and accessed as separate drives. Appendix D has more details on this type of software. Under DOS 3.3, you can now set up what is known as the primary partition, and then set up extended partitions. The primary partition becomes drive C and all extended partitions are referred to with drive letters starting at D.

Hard Drive Performance Considerations

You've seen how hard drives operate and how DOS takes advantage of their physical properties. The 522,239 bytes per second transfer rate is actually very close to the maximum transfer rate of the IBM 8088 based PC bus with standard RAM chips. In other words, the computer itself cannot move data through its own data transfer lines much faster than it can be transferred from the drive. But, keep in mind that this figure is the optimum transfer rate if data were stored sequentially on the tracks. In reality, this is never the case. Sequentially stored files are usually only found on freshly formatted drives.

There are factors that come into play that will slow a drive down considerably. First of all, the data transfer rate described earlier occurs once the heads are positioned in the right track. The time required to get the head to that track, the "seek" time, must also be considered. The time required to physically move the read/write head is large when compared to the processing time of your computer. Once the head arrives at the right track, it must settle in before it can begin reading or writing data. This is known as the "settle" time. "Latency" refers to the time it takes for the proper sector to swing around to the head position. All of these factors account for mere microseconds of time, but when averaged together into the "average access time", determine the difference in speed from one drive to another.

The average access time is hardware dependant for the most part. How fast the head can move to a track is dependent on the technology used in the read/write head arm. Older "stepper motor" heads rely on a largely mechanical process where the heads make incremental steps from one track to the next. Newer "voice-coil" drives use read/write armatures that rely on a less mechanical, smooth-action process that helps to decrease the average access time. Average access times of voice-coil drives is anywhere from 18 to 40 milliseconds, whereas older stepper-motor drives have access times of 60 milliseconds and up.

Another factor that will reduce the read/write efficiency of a drive, especially over time, has to do with file fragmentation, as discussed earlier. As random clusters are made available throughout the disk due to erased files, new files are divided among them, making them both harder to write and read. The problem increases over time. This is where a fast access drive is really advantageous, even on a PC that normally can't handle the faster data transfer rate available from a fast drive. As file fragmentation increases, superior drives such as the voice coil variety will deliver better performance since they can jump from sector to sector much faster.

So one way to get better performance in your system is to use a voice-coil drive. A second way to gain speed from a hard drive is possibly the strangest, or so it seems at first. Buying a hard drive of extremely high capacity such as a 70 or 130 megabytes will dramatically increase hard drive performance. The reason for this is simple. Drives of this size typically use up to 5 platters. That means that up to 10 tracks of data can be stored in a single cylinder, translating into anywhere from 60 to 80K of data. That means that you could theoretically access a 60K to 80K file in a single cylinder without even moving the heads. The average access time for high capacity drives can be in the 15ms to 30ms range, an ideal choice for 80286 and 80386 class machines that have full 16 bit data paths to the hard drive.

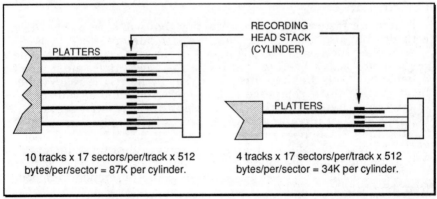

10 tracks x 17 sectors/per/track x 512 bytes/per/sector = 87K per cylinder.

4 tracks x 17 sectors/per/track x 512 bytes/per/sector = 34K per cylinder.

Figure 12-7. The more platters there are, the less the heads have to move from track to track, decreasing average access time. With the drive on the left, DOS can write up to 87K of data before moving to a new track.

This brings up an important point about the difference in speed of 80286 and 80386 machines over their 8088 based predecessors. If you compare the bus slots (the slots where expansion cards are plugged in), you will notice that some slots on the newer models are actually wider than those on the 8088 machine. These slots are full 16 bit ports into the microprocessor that allow almost twice as much information to be transferred at any time. That means you can grab up to twice as much information from a hard drive in the same amount of time. The performance difference can be compared to the difference between an 8 lane and a 16 lane freeway.

New Coding Techniques

Another way to get a really effective increase in the data transfer rate *and* the storage capacity of a hard drive is to use a drive and a controller card that take advantage of a data coding scheme known as Run Length Limited (RLL) encoding. RLL encodes the data in a way that essentially squeezes from 50% to 100% more information in the same amount of space. Making use of the braille analogy again, assume that we can place more text on a braille sheet by reducing the size of the holes and the spacing between them. This brings up another problem, however. Now, the holes are smaller and the fingers of the person reading the text may not be able to distinguish them as well. One way to get around this is to establish a scheme where there are never less than two spaces between one of the holes. In this way, two holes side-by-side would be less likely to be misread as a single hole.

RLL works in a similar way. Think of each 1 bit in the 1's and 0's coding scheme as a tiny bump (actually magnetic fluctuations) on the disk surface that are detected by the read/write head. Since the read/write head is somewhat enormous compared to these bits, there are only so many bits that can be packed per inch before the head can no longer detect them accurately, especially if they are close to one another. It follows then, that the fewer changes in state there are, the easier it is for the head to determine their state. RLL encodes each 8 bit pattern (byte) into a new code that is 16 bits long and has between two and seven zeros between each magnetic fluctuation. RLL actually *increases* the number of bits it takes to store a piece of data, but the bit pattern requires less space. Consequently, up to 50% more data can be stored and the speed of reading that data increases. RLL allows 25 sectors per track instead of the standard 17 sectors.

RLL is a well-established technology in the mainframe world that has been adapted to the world of microcomputers by companies like Adaptec. The RLL coding scheme (officially known as 2,7 RLL) was originally developed by IBM around 15 years ago and has since been licensed into the micro-world. Because of advances in platter coating techniques (thin film) and new drive read/write head technology. RLL is beginning to replace the original MFM coding scheme used on almost all early IBM XT and AT systems. MFM or Modified Frequency Modulation established the 17 sectors per track format; RLL increases the number of sectors to 26. That means that over 13,312 bytes (characters) of data can be stored per track instead of 8,704 bytes as was the case with MFM. Storage capacities increase by 50 percent, but that is not all. There is also a gain in access time from 5Mbits per second to 7.5 Mbits per second since more bits are passing under the read/write heads at the same platter rotation speed.

An even newer method of squeezing speed and capacity from hard drives known as Advanced Run Length Limited (ARLL) was recently pioneered by Adaptec. This method uses an even tighter coding scheme to increase both storage and data transfer rate by 100% compared to older MFM drives. This is possible due to newer electronics that allow even faster reading of data. The bit window of ARLL becomes smaller, from the 100 nanoseconds of MFM to 50 nanoseconds. (Imagine a "bit window" as you would a shutter on a camera, opening and closing at high speed to record the bits as they pass by.) ARLL capable drives will deliver data at up to 10Mbits/second. At the same time, ARLL capable drives can be divided into 34 sectors per track instead of the 17 sectors of MFM drives.

If you want to take advantage of RLL and ARLL, you'll probably need to upgrade your drive to one that supports RLL or ARLL. In addition, only certain controller cards contain the RLL or ARLL electronics. If you own an 80286 AT type machine that comes with a hard disk controller card, you may need to upgrade. Keep in mind that RLL and ARLL performance increases will not be fully realized on 8088 based machines because of the narrow data bus. Your best bet is to purchase a drive and controller that have been tested and packaged together for AT class machines. RLL and ARLL require tighter tolerances in drives, so make sure you know the specifications of the drives you are buying. Table 12-2 list the basic drive requirements.

Requirements	MFM	2,7 RLL	ARLL
Data Transfer	5 Mbit/sec	7.5 Mbit/sec	10 Mbit/sec
Data Clock	10 MHz	15 MHz	20 MHz
Data Window Bit	100 ns	66.7 ns	50 ns
Drive Margin	±40 ns	±27 ns	±21 ns
Read/Write Channel	2.5 MHz - 5 MHz	1.875 MHz - 5 MHz	2.5 MHz - 6.67 MHz

Table 12-2. RLL and ARLL drive requirements. Table courtesy of Adaptec

Hard Drive Interfaces

As you can see, there are a number of factors that can speed up the access to data on the hard drive. Getting that data to the memory and processor in your computer is another matter, however. The type of computer system you have, the controller type and the interface standard are the primary factors in determining the data transfer rate from hard drive to final processing or vice-versa. The most common interface for PC, XT and AT type machines is the ST506/412, which specifies a transfer rate of 5 million bits per second (5 Mhz). The PC and XT will not be able to keep up with this transfer rate. The AT, however, does a good job with its full 16 bit data bus and faster processing speed. Two other interfaces are beginning to appear on the market. Both are designed for AT or 80386 class machines and require the replacement of the existing hard drive controller in AT machines.

Small Computer Systems Interface (SCSI)

The SCSI or Small Computer Systems Interface is providing, among other things, a way to daisy chain other devices off of the back of your computer system without adding extra expansion cards. A SCSI hard drive controller card typically replaces the existing hard drive controller in AT type machines and simply plugs into an available slot in PC and XT type machines. Once the card is in place, a cable is attached to a SCSI compatible hard drive mounted inside the computer. That is where the similarity to other hard drive systems ends.

You can think of the SCSI card as the beginning of a long chain of devices that attach to each other in a daisy chain fashion. In most cases, the first device is an internal hard drive unit. For example, you can plug a SCSI compatible tape drive backup unit into the hard drive SCSI card. There is no need to purchase a separate card for the tape unit. You can continue to daisy-chain other SCSI devices, like an optical disk or even another PC. In fact, you can plug up to eight compatible devices into the SCSI chain. Each device works independently of the others and there is no slow down in processing.

SCSI devices can communicate at up to 12Mbits per second compared to the 5Mbits data transfer rate for standard MFM hard drives. A single SCSI card, often referred to as the host adapter can function at this peak performance level with all eight devices connected. You can even place a second card in a second expansion slot to double the number of devices available if eight isn't enough. Adding new devices to the chain is as simple as plugging them into the SCSI chain. Each device comes with it own built-in electronics and is ready to be attached. All you need to do is install the front end software.

The Small Computer System Interface is in many ways like a network. Each device can be accessed at any time, no matter where it is in the chain. Other computers can be connected into the chain so that hard drives can be shared as they are in most networks. As more computers are added and set up to share the existing hard drives in the SCSI chain, newer, larger drives may be required. That becomes a simple matter of attaching the drive to the SCSI chain. Since SCSI is a fairly intelligent stand-alone interface, much of the processing can be done outside of the actual computer, freing it to perform more important tasks on its own, like backups to a SCSI tape device.

Because it is relatively simple to design and market products for the SCSI system, it will become a standard and more and more SCSI compatible products will become available.

Enhanced Small Device Interface (ESDI)

The Enhanced Small Device Interface is gaining in popularity, especially since IBM has integrated it into its high performance Personal System/2 model 60 and 80 machines and Compaq uses it in its 80386 based Deskpro. The ESDI interface requires replacement of the existing controller card in AT type machines, the same as SCSI. A transfer rate of up to 10Mbits per second has been specified.

Optimizing Your System

More Speed From Your Hard Drive

The software structure you designed in the first part of this book is essential to the operation of your computer. Building the right directory structure and creating the user menus can make your interaction with the computer more convenient. It can also help make your system faster and more efficient to use. There is one aspect of hard drive use that requires constant monitoring, however. As you use your hard drive, it tends to become slower and slower due to the way DOS must handle files it stores on the hard drive. Understanding how and why the performance of your system degenerates over time will help you minimize the effects of this process. That is part of the subject of this chapter.

In addition to helping you improve the efficiency of DOS's file handling, this chapter will also help you speed up your system in other areas. You can improve performance by properly setting various parameters in DOS, like the PATH and BUFFERS command, or setting up the DISKCACHE utility provided with IBM Personal System/2 machines. Last, I'll cover various hardware modifications and additions you can perform.

File Fragmentation

File fragmentation is the biggest nightmare of almost every operating systems, not just DOS. In a nutshell, file fragmentation has to do with the inability of DOS to store a complete file in one single place on a disk, on a regular basis. If you recall from the previous chapter, DOS stores files in sectors of 512K bytes each. That means that a file containing about 512 characters will fit nicely in one sector. Most files, however, are bigger than 512 bytes, and so will require two or more sectors for storage. Ideally, DOS would like to store every file in what are commonly called contiguous sectors, or sectors that are next to each other. Since this is rarely the case on systems that have been in use for a period of time, DOS will break the file up and store it on sectors "scattered" throughout the disk. This is where degradation in both read and write performance occurs, increasing the average access time.

Let's look at a situation where files are written to a new disk, some are erased and then more added. Figure 13-1 illustrates the platter of a hard drive. For this example, several assumptions must be made. First, the illustration only shows one side of the platter. Second, the interleave factor as discussed in Chapter 12 is disregarded for clarity of this subject. Remember that interleave lets DOS naturally skip over sectors to compensate for computers that cannot absorb data as fast as the drive sends it. DOS still sees these sectors as being next to each other, even though it has to skip over others to get to them. Illustration 13-1 does not show interleaved sectors. Also, remember that a circular track on a hard drive is referred to as a cylinder when discussing tracks on all sides of all platters. We use the term cylinder in this discussion.

Remember the rule from Chapter 12 that says DOS will always attempt to store a file in cylinders as close to the outer edge of the disk as possible. That means on a new drive, programs and data files are written to the outer cylinders first and on into the inner cylinders as more and more files are added. Figure 13-1A shows how new files are placed contiguously from the outer cylinders to the inner cylinders. In Figure 13-1B, files have been deleted as can be seen by the opened sectors. In 13-1C, a new file that spans several sectors is written to disk. DOS follows its rule of filling outer cylinders first, and "fragments" the new file by placing parts of it in the opened sectors freed by the previously erased file and the remainder of the file in the next available cylinder.

DOS does not have any problem keeping track of where each fragment of the file is located on the disk. The information is located in the File Allocation Table (FAT). The FAT actually keeps track of a group of sectors known as a cluster, but for this example, that is not important. Problems begin to arise as more and more files are fragmented due to free space made available by erased files.

The moving mass of the read/write head must work harder to read or write fragmented files that are scattered over the disk surface. You can check the contiguity of the files on your hard drive by using the CHKDSK command:

```
C:\>CHKDSK *.*↵
```

Each file that is fragmented over several sectors will be listed. When fragmentation becomes excessive, you will need to perform the cleanup procedures described here.

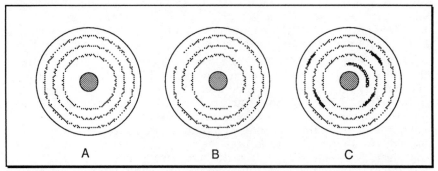

Figure 13-1. File fragmentation can degrade the performance of a hard drive. In A, the files are stored contiguously. In B, erased files leave "holes." In C, DOS fills the holes before continuing to write on a new track. The file is "fragmented" and harder to read.

Unfortunately, DOS does not have facilities to correct the fragmentation problem automatically. In fact, the fragmentation problem tends to grow as you use your drive. Files are constantly erased and new files are then written to the available sectors. The average access time degrades more and more and the drive is subjected to excess wear and tear since the read/write head armature must constantly jump from sector to sector. The life expectancy of the drive falls off.

Optimizing the Hard Drive

There are several ways you can "optimize" your hard disk filing system. Since a hard drive tends to fragment through normal use, you will have to perform these optimizing routines on a regular basis, depending on how much you use your system. As an alternative, you can buy commercial software to make the process easier and more automatic. The first method is to simply back up the entire hard disk and then restore the files. The second method is simpler and faster, but requires that you purchase third party software packages. I'll cover the least expensive process first.

Optimizing with BACKUP and RESTORE

This method involves backing up your entire hard drive, formatting the disk and then restoring all of the files. The reason this optimizes your drive is that files restored to a freshly formatted disk are placed in contiguous sectors. DOS does not care how they were stored on the disk previously. Chapter 10 covers the DOS BACKUP and RESTORE commands in detail. In fact, you may want to integrate your optimizing routines in with your back up routines.

When performing a normal backup as described in Chapter 10, the entire hard drive is copied to a set of diskettes on a regular basis, usually once a week or once a month, depending on system requirements. Between these backup sessions, intermediate sets of backup diskettes are used to collect files that may have changed or been added since the last major backup. When a restore is required, the major backup is first restored and then the intermediate sets are restored. Unless the hard drive goes down, a RESTORE is usually not part of this procedure. You can make it part of your backup procedure, however, if you want to optimize your hard drive every time you do a backup.

If you decide to add the optimizing routine to your normal backup, the following procedures can be used:

1. Manually scan through your file structure and remove all unnecessary files. EDLIN and some word processors create BAK (back up) files every time you alter an existing file. Often, these can be deleted. Look for files you no longer need, or files that can be copied to a diskette for archive purposes. Performing this cleanup task will reduce the time and the number of diskettes required for a backup. Clearing these files off also makes your system run more efficiently. Keep in mind that you may need to **uninstall** copy protected software before backing up.

2. Perform the major hard drive backup at the predetermined interval. Don't forget to type VERIFY ON before starting. This will make DOS double check the copies for accuracy. You will be completely erasing the hard drive, so the backup set must be good. Chapter 10 discusses a procedure for maintaining two backup sets. If your directory structure uses data directories, as discussed in Chapter 5, you will only need to back up these directories. You'll be able to restore your program files from their original diskettes.

3. Reinitialize the hard drive using the DOS FORMAT command to clear all files and data. This command is covered in Chapter 2. The /S parameter should be used so that the DOS system files will be copied after the format is complete. At this point, you may want to run a program that scans the entire drive and marks bad sectors so that DOS does not attempt to write data to them. There are several third party programs listed in Appendix C that perform this function.

4. Once the drive is ready to accept files, you can use RESTORE to copy the files back to the hard drive. All files will be restored contiguously on the disk.

5. Place the backup set in a safe place and perform intermediate backups until the next major backup session, as discussed in Chapter 10.

Restoring the Software

Once the drive is formatted, you can begin reinstalling the software and data files. If you backed up only the data files and are restoring programs from original diskettes, restore the programs first, then restore the backup sets. The RESTORE command is shown below:

`RESTORE A: C: /S`

As files are restored to your hard drive, they are placed in contiguous sectors on the disk. You should notice an immediate improvement in speed if your drive was badly fragmented.

There are certain advantages to using data directories as discussed in Chapter 5. This is the organization scheme that places data files in their own directories, separate from program files. Separating your program and data files gives you more control over where they are placed on the drive. You can copy your program files to the disk before data files, ensuring that they are placed in permanent sectors. The data files can then be copied to areas of the drive where file fragmentation is allowed to take place.

One thing to keep in mind is that DOS's BACKUP command stores each file on the back up sets with their complete path name. When these files are restored with the RESTORE command, DOS automatically recreated the directories that the files previously occupied. That means you won't be able to reorganize your directory structure in a different way. If that is what you want to do, you should reorganize first, then perform the backup and restore procedures.

Third Party Optimizer Programs

If the procedures outlined for optimizing your drive with BACKUP and RESTORE sound like a lot of work, you may want to consider various software programs on the market that unfragment hard drives more or less automatically without the need to backup, although backup is recommended before running any program that drastically alters the structure of your drive. These disk optimizer programs temporarily copy whole clusters of data to unused portions of your hard drive, determine the best way to reorganize and unfragment the disk and then restore the files in the best way.

Some programs contain features that analyze your drive and inform you of the best time to optimize. Other programs will automatically place COM, EXE and SYS files in the beginning clusters of your drive to increase performance. One program places all files that were originally contiguous in the beginning clusters, assuming that these files are never altered. For a listing of disk optimizing programs, refer to Appendix C.

Other Optimizing Tricks

Many factors effect the performance of your PC or AT's disk performance. The file fragmentation problem discussed earlier is the biggest contributor to a loss in drive performance. This does not take into consideration the hardware performance of the drive, such as its average access time. There are a number of other ways you can "tweek" your system to get just a little more performance.

The PATH Command

Take a minute to evaluate the path you set when executing the PATH command in your AUTOEXEC.BAT file. This command specifies the search order DOS will follow when looking for commands and batch files. The subdirectory that contains the commands and batch files you use most often should be the first subdirectory specified in your command. Subdirectories of decreasing priority should then be specified. DOS will search through each subdirectory in the path until it finds the program or batch file it is looking for.

IBM PC DOS 3.3 introduced a new command called FASTOPEN to keep track of the location of files or directories in a memory list. When you request a file, DOS will look into the memory list to help it locate the file, thus improving the access time, especially when using complex directory structures. FASTOPEN will keep track of directories and recently opened files. You can specify the number of files to be remembered which can be anywhere from 10 to 999, the default being 34. DOS 4 users should refer to Appendix E.

Using Buffers

Setting the correct number of buffers is one of the most important things you can do to speed up hard drive access. The BUFFERS command, which is placed in the CONFIG.SYS file as covered in Chapter 3, tells DOS how much memory to set aside as a temporary holding area for data going to and from your hard drive. If DOS reads a block of data, it is placed in the buffer. The next time the same block of data is requested, DOS goes to the buffer instead of the hard drive, saving time and wear and tear on the drive.

The more buffers you have, the more data DOS can keep in memory. If you fill up the buffers, DOS will begin to swap out the oldest or least accessed blocks for new blocks from the hard drive. All of this takes place in the background.

Each buffer holds 512 bytes which corresponds in size to a disk sector. Setting BUFFERS=10 would allocate about 5K of memory space. If you have a 640K system, this is a very small amount and well worth the trade-off in speed. A good place to set buffers is about 25 or 30. If you are working with a disk intensive application like a database, however, you may want to set buffers higher, say to 50 or 60. Keep in mind that the more buffers you have the more memory is used. Setting BUFFERS=50 takes about 25K of memory. Setting buffers higher than 90 may tend to bog the system down since so much time would be used to search through and manage the buffers. DOS 4 users should refer to Appendix E.

The applications you are using should be considered when setting buffers. A very large spreadsheet that requires a lot of memory and little disk access has no need for buffers. A data base application that performs a lot of disk reads and writes can benefit from a large buffer setting.

Disk Caching

One step up from using buffers is the use of a disk caching program (pronounced "cash"). Although very similar to BUFFERS, a disk cache works more efficiently than DOS BUFFERS and provides a few extra features. You can actively control the amount of memory you want set aside for buffers more easily with most caching programs than can be done with the DOS BUFFER command. Because DOS requires buffers to be set from CONFIG.SYS at boot time, you cannot change buffer settings without rebooting.

Many cache programs also support extended memory beyond

640K for those systems that have expanded or above-board memory installed. This is a major advantage for programs that require a lot of memory that might be tied up by DOS's BUFFERS command. With some programs you can specify that certain blocks of data be kept in the cache no matter what. You can also prevent certain blocks from being inserted in the buffer. Appendix C has more information on disk caching programs.

Changing the Interleave

Recall from the last chapter that older PC's often cannot "process" data going to or coming from the disk fast enough. The disk continues to spin, bringing the next sector under the heads even though the PC is not ready to receive the data because it is still handling data from the previous sector. Interleave is a factor that lets DOS skip over the next one, two or three sectors so it can catch up. It begins reading or writing again at the third or fourth sector, when it is ready to handle more data transfers. This is pictured in Figure 12-6. Newer hard drives will transfer data at even faster rates than those installed in early PC's, so their potential speed is lost if installed in a PC.

Fortunately, newer AT class machines, and some 8086 type computers are able to handle hard drive data transfers at faster speeds due to higher internal clock rates or wider data buses. The bad news is that you may still be working with the interleave factor set for the old PC's and so are not realizing the potential speed of the drive. If this is the case, you will want to take various steps to set an interleave factor that is best for your system. There are several programs that will perform a series of tests on your specific equipment and suggest an optimum interleave factor. *HTEST/HFORMAT* from Paul Mace Utilities and *SpeedStor* by Storage Dimensions are two programs that will do this. They will also reset the interleave if you wish as well as perform extensive tests on your hard drive.

WARNING: Before attempting to change the interleave factor on any drive, you must first back up the data on the hard drive. Since a radical change is made to the filing structure of the drive, the sector mapping that describes the location of files will become useless. After altering the interleave, you will need to reformat the drive and then reinstall the software.

Owners of IBM Advanced Diagnostics can set their own interleave factor using the setup program on the disk. If your system will handle fastest data transfer rates, you can simply set a 1 to 1 interleave. XT type machines may have a routine in the "auto-configure" programs of the controller card (see Appendix A) to set interleave.

Picking the wrong interleave, however, can slow your system even more. There exist an ideal interleave for your system that is different from one machines to the next. Although a 1 to 1 interleave is often best for AT type machines, PC and XT machines will differ quite a bit depending on the hard drive. It is best to use a program that performs an interleave evaluation, like the two described above, before changing it.

RAM Disks

A RAM disk is an area of memory that has been set aside to act like a disk drive. You can even refer to a RAM disk as you would a regular drive by giving it a drive letter. Under DOS 3, the VDISK command can be used to set up RAM drive of almost any size in memory, as covered in Chapter 9.

There is a big difference between buffers, caches and RAM drives. When using buffers and cache programs, changes made to the data are almost instantly written to the permanent disk file as soon as they occur. Changes made in a RAM drive are made in memory only— if the power goes down, you lose your data. I do not recommend that you work with any data files in a RAM drive unless you constantly save updated information to a permanent drive. This can be impractical. A better use of a RAM drive is to copy just the program files to it. These are the files that must be accessed often as you run the application. Since they are never altered and an original copy is permanent on disk, you can safely store them in a RAM drive. While running the applications, all data can be written to permanent storage.

DOS Upgrade

As mentioned in the last chapter, there are differences in the way DOS-2 and DOS-3 store files. A cluster is the smallest unit of storage that both version of DOS will use when writing a file to disk. DOS-2 allocates 8 sectors to a cluster and DOS-3 allocated 4 sectors. Since there are 512 bytes in a sector, the minimum file size for DOS-2 is 4K and for DOS-3 is 2K. Obviously, there are advantages to using DOS-3, especially if you create a lot of small files (under 2K in size). In fact, that would be the main reason for upgrading due to cluster size. Large files will spread out over many clusters; only the last sector may have extra space. Many small files that leave extra room in clusters waste a lot of disk space in DOS-2.

If you decide to upgrade, you can't simply copy the new system files to the hard drive. The drive would still be formatted using the DOS-2 cluster size. You will need to completely back up your hard drive, reformat under the new DOS and then restore the files. Make sure you don't restore the old DOS system files.

Note: You can determine the cluster size of your system and its minimum file size by noting the available disk space before and after creating a file. First, run the DIR command and make a note of the bytes available at the end of the listing. Next, create a simple file called TEST that contains nothing but a carriage return:

```
C:\>COPY CON TEST↵
↵
<F6>
C:\>
```

After creating the file, you can check how much room it takes on the disk by running the DIR command again and noting the decrease in available disk space. DOS-2 will use 4K and DOS-3 will use 2K of space for the nearly-empty file.

Optimizing with Hardware Options

Buy a New Machine

There are a number of ways to gain speed and efficiency from a computer system but you need to evaluate the cost of upgrading an essentially old technology machines. It may be more cost-effective to simply upgrade to a better computer. I'll admit that buying a new system is not the most practical solution to gaining more speed, but if your system requirements are growing, trading up is the only way to go. There are big differences between the 8088 bases PC and XT type machines, the 80286 AT, the 80386 Compaq Deskpro and Personal System/2 machines.

The speed enhancements of the new, advanced machines are often put in terms of the *throughput* of the machine. Throughput is a combination of speed gains obtained from faster processors, wider data busses, better and faster memory, coprocessors and high speed drives. The new Personal System/2 machines from IBM offer a considerable increase in speed over previous models. The throughput of the model 60 and 80 is from 2 to 3 1/2 times faster than the IBM AT.

IBM has announced an entirely new data bus architecture called the *microchannel bus* in its new Personal System/2 line that offers increased performance far beyond the bus design of the original IBM PC's and AT's. Microchannel is designed for multitasking operations. It allows several processes to operate at the same time and will handle more "traffic" on the line. Traffic refers to its ability to send more than one packet of information over the lines at a time, as the old machines were limeted to. If a process has the need to send a "burst" of information quickly to the hard drive or some other device, microchannel will free the lines for that task. Microchannel opens the world of extremely fast storage devices (SCSI and ESDI) to the PC world.

Improve the Drive Type

It is possible to improve the speed of early PC's by upgrading to the newer technology RLL and voice coil drives. The speed improvement will only help alleviate the fragmentation problem, however, since the drives can access badly fragmented files more efficiently. The throughput of the system will still bog down the improved transfer rate of the new drives.

If you own an 80286 AT class machines, you will gain an immediate speed improvement by upgrading to RLL and voice coil drives. Not only does RLL increase performance, it also boost storage capacity by 50% for a minimal increase in price. On both the PC and AT class machines, you will need to upgrade the controller card to take advantage of these features, however.

The drive interleave factor, as discussed in Chapter 12 is one element that can be changed improve performance. IBM originally set its PC XT hard drive interleave factor at 6 to 1. That meant that 6 sectors would be skipped before data was read or written again. On new faster PC and XT clones, this interleave can be decreased to gain a significant decrease in the read/write time. Appendix C list several products that can help you determine and set the best interleave factor for your system.

Clock Chips

There are several things you can do to speed up your computer that are not directly related to your hard drive. If you own an IBM AT, you can replace the clock crystal in your system with a faster one, but it will void the warranty. Purchase the appropriate clock crystal from an electronics parts dealer who is familiar with what you want to do. Other people have probably purchased the same chips from him for the same reasons. A clock crystal is rated at twice the target CPU speed. In other words, a 8MHz CPU target clock speed translates to a 16MHz frequency crystal; a 10MHz CPU clock speed would require a 20MHz crystal and so on.

To install the crystal, locate the old crystal on the motherboard just above and to the left of the 80286 processor when looking from the front of the machine. Ground yourself first by touching the chassis of the machines, then remove the chip with either a chip puller or very carefully with a small, flat head screwdriver. Install the new crystal. If your system doesn't work properly, you may need to step down to the next crystal speed.

Coprocessor Boards

A coprocessor board is actually a whole new computer that you plug into one of the slots of your existing computer. This board contains a new, upgraded microprocessor like the 8086 or 80286 and may even have its own bank of memory on board to increase speed further. The concept of using a coprocessor board comes from the fact that you already have most of the equipment you need to make a faster machine, like the keyboard, screen, printer and even the software. It makes sense to simply upgrade the microprocessor by installing a co-processor board.

There are several drawbacks in using coprocessor boards. If you intend to upgrade a PC type machine with an 80286 coprocessor, the full potential of that processor can never be realized since it will be "choked off" by the small 8 bit data bus of the PC. The 80286 microprocessors work best with wider, faster 16 bit data buses that are only available in machines like the IBM AT. These boards, when installed in a PC type machine, do offer greatly improved processing speed for spreadsheets and programs that operate in memory. If you already own an AT type machines, you can take full advantage of its 16 bit bus by adding advanced coprocessor boards using the new Intel 80386 processor.

Selecting a Hard Drive System

The purpose of this chapter is to help you select a hard drive or hard drive system that is right for you. When everything else is considered, the performance of the hard drive is one of the most important factors contributing to the overall speed of your computer. You should look carefully at the specifications of the hard drive you intend to install in your existing system or the one that comes with a computer you intend to buy.

Don't think that because you have or are about to purchase an 8088 or 8086 based PC that you can't benefit from the newer RLL and SCSI drives discussed in Chapter 12. The slow throughput of PC's has led many to believe that fast hard drives don't do much good. While this is somewhat true, the problems associated with file fragmentation can be alleviated to some extent with a fast drive. There are also advantages in capacity and physical size.

Selecting A Drive

For the most part, hard drives are mounted in the internal bays of most microcomputer systems. On an IBM XT, the hard drive is mounted in the right bay, with a full height or two half height floppy drives mounted in the left bay. Since hard drives are available in half-height sizes as well as full height sizes, it is possible to fit two half-height hard drives in a single full-height bay. Most computers manufactured by Compaq take advantage of growth potential in using half-height drives.

The IBM AT comes equipped standard with a half-height 1.2 megabyte floppy drive. It also has a designated slot for either a full or half-height hard drive to the left of the floppy drive bay. A second floppy drive can be installed under the first floppy drive and a half-height hard drive may be installed under this. Or, a full height drive may be installed under the 1.2MB floppy drive. The AT, however, only provides front panel access to two half-height devices.

The new IBM Personal System/2 and Compaq 386 machines are, for the most part, being shipped with hard drives already installed. This limits your selection although the IBM Personal System/2 Model 60 and 80 and the Compaq 386 models come with very fast and efficient hard drives using the latest technology on both the controller and drive.

There are many combinations of half-height and full-height drives that can be mounted in XT and AT clones. Before deciding, you should determine the optimum setup for your needs. Keep in mind that half-height drives are always best if you are not sure of your future needs or power requirements. If you need large capacity drives, you'll probably need to go with a full-height drive. Don't forget to leave a bay open for future expansions like tape backups.

Hard drives for 8088 and 8086 based PC's will usually require the addition of a hard disk controller in one of the card slots. Make sure that you have an available slot before making your decision. If you are running short of mounting bays, you might consider the use of a "hard-card." This is a hard disk mounted directly to the controller card that fits into one of your card slots. Hard-Cards are available in 10, 20 and even 30MB capacities.

In addition to internal hard drives and hard-cards, you can select among a variety of external drives that run off separate power supplies and connect via special hard drive adapters. One brand of drive in particular, the Bernoulli Box, made by Iomega, features a removable disk pack. The hard drive platter itself is contained within a plastic housing that seals itself when you remove it from the drive. In this way, your hard drive capacity is limited only to the number of disk packs you have available. The drives are available in 10MB or 20MB single or dual configurations. The dual drives allow you to copy and backup from one cartridge to another.

Features to watch for when selecting a hard drive include its ability to self-boot and self-park. Self-booting simply means that you can start your computer from the hard drive without having to place a special start-up disk in the floppy drive. This is not so much a problem these days since newer computers contain this self-boot procedure in ROM. The hard drive and controller must be able to tie into this logic, however. Drives that are self-parking will move the read/write heads to an unused "parking-zone" when you turn the power off. This alleviates head crashes onto valuable data areas of the drive platters. If you are going to move your hard drive system around or plan to install a hard drive in a portable computer, you should consider a "shock-mounted" unit. These drives are usually smaller 3 1/2" drives mounted with rubber grommets within a metal frame.

If by chance, you own an older PC, you may need to upgrade one of the ROM chips on your system with a newer chips that recognize and self-boot hard drives. For IBM systems, this replacement is available from authorized dealers for a minimum price (about $35 to $50). You will need to bring in your old chip for exchange, so call your dealer for details. Older PC's also suffer from power supply constraints. Make sure that the drive you buy is a low power consumption model that will work in your system, especially if you have it loaded with a lot of expansion boards.

Last, but not least, you'll need a mounting kit that's right for your computer. Usually, this will come with the hard drive, but if you own a clone, you had better do the right research to procure the mounting hardware before buying the drive. Mounting kits include extra cables, if needed, screws and mounting rails used to hold the drive in the bay.

Making the Right Selection

One of the main reasons for replacing or adding a hard drive to any system, or researching the hard drive in the computer you intend to buy, is to gain greater speed and access to your programs and data. The following is a recap of the features most important to making the proper decision.

The flow chart in Figure 14-1 and drive selection Table 14-1 can help in your drive decision. Most of the drives listed with access times of 30 milliseconds or less are voice-coil drives. Although each manufacturer listed makes a large selection of drive types, I chose those in the 21MB, 32MB, 60MB and 120MB range for this table.

- **Drive Size**. The larger the drive, the faster its performance. A 70MB or 130MB drive has more platters and thus more data tracks to record on before moving the read/write heads.

- **Read/Write Head Type**. The voice-coil type read/write head mechanism offers one of the biggest increases in drive performance. Older stepper motor designs like those used in early XT models are clunky by comparison. One of the main reasons for adding a higher performance hard drive to a PC or XT type machines is to counter the sluggishness caused by excessive head movement of badly fragmented drives. The only effective way to do this is to use a voice-coil drive that can perform quick track to track reads and writes.

- **RLL Encoding**. Not only does RLL encoding pack 50% more information than standard MFM encoding, but a significant increase in read/write performance is also realized. RLL encoding typically provides transfer rates of 7 Mbits per second compared to 5 Mbits per second MFM drives.

- **Bus Size**. This is entirely dependent on your computer. AT type machines have a full size 16 bit bus, whereas older PC and XT machines use an 8 bit bus. If you move up to an AT machines, you will be able to take advantage of the full performance of RLL and voice-coil drives.

- **Interface Type**. The interface type you choose will greatly determine the transfer rate of data to and from the drive. If you are placing a drive in a PC or XT type machines, you will need to use the ST506/412 interface. This interface is also standard equipment on AT type machines. You can, however switch to a different interface on AT's. The SCSI or ESDI interface standard offer considerable improvements in features and transfer rates.

DRIVE TYPE	A	B	C	D	E	F
SEAGATE ST125	21	30	8	70	MFM	ST412
SEAGATE ST225N	21	65	20	150	MFM	SCSI
MINISCRIBE 8425S	21	68	15	150	RLL	SCSI
MINISCRIBE 3425	21	85	15	190	MFM	ST412
RODIME RO5040	32	28	5	55	MFM	ST412
SEAGATE ST138R	32	30	8	70	RLL	ST412
SEAGATE ST138N	32	30	8	70	RLL	SCSI
SEAGATE ST138	32	30	8	70	MFM	ST412
MINISCRIBE 3438	32	85	15	190	RLL	ST412
CMS K-30	33	55	8	130	MFM	ST412
RODIME RO3045	35	28	7	60	MFM	ST412
CMS K-60	60	28	6	62	MFM	ST412
RODIME 5075S	64	28	5	55	RLL	SCSI
SEAGATE ST4077N	67	28	6	55	RLL	SCSI
SEAGATE ST4077R	68	28	6	55	RLL	ST412
SEAGATE ST4144R	122	28	6	55	RLL	ST412
SEAGATE ST4144N	122	28	6	55	RLL	SCSI
RODIME 5125S	128	28	5	55	RLL	SCSI

Table 14-1. Hard drive sampling.

A: CAPACITY   B: AVERAGE ACCESS TIME
C: TRACK TO TRACK ACCESS   D: MAXIMUM ACCESS TIME
E: RECORDING METHOD   F: INTERFACE TYPE

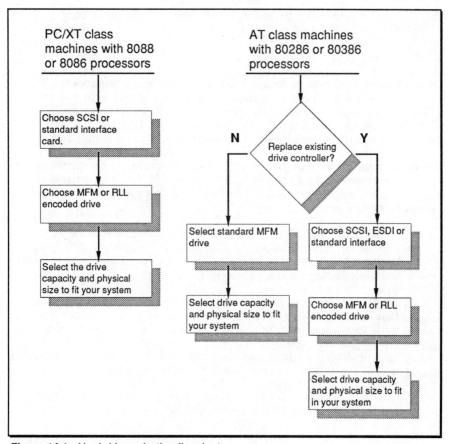

Figure 14-1. Hard drive selection flowchart.

- **Capacity**. The drive capacity is purely a personal choice that depends on the number of programs and the amount of data you will need to store on the drive. Most 20MB and 30MB drives use two platters and are of the half-height variety. Larger drives may come in both half-height and full-height capacities. You will find that the price per Megabyte of RLL drives is close to that of MFM drives, since there is not much difference in the physical aspect of the drives.

- **Average access time**. The average access time is based on how long it takes for the head to seek and position itself over the proper track, and how long it takes for the proper sector to swing around under the head. The starting position of the head and the location of the data it needs makes comparisons between different drives vary. Each manufacturer may rate their drives using different parameters, but, for the most part, average access time can be used as a rough comparison guide.

- **Track to track access**. This figure becomes important when you consider that files on drives become fragmented over time. When the read/write heads need to move to multiple tracks to read a single file, the speed at which the head mechanism can make track to track moves is important.

- **Maximum access time**. This figure is obtained by measuring the time it takes for the heads to read from the furthest tracks, and is an indication of the maximum time it will take to read a file.

- **Recording Method**. If a drives performance seems exceptional, it is probably an RLL drive. The packing density increases the read/write performance and allows you to store up to 50% more data.

- **Interface Type**. There is really not much use in purchasing a fast drive if it doesn't have the proper interface to get the data to your computer. The SCSI interface is an excellent choice for AT type systems since it can deliver data from the fastest drives at their full rate. An RLL drive will transfer data at 7.5 Mbits per second which is easily handled by the 12 Mbits per second rating of the SCSI interface. The ESDI (Enhanced Small Device Interface) is a feature of the IBM Personal System/2 models 60 and 80.

The following table lists the hard drive specifications of the new IBM Personal System/2 computer systems and can be used as a comparison guide when selecting a system or hard drive.

	Mod 30	Mod 50	Mod 60 & 80 44Mb capacity	Mod 60 & 80 70Mb capacity	Mod 80 115Mb
Formatted Capacity	21Mb	20Mb	44Mb	70Mb	115Mb
Bytes per sector	512	512	512	512	512
Sectors per track	17	17	17	36	36
Number of cylinders	612	612	733	583	915
Transfer Rate	5.0 Mbits	5.0 Mbits	5.0 Mbits	10 Mbits	10 Mbits
Access Time					
track to track	15ms	15ms	10ms		
single cylinder				5ms	6ms
average	80ms	80ms	40ms	30ms	28ms
maximum	180ms	180ms	80ms	60ms	60ms
Power on time	15 sec	15 sec	25 sec	25 sec	25 sec
Interleave	3:1	1:1	1:1	1:1	1:1
Adapter type	PC Bus	ST506	ST506	ESDI	ESDI
Bus Type	PC Bus	---------------------------------- Microchannel ----------------------------			

Table 14-2. The hard drive specifications for the new IBM Personal System/2 series.

15

Optical Disk Technologies

A discussion of optical or laser disk technologies is appropriate for this book because optical disk storage will almost certainly figure into the scheme of almost all microcomputer storage techniques in the next few years. Optical drive technology is a relatively new concept in information storage on microcomputers. Through the use of focused beams of laser light, information can be stored on small, portable disks in an extremely dense form. These disks, similar to the Compact Audio Disk that has become so popular in the music world, are durable and not prone to accidental erasure or contamination.

Not only can optical storage be used as an alternative to the hard drive as a means of storing and retrieving information quickly, but it also figures well into data backup schemes. A typical optical disk can hold anywhere from 200MB to 500MB of information. That means you could backup your entire 20MB hard drive anywhere from 10 to 25 times onto a single disk that costs about $25. Besides the potential for archiving all of your data, the optical disk offers a large amount of data security since you can simply slip it in your briefcase. This portable disk can hold all of your data so that you don't have to leave it behind where other people can have access to it.

When data is written to an optical disk, an actual "pit" is burned into the media. That means that once data is written, it is permanent, but that permanence just happens to be one of the most attractive features that the optical disk has over standard magnetic media, as you'll see. Each pit is burned in a spiral fashion from the inner to the outer hub of the disk. The pits and the spiral rings they form are so minute that a density of 16,000 ring or tracks per inch is achieved. Binary information is stored by burning pits and leaving blank spaces between them, known as "lands." A typical optical disk might contain up to 2 billion pits.

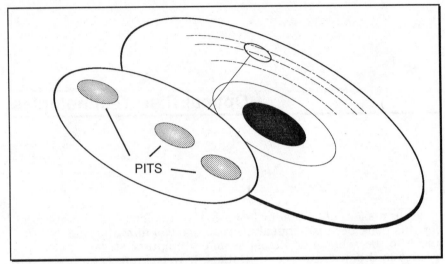

Figure 15-1. Pits and lands of an optical disk.

Storage potentials of up to 500MB translates into about 150,000 pages of text information. That also translates to the storage equivalent of about 1300 floppy diskettes. Imagine manipulating that many diskettes in an out of your floppy drive, let alone trying to find a place to store them safely. Because of the potential capacity, the optical disk finally opens up the possibility of storing data, text, audio and visual information in one place with plenty of room to effectively use that information.

If you are having trouble visualizing how optical disks can be used or how they will fit into your future, stop for a minute to think about all of the information and data that you don't have available on your computer at this moment. Because the potential storage capacity of optical disks is so high, a whole new era of instantly available information is upon us. For example, if you are an attorney or doctor, you can purchase legal or medical data bases at a minimum charge. The data is made available at a subscription rate with monthly or yearly updates. In the past, this type of service was never really feasible because too many diskettes were required to get the data base to the end users computer system. On-line communications services using slow phone modems were used occasionally.

Just look around your office or home. You'll begin to realize the potential for optical storage. As an example, take a look through your phone book. Here is an extremely large data base that also includes the yellow pages business directory. The phone company must update this book on a regular basis, and then reprint it at great expense. Obviously, the phone company wouldn't consider putting the phone book on optical disk unless everyone had a way to read that disk and the disk were cheap to reproduce. Those possibilities, however, may not be far away. The CD-ROM optical disk format, discussed in a minute, is similar to the Compact Audio Disk format that has become extremely popular. Disk players are already being developed that will read both the audio disk and data disk, allowing you to plug the unit into your stereo and your computer.

The manufacturing process for CD-ROM's, as well as the audio variety is becoming more streamlined and disks are becoming cheaper, thanks to the popularity of the of the audio variety. Once a master is made, duplicates can be stamped out almost endlessly, and cheaply. Compare this to the copying of magnetic media, where each disk or tape must be recorded. If the phone company, or even your own company, decides to mass produce a data base, the expense will be minimal compared to the value of the data.

Optical disks also offer a more reliable means of getting data from one place to another. They are not subject to external magnetic fluctuations and electrical discharges that can wipe out whole clusters of data on normal magnetic media. Each disk is covered with a durable plastic that can even be scratched to some extent, and not affect the integrity of the data. I have restored a scratched Compact Audio Disk by cleaning it with a well known car dashboard reconditioner. Since the disk is read by a beam of light, there is never a possibility of head crash.

Speaking of data integrity, the optical disk offers one of the best and most reliable error correction techniques possible. Because there is so much available room, extra bits are used for error correction codes. That means that each piece of information is backed up by extra coding that ensures that it will be read correct every time. For example, a typical CD-ROM disk stores about 2000 characters of information in one sector. This is backed up by about 300 bytes of error correction information.

The optical disks potential is not limited to commercially available data bases. Write Once-Read Many (WORM) drives allow you to write to an optical disk once and then read that information many times. You can create your own data bases for distribution throughout your company or for resale. The WORM drive also allows you to backup existing hard drives. A typical personal computer system using a optical drive would also use a magnetic hard drive. Since the hard drive can be written to many times and then erased, it would be used to prepare the data for eventual storage to the optical disk. Once the data base is complete and updated, it can then be copied to the optical disk.

Besides data and text storage, you can store pictures as well as audio information on the same disk as your text, provided you have the right software. An immediate application can be seen in the real estate office, where pictures of properties can be stored along with descriptive text. With the proliferation of desktop scanners that transfer photographs and drawings into computer memory and because the optical disk can hold so much information, this is becoming more and more feasible. A typical scanned photograph needs up to 1MB of memory. If you include some text with each picture, it is possible to store anywhere from 200 to 500 properties on one optical disk. Many scanners allow cropping of pictures, as well as resolution selection, allowing you to store pictures in less memory. This could increase the storage potential up into the thousands of images.

Basically, optical disks and drives come in two varieties. The first is the CD-ROM, or Compact Disk-Read Only Medium. This disk technology is read-only; you cannot write to the disk yourself. The second major variety is the WORM drive, or Write Once, Read Many. This technology allows data to be written once and read many times. The disk cannot be erased, however. The WORM is of the most interest in this article since it allows you to develop an alternate means of data storage other than you hard drive and also allows you to archive data from your hard drive.

CD-ROM Drives

CD-ROM has become a standard throughout the industry and is supported by many important companies, including Microsoft. Over the next 5 years, the use of CD-ROM's should increase dramatically as more and more information becomes available on disk. An entire industry that peddles information data bases will blossom as more and more CD-ROM drives come into use. If your company has its own database that is either marketable or needs to be accessed by offices throughout the country, you can even have your own CD-ROM disk pressed by these optical disk publishing houses.

Currently, CD-ROM is a standard that was originally set by a group of major manufacturers known as the High Sierra Group. This group consisted of such major companies as Microsoft, Apple, 3M, Philips and Hitachi, among others. CD-ROM stores up to 540 million bytes of ASCII characters in one or more files. The disk is the standard Compact Audio Disk variety that measures 4.72 inches across and weighs 0.7 ounces. Portability and convenience are the key here. As mentioned earlier, the information is stored as pits and lands in a spiral ring that stretches from the inner hub to the outer edge. The disk is then completely enclosed in a hard plastic coating.

Since CD-ROM contains read-only data, all information is "pressed" on the disk at the factory from a master disk. This master disk is created by the publisher from data that has often been manipulated with magnetic media type storage systems such as a hard drive or tape. Because magnetic media is erasable and changeable, it will continue to be a major part of the process in creating the data bases and other information stored on optical drives.

You will probably continue to use magnetic hard drives with your computer system over the next few years, even after purchasing a CD-ROM drive. The CD-ROM would become the device you use to retrieve information, while still working with your hard drive as a data storage unit. For example, you may use a data base program that read and writes data to your hard drive and uses the CD-ROM drive to look up secondary information, such as zip code data or inventory part descriptions.

WORM Drives

The WORM (Write Once, Read Many) drive is one of the best additions you can make to your computer system if you need to work with large amounts of data. As the name implies, you can only write to the disk once. A hole burned into the disk material cannot be removed. This, however, is one of the major advantages of optical disks since it ensures the protection of your data. A WORM drive is as excellent alternative to tape or diskette backup methods for hard drives. You can backup an entire hard disk multiple times and retain a permanent record of all of your disk files.

You may be wondering why you would even need a hard drive after installing a WORM drive. In reality, a hard drive and an optical disk make an excellent combination. You can create and manipulate your data using the changeable magnetic media of the hard drive and then copy the final version of the data to the optical drive, where it can be referenced as a read-only data base. As of this writing, many WORM drives are still slow compared to current models of magnetic hard drives. A considerable amount of time is required to write to a WORM drive because the holes must be burned. The real speed advantage comes in the retrieval of large amounts of information that would normally be archived to paper or backup diskettes.

One aspect of WORM drives that is disconcerting at this time is that there is little standardization in the disk specifications as there is with the CD-ROM format. That means you may not be able to take a disk written on one drive and read it on another. This will cause major problems in the future unless one manufacturers WORM drive becomes standard throughout the industry. In April of 1987, IBM announced its first optical disk for microcomputers, the model 3353. Although the storage capacity of this drive is rather small (200MB), it could prove to be a standard setting device. As an example of a WORM drive, I will describe its features here.

The model 3353 is a mass storage device designed specifically for IBM PC's, XT's, AT's and the new Personal System/2 machines. IBM wishes to view the device as a supplement to a fixed disk, and for applications where removability of the disk is important, as in security, archiving and backup. The drive uses a 5.25 inch write once, removable optical disk that is housed in a protective cartridge. It records on one side and has a capacity of 200 million bytes. Up to eight of the drives may be installed at one time.

The drive utilizes the typical spiral format. Each sector holds 512 bytes of data and there are 23 sectors per track with 17,100 tracks per disk. The drive has a burst data rate of up to 2.5 Megabits per second and an average seek time of less than 230ms (up to 101 tracks in less than 45ms). The drive supports files larger than 32MB and a file versioning technique that allows users to retrieve prior version of files with the same name.

Optical Disk Format Types

There is a big difference between the way magnetic floppy diskettes and hard drives place data on the disk platters and the way data is stored to an optical disk. Obviously, there is a big difference in the number of data tracks available between all of the formats. But this is not the point. With typical magnetic media, each track contains the same number of sectors. If you think about the tracks as being rings around the disk, you can imagine that the outer rings are larger than those closest to the center of the disk. Even though the outer rings are larger and could conceivably hold more sectors, the sectors count of the outer track is the same as the inner track. This means that the space between sectors on the outer tracks is greater than the space between sectors of inner tracks.

To read a floppy or hard drive, a read and write scheme known as Constant Angular Velocity (CAV) is used. Under this scheme, the drive rotates at a constant speed under the drive. Since the sector count and size is consistent between inner and outer tracks, the drives read and write head can jump from track to track and sector to sector without having to make an adjustment for differences in the size of the tracks. Except for the fact that it must take into account the larger spacing between sectors on outer tracks, there are no other changes required when the head moves between tracks.

Reading and writing optical drives is another story entirely. A scheme known as Constant Linear Velocity (CLV) is used to read data along the continuous spiral track that stretches for nearly 3 miles on the disk. Each block of data holds a little over 2000 bytes and is exactly the same size as every other block in the spiral. Since the outer edge of the continuous data spiral contains more data blocks than the inner spiral, and since these data blocks must all be read at the same speed, the disk will need to spin slower when a read or write occurs on the inner portion of the spiral.

Consider the Compact Audio Disk. The player begins reading the disk at the center and follows the continuous spiral all the way to the outside edge of the disk. There is no random jumping, just a continuous read, unless you request a song in the middle of the disk. When the head moves to another part of the disk, either inward or outward, a change in the speed of the disk spin must be made by the drive circuitry. This is really not much of a problem with music disks, since most people can tolerate a short pause between songs. This speed adjustment can cause major problems, however, when an optical disk is being used for data storage. If you are searching through several files that are not next to each other, the drive will need to make numerous adjustments to its speed, significantly slowing it down.

As of this writing, new optical drives that utilize the CAV scheme are being developed. These drives offer a significant increase in speed, but waste a lot of space. You should note, however that the CLV scheme is perfectly acceptable for audio disks where jumps to other parts of the disk are rare. This scheme is also acceptable for disks that contain text information that is read sequentially or does not need to be accessed constantly.

Software Interface

Because of the huge amount of data that can be stored on an optical disk, a special software menuing system is essential. For the most part, this front end is usually similar to the hierarchical filing system of DOS. Many CD-ROM disks come with a front end program for interacting with data, but it may not be consistent with programs from other manufacturers. Each publisher prefers to use their own program and different types of data bases often require different menuing systems anyway.

Operating System/2

In early 1987 IBM announced Operating System/2, the successor to DOS, its standard operating system for over 6 years. OS/2 was developed in conjunction with the Microsoft Corporation, just as the early DOS was. At the same time OS/2 was announced, IBM launched a new generation of computers known as Personal System/2. These new machines are based on 8086, 80286 and 80386 processors from Intel and include enhanced features like expanded memory, on-board video and disk controllers, and new hard drives with 1-to-1 interleave and ESDI interfaces (Table 14-2 lists the specifications for the new drives and interfaces).

The 80286 and 80386 machines include a new 16/32-bit Micro Channel architecture bus structure that greatly improves data throughput. Throughput refers to the speed associated with a number of factors, including disk and memory access, processor speed and bus size. Operating System/2 was designed to take advantage of this new bus, which allows multitasking (the ability to run several tasks at once) and multiuser capabilities (the ability to have several users accessing the system at once). In addition, OS/2 will run on the IBM AT and XT-286 machines. It uses 16-megabytes of memory and will run DOS applications in what is known as "compatibility mode."

Operating System/2 comes in several different forms. Since OS/2 is not strictly an IBM/Microsoft product, other hardware vendors can market the operating system with their products. The main part of OS/2 is the same no matter what machines it is running on. This *kernel* handles most of the file input and output, keyboard and mouse input, character mode display output, multitasking and communications between processes.

The starting edition is called "Standard Edition" by IBM and "MS Operating System/2 (MS OS/2)" by Microsoft. The OS/2 Windows Presentation Manager is an addition to the operating system that provides a front end menuing system that can be used in place of the menuing system described in the front of this book. IBM is including its windows manager in its OS/2, Version 1.1. Although OS/2 will run without the Windows Presentation Manager, both IBM and Microsoft consider it a vital part of the operating system. The Presentation Manager is actually an offshoot of Microsoft Windows. Both MS OS/2 and the Windows Presentation Manager are in compliance with IBM's Systems Applications Architecture (SAA), a set of common specifications created to promote "consistent" applications development across the entire line of IBM computers.

A LAN (Local Area Network) Manager is also available for OS/2. This component offers network support so PC's can communicate across communications lines to other PC's. IBM's version of the LAN Manager is called OS/2 Extended Edition and includes support for communications among various IBM mainframe and minicomputers, as well as the LAN manager.

DOS-Like Interface

To the DOS user, most of the features of OS/2 will be familiar. The command line and the way it is used is the same. Most of the existing DOS commands have been duplicated to the new operating system. The big difference is that you don't have to wait for one command to end before you start another. When several tasks are running simultaneously, each task becomes known as a session. Switching between each of these session to see what is happening in each is a simple matter of pressing the Alt-Esc key sequence. This clears the screen and displays the Session Manager, which lists all current activities identified by the names of the programs running in them. You can use the cursor keys to move between them to make a selection. To move between the session automatically, simply hold down the Alt key while pressing Esc. One of the biggest advantages of this feature is the ability to switch between several different programs without exiting out of one and loading another.

DOS Compatibility Box

One of the sessions available under OS/2 is called the DOS Compatibility Box. This is the "environment" where you can run existing DOS applications as if you had a 640K 8086 based PC. Compatibility mode allows one MS DOS/PC DOS application to execute in the foreground. Any applications that might be running in the background are temporarily suspended, but may be resumed at any time by switching to their sessions. Programs running in the compatibility mode can only run in the foreground and are suspended when running other sessions.

Most existing DOS applications will not gain much in speed by running under this mode when compared to running the same application under DOS. Some programs that directly access hardware will not run in this mode.

Multitasking

Every version of MS DOS or PC DOS, including DOS 3.3 have been a single-process operating system. In other words, they have only been able to execute one application at a time. This is mainly a fault in the 8088/8086 architecture of early systems, which are limited to 1MB of memory and offer no support for protecting memory. Protecting memory is required when running multiple applications. One program cannot use the same memory locations as another. The new Operating System/2 will not allow multiple applications to run in the compatibility box, however, you can still run an application in the box while others run in the other sessions of OS/2.

Because of the limitations of early PC's using 8088/8086 processors and the limitations of the Disk Operating System designed around them, both Microsoft and IBM decided to invest in a new operating system that would take advantage of newer hardware like the 80286 processor available in the IBM AT. The new operating system would take advantage of the new hardware, allow multitasking and break the 640K barrier.

Future Plans

OS/2 has a future in the world of IBM Personal Computers. Microsoft intends to move the operating system into an 80386 version and hopes that the foundations established by OS/2 will become the standards for personal computer operating systems for years to come. Software developers need an established operating system that also takes advantage of state-of-the-art hardware so they can develop future applications.

In time, as software developers become skilled with the new environment of OS/2, new, more powerful applications will become available. Microsoft has included many features that make the job of programming to the new system easy. With new hardware that eliminates many of the bottlenecks of the old equipment, Operating System/2, programmers will be more than willing to invest their time and energy into the new operating system.

Hard Drive Installation

This appendix will help you physically install a hard drive in your PC, XT or AT type system. The procedures described here cover the mounting of the hard drive and the determination of either switch settings or drive types to be used in software setup programs. PC and XT class machines and AT class machines are covered separately since the installation process is different.

Physical Installation of Hard Drives: PC and XT Type Machines

Most PC/XT drives are selected through switch settings on the hard drive controller card. Many cards use a ROM based installation program that is accessed through the DOS DEBUG command or a program supplied by the hard drive or controller manufacturer. These installation programs allow you to set the drive type, and in some cases, the interleave factor and partition size. A program called **SpeedStor** from Storage Dimensions is an excellent utility for those installing their own hard drives. It assists not only with installation and partitioning, but also testing of the hard drive.

In order to install a hard drive on a PC XT type machines, you will need the following:

- A hard disk controller, such as:

  Western Digital SW1002S-WX1 or WD1002S-WX2
  Adaptec 2002A or 2010A
  OMTI 5510-7
  Data Technology Corporation DTC-5150BX
  NDC Centan 5026

- A hard drive suitable for PC XT class machines

  The power supply in PC type machines may not be sufficient to a hard drive. You may need to upgrade it to a minimum 135 watt unit. Most half height drives will operate with the original PC power supply, however. The XT is equipped with a sufficient power supply.

- Minimum of 192K of memory

- A version of DOS higher than 2.0

- Appropriate hard drive mounting and connection hardware, including mounting rails and cables.

- The instruction manual for the controller and hard drive so you can properly set the jumper and dip switches.

Note: Early PCs and Compaqs with 64K motherboards may require a ROM upgrade in order to access a hard drive properly. For IBM PCs, you should obtain ROM BIOS #1501476 from an authorized dealer so that you can self-boot your system from the hard drive.

The rest of this section covers the physical installation of the hard drive and its controller, as well as the setting of various switches or software selectable features.

1. Set the switches on your hard drive controller. On most controllers, this can be done one of two ways. You can select an auto-configure mode that sets switches according to a self-running program, or you can set the switches on the board to match the drive type you may have, which can be determined from Table A-1. PC and XT machines will handle up to two hard drives, so most controllers must have their switches set for one or two drives. Refer to your controller manual for the proper switch setting to match your drive. If you don't have this manual, you should contact the manufacturer or refer to Appendix D. Further information is available in Appendix E.

   If you are not sure of the specifications of your hard drive needed to determine the drive type, you can refer to Appendix D for a fairly complete list. If your hard drive is larger than 32MB, you will need a program that automatically partitions the drive and configures it for your controller card. *SpeedStor* is an excellent program for this.

	TYPE	CYLINDERS	HEADS	CAP (MB)
OLD XT	0	306	2	5.3
	1	375	8	26.1
	2	306	6	15.9
	3	306	4	10.6
NEW XT	0	306	4	10.6
	1	615	4	21.4
	2	306	8	21.2
	3	612	4	21.3

Table A-1. IBM PC and XT drive types.

2. Turn off the system and remove the power cord.

3. Remove the cover by undoing the 5 screws in the corners and top middle of the backplate on your system unit.

4. Plug the 34 and 20 pin conductor cable onto the correct plug of the controller card. The pin numbers or color striping must match. Do not install the card in the system unit yet.

5. Remove either the blank panel or the floppy drive from the bay you intend to install the hard drive in.

6. Slide the hard drive into the bay from the front panel.

7. Place the 34 pin and 20 pin conductor cables on the hard drive connectors, making sure that the orientation is correct.

8. Slide the power connector from the hard drive onto the power supply connector.

9. Install three mounting screws. Two are secured on the side of the drive next to the controller cards. One comes up from underneath the drive and system unit.

10. Plug the controller into one of the empty slots of your system, preferably as close to the hard drive as possible.

11. Replace the cover and power cord.

If you installed a half-height hard drive in your system, you may still have room to install another on top or below it. You will need a "Y" connector for the power supply cable and additional cables to go from the hard drive to the controller. In addition, you will need to remove the "terminating resister" from the second drive (the D drive).

At this point, you can proceed with the auto-configuration of your hard drive as covered in the instruction manual. This may involve using the DEBUG program to set the internal memory switches on your controller card to the drive type, interleave and other settings. After this step, you can run a hard disk partitioning programs if your drive is larger than 32MB. You can then proceed with the FDISK and FORMAT instructions as covered in Chapter 2.

Physical Installation of Hard Drives: AT Type Machines

Most drives for AT class machines are selected by running the SETUP program on the diagnostics disk supplied with the system. A program called *SpeedStor* from Storage Dimensions is an excellent utility for those installing their own hard drives. It assists not only with installation and partitioning, but also testing of the hard drive.

In order to install a hard drive on a PC AT type machines, you will need the following:

- A hard disk controller, such as:

  The original controller supplied with all AT type machines.
  Western Digital WD1002-WA2 (or WD1003) (fixed disk and floppy drive)
  Western Digital SW1002-WAH (or WD1003) (fixed disk only)
  Data Technology Corporation DTC-5290 (Fixed disk/floppy controller)
  NDC Centan 5025 (Fixed disk/floppy controller)

- A hard drive suitable for PC AT class machines
- Minimum of 192K of memory
- A version of DOS higher than 3.0
- Appropriate hard drive mounting and connection hardware, including mounting rails and cables.
- The instruction manual for the controller and hard drive so you can properly set the jumper and dip switches.

The rest of this section covers the physical installation of the hard drive and its controller, as well as the setting of various switches or software selectable features.

1. Determine the drive type of your hard drive by referring to Tables A-2 and A-3. If you are not sure of the specifications of your hard drive needed to determine the drive type, you can refer to Appendix D for a fairly complete list. If your hard drive is larger than 32MB, you will need a program that automatically partitions the drive and configures it for your controller card. *SpeedStor* is an excellent program for this.

2. Turn off the system and remove the power cord.

3. Remove the cover by undoing the 5 screws in the corners and top middle of the backplate on your system unit. The cover slides forward.

4. Remove the two fixed disk restraining screws and clips from the AT front panel.

5. Remove the power supply load resistor, if present, located in the mounting bay.

6. Attach the mounting rails supplied with your system to the sides of the drive and slide the drive into the bay.

7. Place the cable labeled "C" coming off of the controller card onto the first hard drive installed on your system.
8. Connect the data cables, making sure to connect them the right way.
9. If you are installing a new controller card, place it in the bus slot at this time.
10. Connect the appropriate cables to the controller card as covered in the instruction manual.
11. Connect the power connector on the drive to the power supply connector.
12. Connect the grounding wire on top of the hard drive.
13. Secure the hard drive with the clips and screws at the front of the system.
14. Replace the cover and power cord.

TYPE	CYLINDERS	HEADS	WRITE PRECOM	LAND ZONE	CAP (mb)
1	306	4	128	305	10.6
2	615	4	300	615	21.4
3	615	6	300	615	32.1
4	940	8	512	940	65.4
5	940	6	512	940	49.0
6	615	4	none	615	21.4
7	462	8	256	511	32.1
8	733	5	none	733	31.9
9	900	15	none	901	117.5
10	820	3	none	820	21.4
11	855	5	none	855	37.2
12	855	7	none	855	52.0
13	306	8	128	319	21.3
14	733	7	none	733	44.6
15	User Definable				
16	612	4	0	663	21.3
17	977	5	300	977	42.5
18	977	7	none	977	59.5
19	1024	7	512	1023	62.3
20	733	5	300	732	31.9
21	733	7	300	732	44.6
22	733	5	300	733	31.9
23	306	4	0	336	10.6

Table A-2. IBM AT drive types.

Note: The capacity may be rounded up or down to match the specifications of your drive.

You can install a second drive in most AT class machines. A slot is provided inside the machine to the left of the first drive. All cables and power supply cords should be in the system. You will need to remove the "terminating resister" from this second drive.

At this point, you can refer to Chapter 2 for formatting and software installation procedures. This will include partitioning drives larger than 32MB into several logical drives. DOS 3.3 performs this task using the FDISK command. You can also use programs like *SpeedStor* by Storage Dimensions. Before doing so you may want to run various software programs that perform extensive hard drive tests. Refer to Appendix C for a list of packages that do this.

TYPE	CYLINDERS	HEADS	WRITE PRECOM	LAND ZONE	CAP (mb)
1	306	4	128	305	37.4
2	615	4	128	638	21.4
3	615	6	128	615	32.1
4	1024	8	512	1023	71.3
5	950	6	512	939	49.6
6	697	5	128	696	30.3
7	462	8	256	511	32.1
8	925	5	128	924	40.2
9	900	15	None	899	117.5
10	980	5	None	980	42.6
11	925	7	128	924	56.3
12	925	9	128	924	72.4
13	612	8	256	611	42.6
14	754	11	None	753	72.2
15	User definable				
16	306	4	128	305	10.6
17	615	4	300	615	21.4
18	615	6	300	615	32.1
19	940	8	512	940	65.4
20	940	6	512	940	49.0
21	615	4	None	615	21.4
22	462	8	256	511	32.1
23	733	5	None	733	31.9
24	900	15	None	901	117.5
25	820	3	None	820	21.4
26	855	5	None	855	37.2
27	855	7	None	855	52.0
28	306	8	128	319	21.3
29	733	7	None	733	44.6

Table A-3. COMPAQ 286 drive types.

Note: The capacities may be rounded up or down.

B

DOS Commands for Hard Drives

DOS Commands for Hard Drive Users

There are a number of DOS commands you will need to use as you work with your computer. These commands are essential to the proper operation of hard drive systems and so I briefly discuss each one here, in alphabetical order. This section is not meant to be a comprehensive guide to DOS commands. The syntax of each command is not listed. You can refer to your DOS manual or elsewhere in this manual for details on executing the command. Instead, this section will help you quickly locate appropriate commands for performing useful tasks.

APPEND

Purpose: Locate data files outside of the current directory, much like the PATH command looks for programs outside of the current directory.

Usefulness:
- Data files can be stored in a single directory, giving you better control over the design of your directory structure.
- Data files can be subdivided into separate categories and placed in distinct subdirectories. They can then be called from any other directory.

Remarks: The PATH command is similar to APPEND, but PATH only finds .COM, .EXE and .BAT files.

WARNING : Some applications do not use APPEND properly. They find the file, but write changes back to the current directory. Experiment with your applications programs.

Announced with: DOS version 3.3

ASSIGN

Purpose: Redirects output meant for one drive to another.

Usefulness:
* Reassign a drive when using a program that insists on saving or retrieving files on a disk other than the one you want to use.

Remarks: ASSIGN was used mainly when DOS was first announced for hard drives. Some applications would not recognize the hard drive or subdirectories and ASSIGN could be used to redirect inputs and outputs outside of the program.

WARNING! Never use this command when using BACKUP, RESTORE, LABEL, JOIN, SUBST, or PRINT.

Announced with: DOS version 2.0

ATTRIB

Purpose: (Attribute) Modifies the read-only and archive status of files.

Usefulness:
* Protects files from accidental erasure by making them read-only.
* Lets you set the archive bit on or off before a backup so you can selectively choose which files are backed up or not

Remarks: Use this command to protect your menu and batch files from accidental erasure by novice users, or by mistakes made at the keyboard.

Announced with: DOS version 3.0
Version 3.2 allows control of the archive bit.
Version 3.3 allows attributes to be set globally and in other directories using wildcard characters.

BACKUP

Purpose: Backup one or more files from one disk to another, primarily used for backing up a hard disk.

Usefulness:
* This command is used for regular backups

Remarks: Chapter 10 covers this command in detail.

Announced with: DOS version 2.0
Version 3.0 allows backup to another fixed disk
Version 3.3 will format diskettes during a backup procedure, will create a log of the backup, will back up according to a specified time and uses a faster, more efficient backup method.

BUFFERS

Purpose: Set the number of memory buffers used by the hard drive.

Usefulness:
- Using BUFFERS increases the performance of the hard drive by storing data in memory that the hard drive might have to retrieve again from disk.

Remarks: The command BUFFERS = X should be placed in the CONFIG.SYS file. X is the number of 512 bytes block of memory to set aside for disk buffering.

Announced with: DOS version 3.0

CHDIR

Purpose: (Change Directory) Move to other directories with this command.

Usefulness:
- CHDIR is the primary command for navigating through your directory structure.

Remarks: CHDIR can be shortened to CD. Chapter 3 covers this command in detail.

Announced with: DOS version 2.0

CHKDSK

Purpose: (Check Disk) Used to analyze files, directories and problems on disk drives.

Usefulness:
- CHKDSK can fix errors in the File Allocation Table caused when files are not completely written due to a power loss or other interruption.
- CHKDSK will attempt to recover parts of lost files.
- CHKDSK can be used to list all files in all directories
- CHKDSK will produce a report showing available disk space and memory usage.

Remarks: You should run the CHKDSK command using the /F option on a regular basis to resolve file allocation problems.

Announced with: DOS version 1.1

COPY	**Purpose:** Copy files to diskettes, directories or makes duplicates of existing files.

Usefulness:
- Copy files between directories and disks
- Copy can also be used to create file at the keyboard and to send files to a printer or another screen.
- COPY can be used to combine several files into a single file.

Remarks: There are a large number of options when copying files. You should refer to your DOS manual for more information.

WARNING! Be careful not to copy over existing files.

Announced with: DOS version 1

FASTOPEN	**Purpose:** Keeps file and directory information in memory for faster searches.

Usefulness:
- Improves the speed of hard drive access by keeping the location of files and directories in memory. DOS does not have to go to disk for this information every time you request a file.

Remarks: A good setting for FASTOPEN is 100 files. Specifying too many files will actually cause the system to slow due to the overhead.

Announced with: DOS version 3.3

FDISK	**Purpose:** Sets up a partition on a hard disk.

Usefulness:
- Used in the initial set up of a hard drive only.
- DOS 3.3 version allows you to set up primary and secondary partitions on drives larger than 32MB.

Announced with: DOS version 2.0
Version 3.3 allows partitioning of drives larger than 32MB.

FORMAT	**Purpose:** Prepares a hard drive and floppy diskettes for use.

Usefulness:
- Format initializes the disk, setting up the file allocation tables and other information required to store files.
- After backing up a hard disk, you can use FORMAT to reinitialize a disk. In the process, sectors that may have bad through use are found and marked as unusable.

WARNING! Do not run this command unless you are sure you want to erase the entire disk.

Announced with: DOS version 1.0

MKDIR

Purpose: (Make Directory) Creates subdirectories on hard drives (and floppy drive if needed).

Usefulness:
• The primary command for building a directory filing system.

Remarks: The MKDIR command can be shortened to MD.

Announced with: DOS version 2.0

PATH

Purpose: Sets a path that DOS will search when you request a command or batch file.

Usefulness:
• You can specify where DOS should look for command and batch files. This allows you to keep only one copy of a program on a hard drive that can be accessed from any other directory.
• PATH gives you more control over your directory filing structure, allowing you to create a system that fits the tasks you perform, as described in Chapter 4.

Remarks: The path is searched in order by DOS after it first searches the current directory for the requested command or batch file. DOS will search for .COM, .EXE and .BAT files in the specified directories.

Announced with: DOS version 2.0

PROMPT

Purpose: Allows alteration of the DOS prompt

Usefulness:
• PROMPT can be used to change the DOS prompt to display the current directory, the time, the date and other information.
• PROMPT can be used to alter keys assignments. See Chapter 9.

Remarks: Refer to your DOS manual for a complete selection of prompts you can assign.
Announced with: DOS version 2.0

RESTORE

Purpose: Restores files from a backup set

Usefulness:
• RESTORE is used to restore the files in the disk set created by the BACKUP command.

- RESTORE can be part of your backup and hard drive optimization scheme, as discussed in Chapter 13.

Announced with: DOS version 2.0
Version 3.3 allows you to restore modified files on or before a given date and time or after a given date and time since the last BACKUP, or restores files that no longer exist on the target drive.

RMDIR

Purpose: Removes directories

Usefulness:
- Allows you to clean up your hard drive by removing directories that are no longer needed.

Remarks: You cannot remove a directory that still contains files and you cannot remove a directory while in it. You must first move to the parent directory before attempting to remove the branching subdirectory.
RMDIR can be shortened to RD.

Announced with: DOS version 2.0

SUBST

Purpose: (Substitute) Allows you to assign a drive specifier to a subdirectory.

Usefulness:
- Applications that do not recognize DOS paths can be fooled into thinking that a directory is a drive.
- Substituting a long directory name with a drive letter (drive D, E, etc.) makes it easier to work with.

Remarks: You may need to set the LASTDRIVE command in your CONFIG.SYS file to specify drives higher than E. LASTDRIVE can be set equal to drive letters A through Z.

WARNING! Use the CD, MD, RD and PATH command with care when working with substituted pathnames.
The following commands should not be used when a substituted directory is in effect:
ASSIGN, BACKUP, DISKCOMP, DISKCOPY, FDISK, FORMAT, JOIN, LABEL, AND RESTORE.

Announced with: DOS version 3.1

TREE

Purpose: Display all directory paths on the specified drive, and optionally list the files in each directory.

Usefulness:
- Allows you to see the directory and branching subdirectory listing of your hard drive.
- A convenient way to scan through a list of files on your hard drive when searching for a file.

Remarks: You can direct the output of the tree command to a file or to a printer. See Chapter 4 for details.

Announced with: DOS version 2.0

XCOPY

Purpose: A selective copy command that can work with both directories and subdirectories.

Usefulness:
- The XCOPY command can be used like BACKUP. The files on the backup sets are useable.
- XCOPY allows you to select each file to be copied from a list.
- XCOPY can copy files by date and archive bit setting

Remarks: XCOPY is a superior COPY command since it gives you more control over the files to be copied.

WARNING! Be careful when using both the XCOPY command and the BACKUP command since both can set the archive bit. Files may not be backed up properly. Refer to Chapter 12 for details.

Announced with: DOS version 3.2

Tools and Utilities for Hard Drives

Disk Partitioning Programs

DOS has a hard disk storage limit of 32MB. Purchasing a drive larger than this limit will require the use of special software to subdivide the drive into what DOS "sees" as several separate disk drives. DOS version 3.3 has this capability built in, as discussed in Chapter 2, but if you are working with an older version of DOS, you will need one of the following programs.

Vfeature by Golden Bow Systems

Vfeature allows you to subdivide your hard drive into separate drives called volumes, or to increase the size of sectors so that DOS will recognize the entire drive as one large disk. Vfeature also offers various volume lockout and protection schemes.

Golden Bow Systems
2870 Fifth Avenue, Suite 201
San Diego, CA 92103

SpeedStor by Storage Dimensions

One of the things that *SpeedStor* does is partition a hard drive. In addition, it performs various tests on the surface of the drive covered under test programs later. *SpeedStor* fully integrates virtually any fixed disk drive into an IBM PC XT, PC AT, or compatible PC DOS or MS DOS personal computer. Disk drive integration can be done with a single command entry to start an unattended batch mode. More sophisticated features can be accessed in the menu-driven mode. Up to 8 partitions can be established and interleave is selectable.

Storage Dimensions
981 University Avenue
Los Gatos, CA 95030

Disk Cache Programs

Disk cache programs provide better buffering of data from the hard drive than the DOS BUFFERS command. Most programs balance the data in memory against that on the hard drive in a better way.

Vcache by Paul Mace Software

Vcache is a disk caching program available on the *Mace Utilities*. The Mace utilities also include the disk optimizing programs *UNfragment* and *Sort/Squeeze,* the file recovery program *UN-Delete* and an unformatting program. All of these useful tools in one package make the Mace Utilities one of my favorates. *Vcache* works in three different type of memory: standard PC/XT/AT memory, expanded memory defined by the Lotus/Intel specification and AT extended memory.

Paul Mace Software
123 N. First Street
Ashland, Oregon 97520

Flash by Software Masters

Flash is a cache that can be used in expanded memory (EMS) and extended memory so that the valuable main memory of your system is not tied up. You can lock some files or disk sectors into the cache, even if you leave the program using those files and come back to them later. Flash will also save various operating modes for later use and can buffer data to a floppy disk as well as a hard drive.

Software Masters
6223 Carrollton Avenue
Indianapolis, IN 46220

Lightning by Personal Computer Support Group

Lightning has many of the features of *Flash,* but tends to work better on system with smaller amounts of memory. A default cache size of 64K is used unless another size is specified. *Lightning* supports expanded memory up to 1.5MB only.

Personal Computer Support Group
11035 Harry Hines Boulevard
Dallas, TX 75229

Optimizers

Disk optimizers improve the speed of your hard drive by relocating files that have been fragmented into contiguous sectors. Files are stored so the hard drive can read them with little or no track-to track head movement.

CONDENSE by Mace Utilities

CONDENSE is included in the Mace Utilities package that includes a set of tools for testing a hard drive, setting up a disk cache and optimizing a hard drive. This package is my favorite because of the features it offers. *CONDENSE* performs a standard defragmentation procedure on a hard drive while displaying a graphic of what is going on. You can specify that *CONDENSE* place non-erasable files such as .COM and batch files together on the outer tracks of the drive. *CONDENSE* takes about 20 minutes to perform its task on a 20MB hard drive.

Paul Mace Software
123 N. First Street
Ashland, Oregon 97520

Disk Optimizer by SoftLogic Solutions

Disk Optimizer performs much of the same tasks as *CONDENSE*. You can scan through the files to determine just how fragmented your drive is. You can also selectively optimize your disk, giving you control over files that will be placed in the "prime" outer tracks of your hard drive, as discussed in Chapter 13.

SoftLogic Solutions, Inc
520 Chestnut Street
Manchester, NH   03101

Disk Testing and Recovery Programs

There are a number of disk test and file recovery programs on the market. The most well known is the Norton Utilities, which provides a set of tools for recovering erased files or files from defective disks. Disk test programs will test the sectors on your hard drive for errors. When errors are found, the sectors are marked as non-usable. Testing programs should be run often to prevent lost data.

Disk Test and the Norton Utilities by Perter Norton

The Norton Utilities are famous in the PC world. They have saved thousands of files from accidental erasure. The *DISK TEST* utility that is part of the package can detect bad sectors and mark them as non-usable. This program should be run on a regular basis in order to detect bad sectors as they fail.

Peter Norton Computing
2210 Wilshire Boulevard
Santa Monica, CA 90403

Disk Technician by Prime Solutions

Disk Technician is the best data protection on the market today. Basically, *Disk Technician* is based on an Artificial Intelligence algorithm that can determine, in advance, when a sector may go bad on your hard drive. It does this by constantly analyzing all sectors on your drive and maintaining a history file for those sectors that begin to show signs of failure. At the appropriate time, *Disk Technician* will tag the file as unusable and move the data to other sectors. *Disk Technician* also comes with an automatic parking program called *SafePark* that moves the heads of your hard drive to a safe zone every few seconds. This will prevent data loss due to head crashes in valuable data areas of the drive. Do yourself a favor and buy this program.

Prime Solutions, Inc.
1940 Garnet Avenue
San Diego, CA 92109

HTEST/HFORMAT by Paul Mace Software

HTEST/HFORMAT is a unique set of utilities for detecting various hard drive problems. *HTEST* is used if the drive has been preformatted. It scans across the entire range of the disk and displays any bad tracks found. *HOPTIMUM* is run to determine the optimal interleave for your drive, which can then be set by *HFORMAT*, which runs a controller level format.

Paul Mace Software, Inc.
123 First Street
Ashland, OR 97520

SpeedStor by Storage Dimensions

SpeedStor was mentioned earlier as a program used to partition a hard drive that is greater than 32MB in size. The program also has various drive testing procedures and makes set-up of hard drive equipment a breeze. *SpeedStor's* powerful diagnostics locate system faults, isolate problems with fixed disk drives and controllers and locates undetected media defects.

Storage Dimensions
981 University Avenue
Los Gatos, CA 95030

Backup, Archive and Compression Software

The DOS BACKUP command is often not a practical way to back up a hard drive. Tape backup systems may not be in the budget. The following software programs offer a compromise.

Fastback by Fifth Generation

Fastback is covered in Chapter 11. The program provides one of the fastest backup and data compression routines on the market, so fast, that the disk drive is left running *while* you switch diskettes.

Fifth Generation System
7942 Picardy Avenue
Baton Rouge, LA 70809

DSBackup by Design Software

DSBackup is also covered in Chapter 11. This program offers a usable menu system that can be bypassed for automatic settings when a backup procedure has been established. Two modes let you backup files in either compressed mode or as usable files on the floppy diskettes.

Design Software Incorporated
2 N. 520 Prince Crossing Road
West Chicago, IL 60185

ARC by System Enhancement Associates

ARC is a file squeezing program that lets you obtain more room on your hard drive. Files are compressed and stored in less space. When the files are needed again, they must be uncompressed. *ARC* is considered an archiving program since files are usually squeezed before they are placed in storage. The program is sold on a "shareware" basis. If you need it and use it, you are asked to send a use fee to the designers.

System Enhancement Associates
21 New Street
Wayne, NJ 07470

Hard Drives Specifications and Manufacturers

The following information can be used when low-level formatting hard drives. Some controllers may require that the information be converted to hexidecimal numbers. If the Write Precomp column is blank, write precompensation is handled by the drive's onboard processor. Some information was not obtainable at the time of this printing. Call the manufacturer if you have further questions.

Column heading descriptions:

Cap	Capacity
Cyls	Cylinders
Hds	Heads
WPC	Write Precompensation
LZ	Landing Zone

Notes:

1	Voice coil head positioner
2	Supports RLL coded data
3	Seagate ST238 RLL only, does not support MFM coding
4	SCSI (Small Computer Systems Interface)
5	ESDI (Enhanced Small Device Interface)
6	WORM (Write Once, Read Many) optical drive

All other drives, unless noted, support ST506/412 interface.

ATASI	Cap.	Cyl.	Hds.	Servo	WPC	LX	Notes
AT3020	17MB	635	3	closed loop	N/A	634	1
AT3033	28MB	635	5	closed loop	N/A	634	1
AT3046	38MB	635	7	closed loop	323	644	1
AT3051	42MB	704	7	closed loop	352	703	1
AT3051+	45MB	733	7	closed loop	368	732	1
AT3085	71MB	1024	8	closed loop	–	1023	1
BULL							
D530	25MB	987	3	closed loop	–	–	1
D550	43MB	987	5	closed loop	–	–	1
D570	60MB	987	7	closed loop	–	–	1
D585	71MB	1166	7	closed loop	–	–	1
CDC							
9415-21	21MB	697	3	closed	–	697	1
9415-25	25MB	612	4	closed	–	612	1
9415-28	28MB	612	4	closed	–	612	1
94155-36	36MB	697	5	embedded	–	697	1
94155-48	48MB	925	5	embedded	–	925	1
94155-51	51MB	989	5	embedded	–	989	1
94155-57	57MB	925	6	embedded	–	925	1
94155-67	67MB	925	7	embedded	–	925	1
94155-72	72MB	925	9	embedded	128	925	1
94155-77	77MB	925	8	embedded	–	925	1
94155-86	86MB	925	9	embedded	128	925	1,5
94155-135	135MB	960	9	embedded	–	959	1,2
94161-101	89MB	969	5	embedded	–	968	1,4
94161-141	124MB	969	7	embedded	–	968	1,4
94161-182	160MB	969	9	embedded	–	968	1,4
94166-101	101MB	969	5	embedded	–	968	1,5
94166-141	141MB	969	7	embedded	–	968	1,5
94166-182	182MB	969	9	embedded	–	968	1,5
94171-312	312MB	1365	9	embedded	–	1364	1,4
94171-344	344MB	1549	9	embedded	–	1548	1,4
94181-574	575MB	1549	15	embedded	–	1548	1,4
94186-383	383MB	1412	13	embedded	–	1411	1,4
94186-442	422MB	1412	15	embedded	–	1411	1,5
94186-383H	383MB	1224	15	embedded	–	1223	1,5
94205-77	77MB	989	5	embedded	–	988	1,2
CMI							
CM3426	20MB	612	4	embedded	300	612	
CM5205	20MB	256	2	embedded	–	256	
CM5410	20MB	256	4	embedded	–	256	
CM5616	20MB	256	6	embedded	–	256	
CM6426	21MB	615	4	embedded	300	615	
CM6426S	20MB	640	4	embedded	256	640	
CM6640	32MB	615	6	embedded	300	615	
CONNER							
CP-340	50MB	980	4	closed	–	980	4
CP-342	50MB	805	4	closed	–	805	1

FUJI	Cap.	Cyl.	Hds.	Servo	WPC	LX	Notes
309-26	26MB	615	4	open-loop	–	615	
305-39	39MB	615	4	open-loop	–	615	2
309-39	39MB	615	4	open-loop	–	615	2
303-52	52MB	615	8	open-loop	–	615	
309-58	58MB	615	6	open-loop	–	615	2
FUJITSU							
M2230AS	5MB	306	2	open loop	–	306	
M2233AS	10MB	306	4	open loop	–	306	
M2234AS	15MB	306	6	open loop	–	306	
M2235AS	20MB	306	8	open loop	–	306	
M2230AT	5MB	306	2	open loop	–	306	
M2233AT	10MB	306	4	open loop	–	306	
M2241AS	26MB	754	4	open loop	375	754	
M2242AS	46MB	754	7	open loop	375	754	
M2243AS	72MB	754	11	open loop	375	754	
HITACHI							
DK511-3	30MB	699	5		300	699	
DK511-5	43MB	699	7		300	699	
DK511-8	72MB	823	10		400	822	
IMI							
5006H	5MB	306	2		128	306	
5012H	10MB	306	4		128	306	
5018H	15MB	306	6		128	306	
LAPINE/KYOCERA							
3062	10MB	306	4	open loop	–	306	
3512	10MB	306	4	open loop	–	306	
3522	10MB	306	4	open loop	–	306	
LT-200	26MB	615	4	open-loop	–	615	
LT-300	39MB	615	4	open-loop	–	615	2
LT-2000	26MB	615	4	open-loop	–	615	
LT-3000	39MB	615	4	open-loop	–	615	2
TITAN20	21MB	615	4	open-loop	–	615	
MAXTOR							
XT800S	800MB	18000	1	closed loop	–	–	4,6
XT1065	57MB	918	7	closed loop	–	1023	1
XT1085	71MB	1024	8	closed loop	–	1023	1
XT1105	88MB	918	11	closed loop	–	1023	1
XT1120R	120MB	1024	8	closed loop	–	1023	1,2
XT1140	120MB	918	15	closed loop	–	1023	1
XT1240R	140MB	1024	15	closed loop	–	1023	1,2
XT2085	75MB	1224	7	closed loop	–	1223	1
XT2085-	62MB	1024	7	closed loop	–	1024	1
XT2140	117MB	1224	11	closed loop	–	1223	1
XT2140-	98MB	1024	11	closed loop	–	1023	1
XT2190	160MB	1224	15	closed loop	–	1223	1
XT2190-	134MB	1224	15	closed loop	–	1223	1
XT3170	150MB	1224	9	closed loop	–	1223	1,4
XT3280	250MB	1224	15	closed loop	–	1223	1,5
XT4170E	170MB	1224	7	closed loop	–	1223	1,5
XT4170S	170MB	1224	7	closed loop	–	1223	1,4
XT4280S	280MB	1224	11	closed loop	–	1223	1,4
XT4380E	380MB	1224	15	closed loop	–	1223	1,5

MAXTOR (cont.)	Cap.	Cyl.	Hds.	Servo	WPC	LX	Notes
XT4380S	380MB	1224	15	closed loop	–	1223	1,4
XT8380E	380MB	1632	8	closed loop	–	1631	5
XT8380S	380MB	1632	8	closed loop	–	1631	4
XT8760E	760MB	1632	15	closed loop	–	1631	5
XT8760S	760MB	1632	15	closed loop	–	1631	5
EXT4175	149MB	1224	7	closed loop	–	1223	1,5
EXT4280	234MB	1224	11	closed loop	–	1223	1,5
EXT4380	382MB	1224	15	closed loop	–	1223	1,5

MICROPOLIS							
1302	22MB	830	3	closed loop	–	829	1
1303	36MB	830	5	closed loop	–	829	1
1304	43MB	830	6	closed loop	–	829	1
1323	42MB	1024	4	closed loop	–	1023	1
1323A	53MB	1024	5	closed loop	–	1023	1
1324	64MB	1024	6	closed loop	–	1023	1
1324A	74MB	1024	7	closed loop	–	1023	1
1325	85MB	1024	8	closed loop	–	1023	1
1333A	53MB	1024	5	closed loop	–	1023	1
1334	64MB	1024	6	closed loop	–	1023	1
1335	85MB	1024	8	closed loop	–	1023	1
1353	85MB	1024	4	closed loop	–	1023	1,5
1353A	106MB	1024	5	closed loop	–	1023	1,5
1354	128MB	1024	6	closed loop	–	1023	1,5
1354A	149MB	1024	7	closed loop	–	1023	1,5
1355	170MB	1024	8	closed loop	–	1023	1,5
1373	85MB	1024	4	closed loop	–	1023	1,4
1373A	106MB	1024	5	closed loop	–	1023	1,4
1374	128MB	1024	6	closed loop	–	1023	1,4
1374A	149MB	1024	7	closed loop	–	1023	1,4
1375	170MB	1024	8	closed loop	–	1023	1,4
1556-11	248MB	1224	11	closed loop	–	1223	1,5
1556-12	270MB	1224	12	closed loop	–	1223	1,5
1556-13	293MB	1224	13	closed loop	–	1223	1,5
1556-14	315MB	1224	14	closed loop	–	1223	1,5
1556-15	270MB	1224	12	closed loop	–	1223	1,5
1576-11	243MB	1220	11	closed loop	–	1219	1,4
1576-12	266MB	1220	12	closed loop	–	1219	1,4
1576-13	287MB	1220	13	closed loop	–	1219	1,4
1576-14	310MB	1220	14	closed loop	–	1219	1,4
1576-15	332MB	1220	15	closed loop	–	1219	1,4

MICROSCIENCE							
HH325	21MB	615	4	embedded	–	615	
HH312	10MB	306	4	embedded	128	306	
HH612	10MB	306	4	embedded	–	306	
HH725	20MB	615	4	embedded	–	615	2
HH1050	53MB	1024	5	embedded	–	1023	1
HH1060	75MB	1024	5	embedded	–	1023	1,2

MINISCRIBE	Cap.	Cyl.	Hds.	Servo	WPC	LX	Notes
1006	5MB	306	2	open loop	–	306	
1012	10MB	306	4	open loop	–	306	
2006	5MB	306	2	open loop	128	306	
2012	10MB	306	4	open loop	128	306	
3012	10MB	612	2	open loop	300	612	
3212	1OMB	612	2	open loop	300	612	
3412	21MB	306	4	open loop	–	615	
3425	32MB	612	4	open loop	300	615	2
3438	32MB	615	4	open loop	128	615	2
4010	8MB	480	2	open loop	128	480	
4020	15MB	480	4	open loop	128	480	
6032	27MB	1024	3	closed loop	–	1023	1
6053	45MB	1024	5	closed loop	–	1023	1
6074	62MB	1024	7	closed loop	–	1023	1
6085	71MB	1024	8	closed loop	–	1023	1
8212	10MB	615	2	closed loop	–	615	
8425	20MB	615	4	closed loop	–	615	

MITSUBISHI							
MR522	21MB	612	4	closed loop	300	612	1
MR533	25MB	971	3	closed loop	–	971	1
MR535	42MB	971	5	closed loop	–	971	1

MMI							
M125	20MB	612	4	open loop	300	612	
M225	20MB	612	4	open loop	300	612	
M325	20MB	612	4	open loop	300	612	

NEC							
5124	11MB	309	4	closedloop	–	664	
5126	21MB	612	4	closedloop	–	664	
5146	43MB	615	8	closedloop	–	664	

NEWBERRY							
NDR320	21MB	615	4	closed loop	–	615	
NDR340	51MB	615	8	closed loop	–	615	
NDR360	79MB	615	8	closed loop	–	615	2
NDR1065	67MB	918	7	closed loop	–	918	1
NDR1085	85MB	1024	8	closed loop	–	1023	
NDR1105	105MB	918	11	closed loop	–	1023	
NDR1140	140MB	918	15	closed loop	–	1023	
NDR1190	191MB	1224	15	closed loop	–	1023	
NDR1190-	191MB	1024	15	closed loop	–	1023	
NDR3170S	147MB	1224	9	closed loop	–	1023	1,4
NDR3280S	244MB	1224	15	closed loop	–	1023	1,4
NDR3380S	319MB	1224	15	closed loop	–	1023	1,4
NDR4175	180MB	1224	7	closed loop	–	1023	1,5
NDR4380	384MB	1224	15	closed loop	–	1023	1,5

PRIAM/VERTEX	Cap.	Cyl.	Hds.	Servo	WPC	LX	Notes
V130	26MB	987	3	closed loop	–	987	1,2
V150	43MB	987	5	closed loop	–	987	1,2
V170	60MB	987	7	closed loop	–	987	1,2
V185	71MB	1166	7	closed loop	–	1165	1,2
V185–	62MB	1024	7	closed loop	–	1023	1,2
519	160MB	1224	15	closed loop	–	1223	1,2
519–	134MB	1024	15	closed loop	–	1023	1,2
I/ED45–	44MB	1018	5	embedded	–	1017	1
I/ED62–	62MB	1018	7	embedded	–	1017	1
I/ED75	74MB	1156	5	embedded	–	1155	1,2
I/ED100	103MB	1156	7	embedded	–	1155	1,2
I/ED130	133MVB	1018	15	embedded	–	1017	1
I/ED230	233MB	1218	15	embedded	–	1217	1,2
ID330–	337MB	1218	15	embedded	–	1217	1,5
OUANTUM							
Q520	18MB	512	4	closed loop	256	512	1
Q530	27MB	512	6	closed loop	256	512	1
Q540	36MB	512	8	closed loop	256	512	1
RMS							
RMS503	3MB	153	2		77	153	
RMS506	5MB	153	4		77	153	
RMS512	10M	153	8		77	153	
RODIME							
RO101	3MB	192	2	open loop	–	192	
RO102	7MB	192	4	open loop	–	192	
RO103	10MB	192	6	open loop	–	192	
RO104	13MB	192	8	open loop	–	192	
RO201	6MB	321	2	open loop	–	321	
RO202	11MB	321	4	open loop	–	321	
RO203	17MB	321	6	open loop	132	321	
RO204	22MB	321	8	open loop	132	321	
RO201E	10MB	640	2	open loop	–	640	
RO202E	20MB	640	4	open loop	–	640	
RO203E	33MB	640	6	open loop	–	640	
RO204E	45MB	640	8	open loop	–	640	
RO252	10MB	306	4	open loop	–	306	
RO352	10MB	306	4	open loop	–	306	
SEAGATE							
ST125	26MB	615	4	closed loop	–	615	
ST138	38MB	615	6	closed loop	–	615	
ST138N	32MB	613	4	closed loop	–	613	4
ST138R	38MB	615	4	closed loop	–	615	2
ST157N	49MB	613	6	closed loop	–	613	4
ST157R	58MB	615	6	closed loop	–	615	2
ST206	5MB	306	2	open loop	128	306	
ST212	10MB	306	4	open loop	128	306	
ST213	11MB	615	2	open loop	300	615	
ST225	26MB	615	4	open loop	300	615	
ST225N	21MB	615	4	closed loop	–	615	4
ST238R	38MB	615	4	open loop	300	625	
ST251	51MB	820	6	open loop	–	820	
ST251-1	51MB	820	6	closed loop	–	820	
ST251-N	43MB	818	4	closed loop	–	818	

SEAGATE	Cap.	Cyl.	Hds.	Servo	WPC	LX	Notes
ST251R	51MB	820	4	closed loop	–	820	2
ST277N	65MB	818	6	closed loop	–	818	4
ST277R	77MB	820	6	closed loop	–	820	2
ST296N	85MB	818	6	closed loop	–	818	4
ST406	5MB	306	2	open loop	128	306	
ST412	11MB	306	4	open loop	128	306	
ST419	15MB	306	6	open loop	128	306	
ST506	5MB	153	4	closed loop	128	153	
ST706	5MB	306	2	closed loop	128	306	
ST4026	21MB	615	4	closed loop	300	615	1
ST4038	38MB	733	5	closed loop	300	733	1
ST4038M	32MB	733	5	closed loop	–	977	1
ST4051	43MB	977	5	closed loop	300	977	1
ST4051N	43MB	977	5	closed loop	–	977	1
ST4053	53MB	1024	5	closed loop	–	1023	1
ST4096	96MB	1024	9	closed loop	–	1023	1
ST4144R	144MB	1024	9	closed loop	–	1023	1,2
ST4192E	191MB	1147	8	closed loop	–	1146	1,5
ST4192N	169MB	1147	8	closed loop	–	1146	1,4
SHUGART							
SA604	6MB	160	4	open loop	–	160	
SA606	8MB	160	6	open loop	–	160	
SA612	10MB	306	4	open loop	128	306	
SA712	11MB	320	4	open loop	128	320	
TANDON							
TM-252	10MB	306	4	open loop	–	306	
TM-353	10MB	306	4	open loop	–	615	
TM-262	21MB	615	4	embedded	–	306	
TM-362	21MB	615	4	embedded	–	615	
TM-501	5MB	306	2		128	306	
TM-502	10MB	306	4		128	306	
TM-503	16MB	306	6		128	306	
TM-602S	5MB	153	4		–	153	
TM-603S	8MB	153	6		–	153	
TM-603SE	12MB	230	6		128	230	
TM-702AT	21MB	615	4	open loop	–	615	1
TM-703	30MB	695	5	open loop	–	695	1
TM-703AT	32MB	733	5	open loop	–	733	1
TM-705	42MB	695	5	open loop	–	695	1
TM-755	43MB	981	5	closed loop	–	981	1,2
TOSHIBA							
MK53F	36MB	830	5	closed loop	512	830	1
MK54F	51MB	830	7	closed loop	512	830	1
MK56F	72MB	830	10	closed loop	–	830	1,2
MKM-0353	72MB	830	10	closed loop	512	830	1
TULIN							
TL226	22MB	640	4	embedded	–	640	
TL238	22MB	640	4	embedded	–	640	
TL240	33MB	640	6	embedded	–	640	
TL258	33MB	640	6	embedded	–	640	
TL326	22MB	640	4	embedded	–	640	
TL340	33MB	640	6	embedded	–	640	

Controller Jumper Settings (for PC and XT type systems)

DTC Controller Card (BXD-06 EPROM)

Capacity	Cylinders	Heads	Switch Block
10MB	306	4	00001111
10MB	612	2	01011111
20MB	612	4	10101111
30MB	640	6	10100000

OMTI Controller Card (5510-3 EPROM)

Capacity	Cylinders	Heads	Jumpers
10MB	306	4	none
10MB	612	2	W1 and W3
20MB	612	4	W2
30MB	640	6	W4

Note: Jumper W10 should always be set.

Western Digital Controller Card (012 or 013 EPROM)

Capacity	Cylinders	Heads	Jumpers
10MB	306	4	none on SW1 block
10MB	612	2	#4 & #2
20MB	612	4	#3 & #1
30MB	640	6	#4 & #2
30MB	612	8	#4 & #2

XEBEC Controller Card (104873X EPROM)

Capacity	Cylinders	Heads	Jumpers
10MB	306	4	#1 & #3
10MB	612	2	#2 & #4
20MB	612	4	none

Using Two Controllers

Most controller cards allow for the use of two hard drives. cables are available for daisy-chaining to the second drive. When using cables without "twists" (cable inverted at the second drive connector), the select switches on the back of the hard drive should be changed from DS1 to DS2. J2 and J3 on the controller card are cabled to the first and second drive respectively.

Low-Level Formatting Drives with DEBUG

You can use a built in (EPROM) low-level format routine on the Western Digital WX2, DTC 5550, and OMTI 5510 controller cards. First, load the DOS DEBUG program, then type **G=C800:5**. On Adaptec controllers, type **G-C800:CCC**. On CMS "K" controllers, type **G=C800:6**. Xebec controllers require the use of Advanced Diagnostics. Answer the questions according to the specifications of your drive, setting the interleave at 3 unless you have determined a preferable interleave.

Manufacturers

Adaptec Inc.
580 Cottonwood Drive
Milpitas, CA 95035
(408) 946-8600

Manufacturers of advanced technology RLL hard drive controller cards.

Alloy Computer Products, Inc.
100 Pennsylvania Ave.
Framingham, MA 01701
(617) 875-6100

125MB, high-speed (30-millisecond average access time) full height hard disk using standard ST506 interface.

Atasi Corporation
2075 Zanker Rd.
San Jose, CA 95130
(408) 995-0335

17MB, 28MB, 38MB, and 42MB hard drives.

Basic Time Inc.
3040 Oakmead Village Dr.
Santa Clara, CA 95051
(408) 727-0877

PC, XT and AT hard drive systems.

Bull Peripherals, Inc.
766 San Aleso Ave.
Sunnyvale, CA 94086
(408) 745-0855

25MB, 43MB, 60MB and 71MB hard drives.

CDC, Control Data Corporation
8100 34th Ave., S
Minneapolis, MN 55440
(612) 931-3131

Full line of PC, XT and AT hard drives.

CMS
3080 Airway Ave.
Costa Mesa, CA 92626
(714) 549-9111

System integration house offering hard drives for PC, XT and AT class machines.

Core International
7171 N. Federal Hwy.
Boca Raton, FL 33431
(305) 997-6055

150MB, high speed full height hard drives with 10MHz ESDI interface and 1 to 1 interleave factors.

Eastman Kodak Co.
Mass Memory Division
343 State St.
Rochester, NY 14650
(800) 445-6325

New cartridge mass storage system based on 5.25" removable media storing 12MB

Emerald Systems Corp.
4757 Morena Blvd.
San Diego, CA 92117
(619) 270-1994

150MB ESDI full height hard drives using 10MHz transfer rates and 1 to 1 interleaves.

Emulex Corporation
3545 Harbor Blvd.
Costa Mesa, CA 92626
(714) 6625600

142MB or 310MB full height hard disk and 60MB cartridge tape backup system using SCSI and ESDI interfaces.

Fujitsu America, Inc.
3055 Orchard Drive
San Jose, CA 95134
(408) 946-8777

21MB, 45MB and 72MB 5.25" full height hard drives for PC and AT class machines.

I^2 Interface Inc
21101 Osborne St.
Canoga Park, CA 91304
(818) 341-7914

Systems integration house supplying hard drives for PC, XT and AT class machines.

IDEAssociates, Inc.
35 Dunham Road
Billerica, MA 01821
(617) 663-6878

120MB full height hard drive using existing AT type controller cards

Iomega Corp.
1821 W. 4000 South
Roy, UT 84067
(801) 778-1000

Removable media hard drives in 20MB side by side units.

Maynard Electronics
460 E. Semoran Blvd.
Casselberry, FL 32707
(305) 331-6402

Hard drives for PC, XT and AT class machines.

Micropolis Corp.
21123 Nordhoff St.
Chatsworth, CA 91311
(818) 709-3300

Full line of PC and AT compatible hard drives.

Microscience International Corp.
575 E. Middlefield Rd.
Mountain View, CA 94043
(415) 961-2212

21MB and 44MB 5.25" half height hard drives for PC and AT machines utilizing thin film technology.

Miniscribe Corp.
1861 Left Hand Circle
Longmont, CO
80501(303) 651-6000

26MB, 44MB and 71MB 5.25" full height hard drives for PC and AT machines

Mountain Computer Inc.
360 El Pueblo Rd.
Scotts Valley, CA 95066
(408) 438-6650

Hard Drives for PC, XT and AT type machines

Plus Development
1778 McCarthy Blvd.
Milpitas, CA 95035
(408) 946-3700

10MB and 20MB hard card type drives for PC and AT class machines.

Priam Systems Division
3052 Orchard Drive
San Jose, CA 95134
(408) 946-4600

130MB full height hard drive using the existing AT type controller cards

Rodime Inc.
901 Broken Sound Pkwy.
Boca Raton, FL 33431
(305) 994-6200

33MB and 44MB 5.25" full and half height drives for AT type machines.

Scientific Micro Systems
339 N. Bernardo Ave.
Mountain View, CA 94043
(415) 964-5700

Manufacturers of advanced RLL technology hard drive controllers.

Seagate Technology
920 Disc Dr.
Scotts Valley, CA 95066
(408) 438-6550

21MB and 31MB 5.25" full and half height RLL compatible drives for AT type machines.

Storage Dimensions
14127 Capri Drive
Los Gatos, CA 95030
(408) 370-3304

160MB full height hard drives using the ST506 interface.

Sysgen Inc.
47853 Warm Springs
Fremont, CA 94539
(800) 821-2151

40MB and 70MB internal hard drives with 1 to 1 interleaves and full track buffering.

Tandon Corp
405 Science Dr.
Moorpark, CA 93021
(805) 378-6081

21MB and 42MB 5.25" and 3.5" half height drives for PC and AT class machines.

DOS 4

DOS 4.0 was announced in the summer of 1988 by IBM and late 1988 by Microsoft. The product offers some additional enhancement to DOS, some of which are beneficial to hard drive users. Changes affecting command relevant to this book have been made in the text. This appendix will provide additional information specific to the IBM version of DOS 4.

IBM DOS 4.0 includes a menu oriented system manager called DOSSHELL that can be run on "shell" over DOS. This menu system offers file handling features especially significant to hard drive users. A graphical directory tree is displayed and movement between directories is a simple matter of selecting the directory in the tree with the arrow keys or a mouse. DOS commands are easier to execute. Pull-down menus allow selection of most file manipulation commands, and the user is prompted for required information. DOSSHELL is loaded by typing DOSSHELL on the command line.

DOS 4 also support the Lotus, Intel, and Microsoft (LIM) Expanded Memory Specification (EMS version 4.0. Two drivers are available for installation of the specification, depending on the type of system available. Because DOS now supports the EMS standard, two commands were modified to work in expanded memory, as listed below:

BUFFERS   Adding the /X parameter to the BUFFERS command in the CONFIG.SYS file installs the buffers in expanded memory, thus freeing conventional memory for programs.

FASTOPEN The /X parameter allows FASTOPEN to perform its file buffering operations in expanded memory, thus freeing conventional memory for programs.

New DOS 4.0 command additions and enhancements are listed below:

INSTALL Provides and efficient means of loading terminate and stay resident commands into the CONFIG.SYS file that were previously placed in the AUTOEXEC.BAT file. The commands are FASTOPEN, KEYB, NLSFUNC, and SHARE.

MEM Displays the amount of memory, unused memory, allocated, and open memory areas, and all programs currently installed in memory.

VDISK The /X parameter specifies that the memory disk should be installed in expanded memory.

XMA2EMS.SYS Provides support for the LIM EMS specification as mentioned above.

XMAEM.SYS Allows 80838 based systems like the IBM Personal System/2 Models 70 and 80 to emulate the IBM Personal System/2 80286 Expanded Memory Adapter/A. The XMA2EMS.SYS command can then be used to provide LIM EMS support.

Additional commands of significance to hard drive users are listed below:

APPEND This command sets a search path for data files outside the current directory. DOS version 4.0 now allows files with the extensions of .COM, .EXE, or .BAT to searched

BACKUP BACKUP now automatically formats diskettes without special parameters, if the diskettes are unformatted.

CHKDSK The CHKDSK command now displays the volume serial number, if one exists, and the allocation units in the status report.

FDISK FDISK now presents a screen to view existing disk partitions. You can also create new ones, or erase existing ones. The command also accepts disk partition sizes in either MB or percentages, instead of cylinders.

TREE   The TREE command now displays its output in a
                        graphical tree format.

Installation of DOS 4.0 on Hard Drives

Installation of DOS 4.0 on a fixed disk is automatic. Place the
Install disk in drive A, then reboot the system. The SELECT
program is started and the installation screen is presented. You are
requested to choose the drive and the directory where DOS should
be installed. If the system has a previous version of DOS, SELECT
saves the existing AUTOEXEC.BAT and CONFIG.SYS files, and
creates new files called AUTOEXEC.400 and CONFIG.400. You may
need to move commands in the existing startup batch files to the
new DOS 4.0 startup files, then erase the existing files and rename
the .400 files with the .BAT extension.

Installing DOS 4.0 to Partitions over 32MB

If you are installing DOS 4.0 to a system with existing partitions
defined at 32MB or smaller and you wish to create larger partitions,
the existing partitions must first be backed up and the partitions
must be redefined. This can be done by starting the system with
the DOS 4.0 *Install* disk. When the initial screen appears, go to the
DOS prompt by pressing Esc and the F3 key. The DOS A prompt
will appear. Place the *Operating* disk (or *Select*) disk in drive A.
The system is now booted with DOS 4 so that the BACKUP
command on the *Operating* or *Select* disk can be used to backup
the hard drive. When the drive is backed up, the FDISK command
on the *Install* disk can be used to repartition the drive. When the
system reboots, the normal DOS 4 installation procedure can be
followed to prepare the drive.

Index